Praise for *Satisfaction*

"J.D. Power's message is clear—customer satisfaction equates to profits. Make no mistake, the world has changed and companies can no longer count on advertising to drive consumer perceptions or behaviors. Don't say this book didn't warn you."   —Alvin Toffler, bestselling author and futurist

"This book shows that customer satisfaction means more than just spending money to make customers happy. . . . The business community should be thankful for it."

—Horst H. Schulze, founding president and COO,
The Ritz-Carlton Hotel Company

"*Satisfaction* is an essential read for anyone focused on the bottom line. It includes at least one hundred different ways to insightfully 'listen better' to those with whom we do business—a key ingredient toward being more successful."
—John Marin, senior adviser, Time Inc. Magazines

"Being successful always means listening to the customers and understanding their needs. J.D. Power and Associates provides us the opportunity to benefit from its experience in methods and techniques of analyzing and identifying customers' expectations."

—Dr. Bernd Pischetsrieder, former chairman of the Board
of Management, Volkswagen AG

ABOUT THE AUTHORS

Chris Denove is a vice president of J.D. Power and Associates, where he specializes in helping businesses improve customer satisfaction and profits through listening to the voice of their customer. He brings a wide range of experience to the firm, having previously held positions managing automobile dealerships and practicing consumer law in his home state of California.

James D. Power IV is an executive vice president and the oldest son of the company founder. Before joining the family business in 1990, he worked for a leading advertising agency and a major automobile manufacturer. Today he represents the company around the world as leader of its international operations.

Both Denove and Power live in Los Angeles, where J.D. Power and Associates is headquartered. For more information, visit www.jdpower.com.

SATISFACTION

How Every Great Company
Listens to the
Voice of the Customer

CHRIS DENOVE and JAMES D. POWER IV

PORTFOLIO

PORTFOLIO

Published by the Penguin Group

Penguin Group (USA) Inc., 375 Hudson Street, New York, New York 10014, U.S.A.
Penguin Group (Canada), 90 Eglinton Avenue East, Suite 700, Toronto, Ontario, Canada M4P 2Y3
(a division of Pearson Penguin Canada Inc.)
Penguin Books Ltd, 80 Strand, London WC2R 0RL, England
Penguin Ireland, 25 St Stephen's Green, Dublin 2, Ireland (a division of Penguin Books Ltd)
Penguin Group (Australia), 250 Camberwell Road, Camberwell, Victoria 3124, Australia (a division of Pearson
Australia Group Pty Ltd)
Penguin Books India Pvt Ltd, 11 Community Centre, Panchsheel Park, New Delhi – 110 017, India
Penguin Group (NZ), 67 Apollo Drive, Mairangi Bay, Auckland 1311, New Zealand (a division of Pearson New
Zealand Ltd)
Penguin Books (South Africa) (Pty) Ltd, 24 Sturdee Avenue, Rosebank, Johannesburg 2196, South Africa

Penguin Books Ltd, Registered Offices:
80 Strand, London WC2R 0RL, England

First published in the United States of America by Portfolio, a member of Penguin Group (USA) Inc. 2006
This paperback edition published 2007

3 5 7 9 10 8 6 4 2

Copyright © J.D. Power and Associates, 2006
All rights reserved

ISBN 1-59184-109-7 (hc.)
ISBN 978-1-59184-164-7 (pbk.)
CIP data available

Printed in the United States of America
Set in Adobe Garamond
Designed by Helene Berinsky

To J. David Power III, our founder, inspirational leader, and father of Jamey Power—and father figure to Chris Denove and hundreds of others at J.D. Power and Associates.

ACKNOWLEDGMENTS

First and foremost, the authors would like to thank consumers everywhere who each and every day for the past thirty-five years took a little time out of their day to share their opinions with us. Neither this book, nor J.D. Power and Associates itself, would exist without their feedback. In return, J.D. Power and Associates pledges to continue to work on your behalf to make your voices heard.

We would also like to thank each and every associate at our firm, for *Satisfaction* is truly a book by everyone who calls J.D. Power and Associates their home. Rather than a company comprised of physical plants and equipment, J.D. Power and Associates is instead an organization whose people, and the various talents they possess, are not only our biggest asset, but also our *only* asset. Led by Steve Goodall, our president, there were literally hundreds of associates who contributed to this project, and we regret the fact there isn't space to thank each one individually.

Outside of our organization, special thanks go to Glenn Rifkin and Joni Evans, two extremely talented and patient individuals who were not only responsible for helping to guide us through this, our first book project, but also were an integral part of helping us turn thirty-five years of data into something that we hope is informative, and occasionally even enjoyable, to read.

We are forever indebted to Adrian Zackheim at Portfolio, who took a chance on us at a time when we lacked a formal manuscript and even the most rudimentary understanding of what it took to write a book. He, and his talented staff, including Bernadette Malone, Will Weisser, and Stephanie Land, patiently endured endless questions on our part and provided the answers and guidance needed to turn this project into reality.

And finally, we would like to thank Ernest Pomerantz and Jerry Pyle, two longtime supporters and former directors of J.D. Power and Associates whose persistence and coaching paid off in convincing us to finally undertake this project.

Chris and Jamey

CONTENTS

FOREWORD BY J.D. POWER III

Good is not good when better is expected.
—THOMAS FULLER

Back in the 1980s, when Peugeot, the French carmaker, was trying to build its market in the United States, I remember one of the engineers getting very upset when we presented our customer satisfaction results. We had showed them that one of the biggest problems reported by their buyers in America was that Peugeots were hard to start. As with all trends, we had investigated this response when we started seeing it appear regularly in the surveys.

Peugeot, it turns out, had developed one of the first fuel injection engines, and its ignition system was different than the conventional engines in other cars. In the United States back then, consumers were accustomed to the conventional carburetors, and before starting their cars they would habitually pump the accelerator a few times, especially during the winter. Though most drivers didn't know why they did it, the action put fuel into the combustion chamber and helped start the engine. With the Peugeot, however, when drivers pumped the accelerator, they were unwittingly flooding the engine so it wouldn't start.

The French engineer responded to our report by slamming his fist on the table and declaring, "We have the best-starting cars in

Europe. What we have to do is train the Americans on how to start the cars." I advised him that Peugeot could spend every cent it had on advertising and promotion to educate consumers on how to start the car but that it wouldn't change anything. "You have to build the ignition and fuel system so that it operates the way American drivers want it to," I told him.

In 1991, not long after our conversation, American consumers stopped buying Peugeot cars entirely, and the company had no choice but to abandon the U.S. market. In a way this was too bad—Peugeot had talented engineers and their designs were excellent. They just had one simple yet significant problem: they could not hear the voice of their customer.

Peugeot's experience, while demoralizing, is hardly unusual. Having spent the better part of my adult life tracking customer satisfaction as the founder of J.D. Power and Associates, I've heard every lament and seen a legion of customers walk away shaking their heads in disappointment. J.D. Power and Associates' awards for quality and customer satisfaction have become a powerful and sought-after recognition in a growing number of industries, from automobiles to hospitality. We also know from our surveys and from our consulting and training services that some companies are not only listening to their customers today but are understanding the huge financial and strategic advantage it gives them. We've had the pleasure of working with organizations like Lexus, Continental Airlines, Progress Energy, and many more that have driven customer satisfaction levels to enviable heights. After nearly forty years in the business, I guess I'll never understand how competitors of these companies have missed the very clear message: listening to the voice of the customer is a winning strategy.

Despite the often disheartening state of customer satisfaction, I remain steadfastly optimistic. I've always believed in the voice of the customer. I'll admit that getting the rest of the world, including many of my own clients, to believe in it as well has been a long, sometimes difficult process. While today the name J.D. Power and Associates has become synonymous with the quest for customer satisfaction, it hasn't always been easy to find believers in what I was preaching.

In January 1980, for example, I was invited to give a talk to the top forty or fifty managers of the Pontiac division of General Motors. The meeting was offsite at a hotel in Northfield, Michigan. It started on Friday afternoon with an early cocktail hour that lasted three hours, followed by dinner. So by the time I got up to talk, it was 10 P.M. and my audience was well-oiled and not particularly in the mood for my message.

I spoke about the Japanese automakers and their quest for quality. I pointed out that the Japanese had been listening to their customers and understood viscerally what satisfied a growing number of buyers. They had concentrated on quality, reliability, and improved gas mileage, all at a low cost. I warned my audience that the domestic carmakers needed to start paying attention or the consequences would be swift and dire. In the last chart of my presentation, I forecast that General Motors, if it were to keep going in its current direction, would find its market share, which was around 48 percent at the time, dwindling to 33 percent by the end of the decade.

Up jumped the general sales manager of Pontiac, shouting at me that what I was saying was a bunch of you know what. A public relations manager added, "We don't have to listen to this." My sense at the time was that their mind-set was representative of the company's, and whether or not the cocktail hour had anything to do with their outburst, it was clear that the General Motors of the 1980s was not seriously interested in the voice of the customer.

To his credit, Bill Hogland, Pontiac's general manager, jumped on the stage and told his colleagues to sit down and be quiet. "What Dave Power is telling us is that we need to change things around here and you should listen to what he says," Hogland admonished.

Bill Hogland was ultimately promoted to group vice president in charge of the Buick-Oldsmobile-Cadillac division, and he invited me back to speak again in 1989. Despite efforts by Bill and others at the company, GM had not shown significant improvement over the decade. When I got up on stage that morning and told the group I believed things were going to get worse, members of the audience began objecting to my findings just as they had a decade before.

Once again Hogland stepped in on my behalf, although this time he was armed with a different message. "Listen," he told his managers, "almost ten years ago Dave Power came in here and told us that GM's market share was going to be down to 33 percent by the end of the decade, and we did everything but throw him out on his ear. Well, it turns out he missed his mark. We actually dropped to 33 percent in 1988, and if we don't do something about it now our share is only going to go lower."

Though I got no pleasure from being the bearer of bad news, I was confident that our surveys had uncovered a deep vein of dissatisfaction among GM customers. As the saying goes, the numbers don't lie. GM's market share as of this writing is under 30 percent. What was remarkable to me was that the world's biggest corporation didn't get it despite the harsh reality that confronted them.

General Motors was hardly alone. From the day I started J.D. Power and Associates with my wife, Julie, at our kitchen table in our Calabasas, California, home in 1968, I had the idea that companies could only improve themselves if they listened to their customers. This was not a new idea, but it was certainly not a credible one in those days.

In fact, when I got out of graduate school in the 1950s, market research was an embryonic field viewed with cynicism and even scorn. I worked for a short time with McCann Erickson, the ad agency for Buick and GMC trucks, and a lot of the research we did was handed over to the client's internal research department. They would then proceed to torture the data until it confessed, the goal being to shape the results into the conclusion they wanted to hear.

Certainly in Detroit, the heroes were the engineers and designers. In their minds, the equation was simple: "If we build it, they will come." And it often worked out that way. When the occasional flop occurred, it was easy to blame it on market research, as Ford did with the notorious Edsel.

Fed up with the car industry, I became director of corporate planning for McCulloch Corporation, a company driven by a hands-on engineer who surrounded himself with other engineers. When I first encountered the company, it was forecasting the sales of chainsaws by looking at the lumber industry and counting the number of trees. My first task was to get them to focus: trees don't buy chainsaws, people do. I spent a year there trying to transform the culture into a market-driven rather than engineering-driven one. It was an exercise in frustration and I started to realize that I could do this better on my own.

It occurred to me that, despite the obstacles, a person could make a good living by listening to the voice of the customer. Offered deep and comprehensive insight into what customers thought and felt about their products, companies would be willing to pay to get such data. Even with three young children and another on the way, Julie and I decided to mortgage our house and take the plunge. I got lucky because one of my first clients was Toyota, then a nearly anonymous Japanese automaker just trying to break into the U.S. market. Back then, in the sixties, the American executives Toyota had hired at its Torrance, California, facility refused to see me. So I sneaked around to the back and found Toyota's embryonic forklift operation, and a Japanese manager there gave me my first job for $600.

I came back to the manager in a few days with a report on the forklift market and a request: introduce me to the Japanese executive on the automotive side. Sure enough, he introduced me to the vice president and general manager of Toyota, who gave me his card. It was Tatsuro Toyoda, a member of the founding family and soon to become my biggest supporter within the organization. When he asked me where I kept my files, I thought for a second—I had been in business for myself for only one month—and then pointed to my head. He laughed and said, "Okay, what can you do for us?" They invited me to Japan for a series of meetings at their headquarters, and my business was off and running. Tatsuro Toyoda went on to become CEO of the entire corporation, a position he held until 1995.

By connecting with a hungry, well-financed organization with designs on a new marketplace, I found myself at the altar of customer satisfaction. Toyota became my biggest client for several years and proved to me beyond any doubt that only if you build it *right* will they come.

Of course, building a business based on measuring customers' perceptions was daunting. Part of the problem lay in the definition of customer satisfaction. What exactly did it mean? Putting parameters around such an esoteric concept was like trying to define the air we breathe. Quality, for example, may well be in the eyes of the beholder.

In the days when J.D. Power and Associates focused almost exclusively on the automotive industry, we would measure customer satisfaction across the entire industry—Mercedes-Benz would be weighed against Subaru. And we were assessing a relative measure: what were the individual customer's expectations when they purchased a car and how did the reality of owning that vehicle meet with those expectations? Mercedes took umbrage at this and complained to us: "Subaru doesn't have as critical or discerning a customer as we do and that's why they can score as high as they do." To a degree, that was true. But more important, the car manufacturers needed to understand that it is they who create the expectations. Their brand attracts a certain type of buyer and they have a great deal of control over whom they sell their vehicles to. In other words, they set the expectations of their own customer base. What we are doing is simply measuring how well they meet those expectations.

Like Peugeot in the example I mentioned earlier, most of the domestic car manufacturers suffered from a similar myopia and they too refused to adapt what customers were demanding. They set their agendas internally and the customer was supposed to be lured to the light. To these engineers and designers in their ivory towers, the consumer was simply not qualified to tell them what was wrong. I was struck by their ability to find excuses. Whether it was poor gas mileage or a bad radio, there was always an excuse. "Well, they just aren't using it right!" they'd say. It was always the consumer's fault.

Back in 1990, J.D. Power and Associates conducted a survey that didn't get much media attention but whose results I found fascinating. We surveyed 5,000 adults, ages 18 and over, and asked them about their satisfaction with 120 categories of products and services, from local and state government to the fire department, supermarkets, department stores, and even public libraries. We asked whether they were getting better overall product value and general service today versus five or ten years ago, or was it the same or getting worse? The majority said their satisfaction levels were getting worse and that their expectations were not being met.

Then we asked them to rate the industry in which they worked, and fully two-thirds thought their industry was doing a good job satisfying the customer. When we asked about the specific company they worked for, the positive response jumped to 75 percent. Finally, when we asked about their own personal contribution to customer satisfaction, nearly 100 percent said they were providing good customer service.

When we analyzed this data further, we could only conclude that these two factions were on a collision course, that expectations were growing faster than our ability to meet them. This startling disconnect between people's perceptions about the magnitude of the problem and their own role in creating the satisfaction chasm set off great concern about the future. What kind of world were we heading into if everyone believed that customer satisfaction was in the toilet but no one was willing to take responsibility for the problem?

The collision we worried about has certainly come to pass over the past fifteen years. The advent of personal computers and the Internet has ushered in the age of the enlightened consumer. We now have more information at our fingertips than we ever dreamed possible and that information has made us more demanding and raised expectations for satisfaction to heretofore unheard-of levels. At the same time, the ability of a whole raft of industries, of products and services, to meet our needs and demands has not kept pace. Has anyone gone through an entire day without complaining or hearing a complaint about some irritating encounter, faulty product, or unmet expectation?

Companies constantly crow, in their advertising and marketing, about being number one in customer satisfaction, but in most cases, they are just paying lip service to the concept. Since part of our mission at J.D. Power is measuring customer satisfaction, we have a pretty good idea who is talking the talk and who is walking the walk.

Technology has spawned a change in the dynamics of customer relationships, and many successful companies, such as Dell, USAA, and others, use technology to help them understand exactly what their customers want. Look no farther than your neighborhood Wal-Mart. Today, Wal-Mart is the world's biggest company—something no one could have imagined in 1990. Despite its size, Wal-Mart often knows more about its customers than the small, family-owned retailers it frequently displaces, and it turns this information into profits by delivering what customers want when they want it.

Peel back the layers of the onion and you will see that it's not just about price—that's just a smoke screen thrown up by competitors. The real key to long-term success is customer satisfaction. Satisfy the needs of your customers and you can charge a price premium. Do a poor job with customer satisfaction and be prepared to have a fire sale. It's that simple.

Unfortunately, a wide array of industries, from the airlines to cable companies to health-care providers to retailers to technology providers to automobile manufacturers, have generally dropped the ball when it comes to satisfying their customers' needs. Sometimes the world in general is so aggravating for consumers that it brings to mind a quote from *Dilbert,* the Scott Adams cartoon: "There are two essential rules to management. One, the customer is always right; and two, they must be punished for their arrogance."

I don't know about you, but as a consumer, I often feel as if I'm being punished—which is why we believe so deeply in getting our clients to not only focus on customer satisfaction but to make it part of the cultural imperative of their organizations.

Much has changed over the decades since we began this journey. We moved from working on a proprietary basis for companies like Toyota to surveying the entire industry and selling our data to anyone interested. By offering objective, quantitative data for the entire industry, our credibility grew. At the same time, we watched closely as the Japanese and European influence increased through the 1980s and set the bar far higher for all automakers when it came to quality and reliability. When the media began to take notice of our work, we realized that we could have a profound effect on a company's reputation and fortunes.

We tried to find new ways to measure and analyze our data, so we measured satisfaction by the age of the customer. We found that the younger the buyer, the lower the satisfaction score. A deeper look revealed that it wasn't an age difference as much as a generation difference. Younger people, say those under forty, had not had the experience that an older generation had had with cars. Cars used to break down a lot. People stranded on the side of the highway was a common sight. Better quality and performance and far higher reliability changed all that, and while older customers felt gratitude,

younger buyers who had not lived through that period felt an enti-
tlement.

Young buyers expect more, and as they get older, their expectations are likely to get higher. As a result, we believe the quality and
customer satisfaction issues are going to get tougher. You give a customer more and they want even more in return. One of the profound lessons I've learned is that customer satisfaction is a moving
target. You never can declare victory.

Also, over time our firm has entered many new industries, such
as home building, hospitality, technology, energy, health care, and
even sports franchises—all having the goal of identifying and hearing that voice of the customer. A J.D. Power and Associates award
for customer satisfaction is now a badge of honor for those who seek
bragging rights for great quality and service.

After nearly four decades of carefully measuring customer satisfaction levels, we have amassed enormous institutional knowledge
about what works and what doesn't. We now consult with and train
clients in methods to improve their customer satisfaction levels. In
so doing, we realize we have a valuable message to share, and this
book is the culmination of our desire to share the insights and the
unconventional wisdom we have gathered over the years.

As my friend and mentor Alvin Toffler wrote in *Powershift,* the
Information Age has shifted power bases in profound ways. The
consumer is no longer the passive recipient of goods but has been
transformed by the Internet and the availability of knowledge into a
power broker. Armed with knowledge and data gleaned from countless sources that were once unavailable, buyers in auto dealerships,
patients in hospitals, and travelers in hotels are now unwilling to
compromise. They have high expectations and the data to back
them up. The customer's voice is louder and clearer than ever and attention must be paid.

It would be nice to believe that companies could be motivated to
embrace these ideas simply because it is the right thing to do. But we

understand the verities of business and the need to satisfy key stake-holders. As you read this book, you will learn from many fascinating case studies and gain the deep insight of our staff. The theme that forms the book's foundation is a simple one: satisfied customers translate into profitable businesses. It is a tenet that is as old as busi-ness itself but seemingly harder and harder to grasp. I hope this book offers you a new way to confront and conquer an old problem.

And to help you evaluate whether your company's culture and infrastructure is set up to maximize customer satisfaction, I invite you to take a free online assessment. Just log onto www.jdpower.com/VOC/test to take an assessment covering the key areas we focus on in the book. You may want to take the assessment now as a quick reality check before you finish, because when it comes to customer satisfaction, what you don't know can hurt you.

J.D. Power III

1

SHOW ME THE MONEY

You would have to search long and hard to find a company that openly declares that customer satisfaction doesn't matter. Just ask any CEO, and we're pretty confident you'll get back a response that sounds something like, "Making sure our customers are satisfied is our highest priority." So why does it seem like being a consumer is such a challenge today? Long lines, broken promises, automated voice trees, and customer service employees who act like their job is anything *but* service. Do senior executives only talk the talk because they are truly skeptics at heart? Or is there an inherent disbelief in the connection between high customer-satisfaction scores and a stronger bottom line?

Over our nearly forty years in this business, we've come to the following important conclusions:

- Despite their rhetoric, most organizations have not made a significant and sustained commitment to customer satisfaction, and

- This lack of attention to customer satisfaction costs companies money because there is *an intractable connection between high levels of customer satisfaction and increased shareholder value.*

Anecdotal evidence abounds to support the theory that high customer satisfaction is important, but we believe that most chief executives need more than a good story to prod them into action. When it comes to spending on intangibles like customer satisfaction, CEOs inevitably return to that memorable line from the film *Jerry Maguire:* "Show me the money!"

And although most executives will agree that it's better to have happy, as opposed to unhappy, customers, they simply do not see the financial benefit in going the extra mile to do everything possible to ensure that theirs are the most satisfied customers in the industry. The reason for this is simple. Most people believe the payoff for high customer satisfaction—if there is a payoff at all—is somewhere far down the road, off in an uncertain future. And, as we've seen all too often, businesses tend to think in terms of the *here and now* and not the *when and if.*

THE BOTTOM LINE

Without a quantifiable link to profits, the push for customer satisfaction is based on nothing more than the moralistic view that "it's nice to be nice." And make no mistake about it: the "nice to be nice" argument just doesn't cut it anymore. Your company is in business to make money, not friends. So, one of the first things we do when we engage a new client is try to understand how customer satisfaction affects their particular business. For most companies, this link is manifested in each of the following:

- **Loyalty**—satisfied customers are significantly more likely to come back to do business with you in the future.

- **Word of Mouth**—satisfied customers not only solicit others to do business with you, but their opinions carry more weight than all your company's advertising combined.
- **Price Premiums**—consumers will pay a hefty premium to do business with companies that have a reputation for high quality and great customer service.
- **Reduced Operating Costs**—high-satisfaction companies have lower warranty expenses and spend less on service recovery in general.
- **Customer Close Rates**—companies that garner high customer satisfaction during the sales experience make a sale to a higher percentage of shoppers.

But even these measures are meaningless in and of themselves. Each is nothing more than an artificial metric companies use to gauge performance. The only true measurement that counts, the one that makes CEOs sit up and take notice, is the one found at the bottom of the corporate financial statement. For unless customer satisfaction pays off in the form of increased profits, it is nothing more than a buzzword destined to be cast out among a long list of business theories that came before it. So, we will postpone the more detailed analysis of *how* customer satisfaction affects business outcomes until the next chapter, and skip right to the bottom line—the literal bottom line, that is: shareholder value.

We recently looked back at all of the customer satisfaction studies we conducted in 2004, and then revisited studies conducted for the same companies five years earlier in 1999. We began with a simple hypothesis: if a company improved its customer satisfaction index (CSI) during that five-year period, that company should have seen improvements in metrics such as loyalty and word of mouth, which should have a corresponding positive impact on the bottom line. This, of course, should in turn have a positive impact on shareholder value.

We were realistic in our expectations. After all, there are dozens of variables besides customer satisfaction that impact shareholder value. But everything we learned over the years told us that customer satisfaction was sufficiently important that we would find at least a visible link between improved satisfaction and shareholder value.

What we discovered surpassed our most optimistic expectations. The relationship between satisfaction and shareholder value wasn't just visible; it was paramount! We divided each company into one of three groups: (1) companies whose customer satisfaction rank within their industry remained constant, (2) those whose rank improved, and (3) those whose satisfaction ranking dropped relative to their industry competitors.* The companies that improved customer satisfaction increased their shareholder value by more than 50 percent! And those whose rank declined actually lost 28 percent of their value over the previous five years.† (See chart on page 5.)

A similar analysis of the automotive industry, which is our legacy playing field, showed an even more impressive relationship between customer satisfaction and the success or failure of individual automotive brands. We surveyed 50,000 people who had owned their current vehicle for three years and asked one simple question: "How satisfied are you with your overall ownership experience?" By "overall" experience, we meant all the ways they experienced their vehicle (dealer service, product quality, performance, etc.). We tabulated the results and once again placed each brand into one of three groups—

*To qualify as "improving" or "declining" in customer satisfaction rank, a company needed to change its ranking position by at least 10 percent. For example, in an industry in which thirty companies were ranked, a company's ranking needed to improve more than three places before it was counted as improving customer satisfaction relative to its competitors.

†The study included twenty-nine separate companies that were both publicly traded and measured using comparable customer satisfaction studies in both 1999 and 2004. The improvement (or decline) of a company was based on its change in rank among its competitors on the satisfaction ranking index. Companies were excluded from the analysis where the attribute upon which satisfaction was measured encompassed only a small part of that company's business. Home builder companies were also excluded from the evaluation due to the overheated nature of the industry during the testing period.

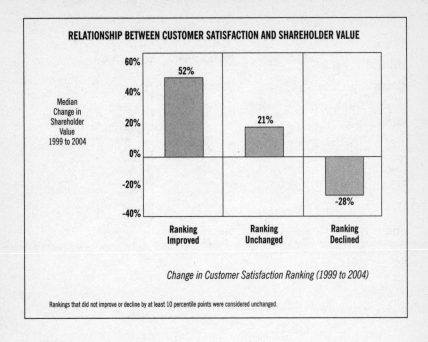

RELATIONSHIP BETWEEN CUSTOMER SATISFACTION AND SHAREHOLDER VALUE

Median Change in Shareholder Value 1999 to 2004

- Ranking Improved: 52%
- Ranking Unchanged: 21%
- Ranking Declined: -28%

Change in Customer Satisfaction Ranking (1999 to 2004)

Rankings that did not improve or decline by at least 10 percentile points were considered unchanged.

low, medium, and high owner satisfaction—to see if the higher-satisfaction companies had grown sales at a faster rate. Once again, the magnitude of the relationship between sales and satisfaction surprised even us. Between 1998 and 2003, sales of the high-satisfaction group *increased by more than 40 percent,* while the low-satisfaction group actually lost sales.*

DOES THE WORLD NEED ANOTHER BOOK ABOUT CUSTOMER SATISFACTION?

No matter where we look, from home building to health care to hotels, the same relationships between customer satisfaction and profitability ring true. This leads to the inevitable question: if the link

---

*The change in sales for each group is defined as the median change in sales of each individual brand within that satisfaction grouping. This prevented any one high-volume brand (e.g., Ford, Toyota) from having a disproportionate impact on the group's average.

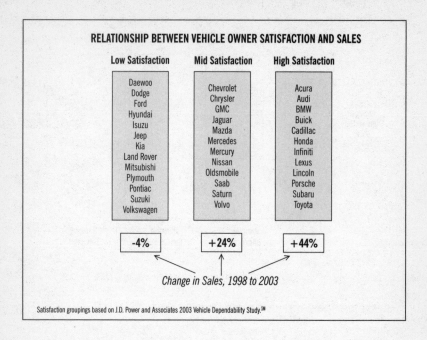

RELATIONSHIP BETWEEN VEHICLE OWNER SATISFACTION AND SALES

Low Satisfaction	Mid Satisfaction	High Satisfaction
Daewoo	Chevrolet	Acura
Dodge	Chrysler	Audi
Ford	GMC	BMW
Hyundai	Jaguar	Buick
Isuzu	Mazda	Cadillac
Jeep	Mercedes	Honda
Kia	Mercury	Infiniti
Land Rover	Nissan	Lexus
Mitsubishi	Oldsmobile	Lincoln
Plymouth	Saab	Porsche
Pontiac	Saturn	Subaru
Suzuki	Volvo	Toyota
Volkswagen		
-4%	**+24%**	**+44%**

Change in Sales, 1998 to 2003

Satisfaction groupings based on J.D. Power and Associates 2003 Vehicle Dependability Study.℠

between satisfaction and profitability is so clear, why do so many companies act as if they are indifferent to their customers' needs? The answer lies in the unfortunate confluence of three critical factors.

The first is awareness. Customer satisfaction problems are insidious. They grow silently within an organization like a cancer, strangling the foundation upon which a brand is built. A company may feel it's firing on all cylinders, moving forward, making sales and profits, and not realize it has a customer satisfaction problem until it's too late. By the time executives recognize the problem, the damage is already done, and a reputation for poor customer service has become part of the fabric of the brand.

The second factor is the length of time it takes to reverse a customer satisfaction problem. Changing widely held perceptions and entrenched consumer attitudes may take years and untold amounts of money. We've watched time and again as companies, upon learning of a serious problem, rush in with a crash program to improve customer satisfaction, only to return to business as usual when the program almost inevitably fails to deliver a payoff at the end of the first fiscal year.

The third factor is the problem we alluded to earlier: too few companies make the effort to truly understand how customer satisfaction impacts their bottom line. Whereas labor costs, accounts receivable, and other line items are conspicuously spelled out across income statements and balance sheets, the benefit of customer satisfaction remains hidden from view.

It is because of this dilemma that J.D. Power and Associates decided to write this book. From day one we wanted to produce a book that executives of companies large or small could use to help them understand not only the *strategic implications* of how customer satisfaction impacts their business, but also the *tactical action plans* they can begin using immediately—a book that would apply equally to large-products manufacturers and small service organizations alike. To do this we knew we needed to do much more than just share our stockpile of customer data. Companies today are inundated with information. What they need is the means by which to turn information into action—specifically, a road map to developing policies and processes that will maximize profits. That, above all else, is our goal.

Therefore, throughout this book we attempt to provide a mixture of what we call the *art* and *science* of customer satisfaction. The science is the easy part because it is data-driven. This includes determining the statistical drivers of satisfaction and linking those drivers to business outcomes: if ABC Company improves satisfaction by X% sales will increase by Y%.

The art of customer satisfaction is less easily defined and focuses on how companies use customer satisfaction information data to their benefit. To get at this "how," we turned back to our research to identify companies that are true leaders in customer satisfaction; companies that quantifiably demonstrate the ability to achieve high customer satisfaction and use it to their advantage; companies that don't just talk the talk, but walk the walk each and every day.

Some of these companies, such as Lexus, DirecTV, and JetBlue, had the advantage of starting with a clean sheet of paper that allowed them to focus on their customers from the beginning. Others, such as Hyundai, Continental Airlines, and Westin Hotels, are turn-around stories in which a company lost its way but found redemption and financial success by reconnecting to the voice of their customer. The key is that we chose each of these companies because they are living proof that the smoothest road to profitability is paved with the legacy of a loyal and committed customer base.

Because great ideas are often born from modest beginnings, we also identified small businesses that have relied on customer satisfaction to dominate their respective markets. We studied Mike Diamond, who discovered that the key to a successful plumbing business isn't just fixing a leak but also providing a professional appearance that includes crisp white shirts and a money-back guarantee if the technician doesn't smell good.

J.D. Power and Associates interviewed countless people at these high-satisfaction companies to learn how they listened to the voice of their customers and, more important, how they turned what they heard into gold. Those interviewed included CEOs, mid-level managers, and even the individual customer-facing employees who fight the battle every day on the front lines. During the course of these interviews we discovered to our own satisfaction that these companies tend to share many key philosophies and processes that impact the way they do business with their customers.

Whether it's a Fortune 100 manufacturer or a local service provider, each of these companies carries a similar outlook on how it approaches business; more important, as a group they approach business differently than the satisfaction also-rans that dot our landscape. By combining this learning with our already existing pool of data, we can identify and share the key basic truths to which every company must adhere if it is to flourish in today's competitive market. These truths, which are covered in detail in the following chapters, include:

- Drawing the financial link between satisfaction and profits
- Understanding the difference between satisfaction and advocacy
- Identifying a company's unique customer touchpoints
- Recognizing the role of customer expectations in determining satisfaction
- Heeding the dangers of overpromising
- Building a culture of customer satisfaction from the top down
- Understanding the role of management versus the role of frontline employees in driving customer satisfaction
- Recognizing the importance of hiring the right people
- Empowering frontline employees to do the right thing
- Using problem resolution as an opportunity to drive advocacy
- Building a community among customers
- Using the Internet to drive customer satisfaction
- Focusing on real customer satisfaction and not just customer satisfaction scores
- Developing an infrastructure built around the voice of the customer

Before a company can use customer satisfaction as a tool to drive profitability, it must first understand what customer satisfaction is and isn't. Customer satisfaction is *not* a goal in itself. A company can not pay down its line of credit or dazzle Wall Street with high satisfaction scores alone. By itself, customer satisfaction is meaningless. It is the by-product that counts, and that by-product is generated by using customer satisfaction (how a customer feels about doing business with a company) as a bridge between what that company does (processes, policies, etc.) and the buying behavior of consumers.

PROCESS	SATISFACTION	BEHAVIOR
What Your Company Did	How Your Customers Felt	What Your Customers Did as a Result

As we will point out many times throughout this book, behavior is key, not feelings. If you say you can show us that the best way to get people out of their chairs and down to your store is to conduct business in a way that goes against their desires, we'll tell you to go for it. Based on our experience, however, this is rarely the case. A company may be able to drive growth over the short term by strong-arming customers or offering poor product quality, but even the lowest-cost providers will soon find that customer *dissatisfaction* catches up with them in the end.

YOU CAN LEAD A HORSE TO WATER

We can provide a company with state-of-the-art measurement tools, a proven road map for success, and even set up shop right on the factory floor, but it won't amount to a hill of beans unless a company *wants* to improve. Here are two more simple truths:

- No organization will improve customer satisfaction unless it truly *wants* to.
- No company will want to make the commitment to improve until it sees the link between customer satisfaction and the bottom line.

Unfortunately, not every company sees this link. To see how this plays out in the real world, we turn your attention to the tripartite relationship between the manufacturers that build cars, the dealers that sell them, and American consumers who dutifully purchase 16 million new vehicles every year.

Despite all the changes and refinements made to automobiles each year, the process of buying a car really hasn't changed much over the past fifty years. Car dealerships remain as the last bastion of horse trading—a place where consumers go to match wits with professional salespeople in a high-stakes game that can mean the difference between paying $3,000 or $4,000 more or less than the last customer who bought the same identical car an hour before. No wonder the thought of haggling over price sends shivers down the spine of most consumers!

Hollywood stereotypes of fast-talking car salesmen dressed in plaid pants and white penny loafers would have us believe that today's automobile dealership is nothing more than a den of thieves. In fact, this stereotype couldn't be further from the truth. In cities and towns across America, the local car dealer is typically one of the pillars of the community, the place that every local Little League turns to first for sponsorship, the outlet where Girl Scouts know they will always find a willing buyer for their cookies.

But while the vast majority of car dealers are honest, they are also in business to make money. And for reasons unique to the car business—specifically, the fact that prices are individually negotiated—there is a very real disconnect between the way dealers go about selling cars and the way that we as consumers *want* to buy them.

Customers ask us every day, "Why won't car dealers just give us a straight answer when we ask 'how much?' Why do they always have to play games?" Instead of giving customers a bottom-line price, America's 200,000 automobile salespeople are conditioned like Pavlov's dog to respond with a question of their own: "I don't know what we can sell it for; *why don't you make me an offer*, and I'll go ask my manager."

Dealers don't put up a smokescreen because they want to frustrate customers. Dealers engage in what some customers see as a distasteful game because they believe in their heart that this is the most effective way to sell a car, even though they realize this isn't the way customers want to buy a car.

From their first day on the job, automobile salespeople are indoctrinated with the notion that customers never really "go home to think about it." Any customer who walks out of the showroom without buying a car is heading to the dealer down the street or across town. Their bosses preach, "Telling a customer your best price is tantamount to giving them a ticket to shop—a starting point for negotiating with the next dealer." In other words, trying to sell a car the way customers want is a one-way ticket to bankruptcy.

We recently attended one manufacturer's annual dealer meeting. The vice president of sales and marketing stood before his dealer council and preached the need to improve their Sales Satisfaction Index (SSI)—the scorecard for how satisfied new-car buyers are with their purchase experience. One of the most successful dealers in the room stood up and asked, "Why?" He went on to say, "If I sold cars the way customers *say* they want to buy them, I'd never sell any!"

The message was clear: the car buying experience is slow to change because the dealers who sell the cars do not see a link between satisfaction and profits. If anything, the dealers at the meeting believed there was an inverse relationship—the dealers who push the hardest will sell the most. This presented us with one of our biggest challenges: convincing America's automobile dealerships that changing their philosophy was not only good for the customer, it was good for their bank account as well.

We first looked to see if there was a correlation between the *size* of a dealership and its sales satisfaction. That theory was quickly deflated. Not only was there very little correlation, some of the largest dealerships in the country received relatively low scores for customer satisfaction. We had to be missing something. Our years of researching customer behavior told us that the most effective sales model could not be one that forced customers to go through a process they perceived as rigid and inflexible. To find the answer, we began by asking *how* a dealer increased sales.

A dealer grows sales by either (1) attracting more people into the showroom, or (2) closing a sale with a higher percentage of shoppers. The number of people a dealership attracts depends largely on its location and how much it spends on advertising—a factor independent of customer satisfaction. This solved part of the problem because we found that those dealers that generated huge volume—despite low satisfaction—tended to spend inordinate sums on advertising to fill the top of the purchase funnel. Now all we needed to do was show that a dealer's close rate was linked to satisfaction.

To find the link between satisfaction and close rates we turned to Nissan, a brand that has always manufactured a quality product, but which, like many Japanese manufacturers, tended to score poorly in customer satisfaction with the dealership sales process. Believe it or

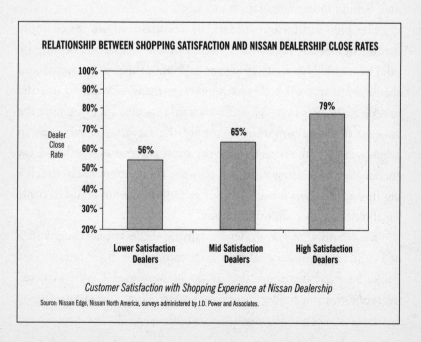

RELATIONSHIP BETWEEN SHOPPING SATISFACTION AND NISSAN DEALERSHIP CLOSE RATES

Dealer Close Rate

- Lower Satisfaction Dealers: 56%
- Mid Satisfaction Dealers: 65%
- High Satisfaction Dealers: 79%

Customer Satisfaction with Shopping Experience at Nissan Dealership

Source: Nissan Edge, Nissan North America, surveys administered by J.D. Power and Associates.

not, measuring close rates was a new concept for dealers, who never focused their attention on the ones who got away, other than the fact that they didn't buy a car. Consequently, few dealers knew why prospective buyers left, whether they were satisfied, or even what percentage of shoppers actually bought a car.

As the chart on page 13 shows, the results of our survey couldn't have been clearer. The Nissan dealers that did the best job satisfying customers ended up making a sale to a higher percentage of people who walked through the door.

We then began looking closely at the high-satisfaction dealers who possess the magical ability to make a sale to almost everyone who walks through the door while still finding a way to put a smile on the faces of even those who walk out. Sure enough, the biggest difference between these dealers and the low satisfaction dealers at the left of the chart is that the customers of the low satisfaction dealers were more likely to say they left because they didn't like the way they were treated; most often mentioned were the sales pressure and rigidity of the negotiation process.

The high-satisfaction dealers, by comparison, are much more flexible in meeting the needs of each individual customer during the sales process: "Not ready to sign today? No problem. Go home and think about it; we'll be here when you're ready." "Want to buy the car for $300 over invoice? Just wait a minute and I'll bring over the book that shows how much we paid the factory for every car in stock." They may not always be the most successful at selling a car on the customer's first visit, but they are much more likely to sell a car in the end. This is because their customers are not afraid to come back in when they are ready to buy.

We found that the underperforming dealers were caught in a self-fulfilling prophecy. When a customer left, they rarely came back. So what did those dealers do in response? They instructed everyone to push harder for the sale *today.* They told salespeople to play it even tighter to the vest and be even more cautious about giving out pricing information. In other words, they made customers even more wary of doing business, which only served to lower close rates even further.

It all looked good on paper, but would survey results be enough to convince low-performing dealers that it could work in the real world? We knew that before we could convince dealers to make fundamental changes in their sales processes we would need to show them concrete examples of instances where improving satisfaction really did increase sales. And for this we turned to Honda, a company for which we had measured sales satisfaction with dealerships for many years. Once again our hypothesis was simple. If a dealership improved its sales satisfaction over time, it should see a corresponding increase in sales. Our hypothesis proved to be correct, and showed once and for all that even for car dealerships, the link be-

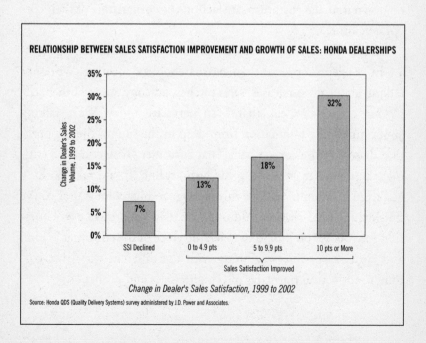

RELATIONSHIP BETWEEN SALES SATISFACTION IMPROVEMENT AND GROWTH OF SALES: HONDA DEALERSHIPS

Change in Dealer's Sales Volume, 1999 to 2002

- SSI Declined: 7%
- 0 to 4.9 pts: 13%
- 5 to 9.9 pts: 18%
- 10 pts or More: 32%

Sales Satisfaction Improved

Change in Dealer's Sales Satisfaction, 1999 to 2002

Source: Honda QDS (Quality Delivery Systems) survey administered by J.D. Power and Associates.

tween customer satisfaction and profits was paramount, in this case driven by higher close rates.

We finally had an effective weapon in the battle to improve the automotive sales process—information that showed that improving customer satisfaction actually improved the bottom line. And we've used this information to help both Honda and Nissan improve customer satisfaction, one dealer at a time. For dealers, seeing this link was critical because *wanting* to improve isn't just half the battle . . . it's closer to *90 percent* of the battle. Once a dealer—or any company—decides it truly *wants* to improve, it just isn't that hard to figure out *how* to improve.

Let's face it, we are all customers and we all yearn for the same thing in our many daily encounters: courtesy, efficiency, empathy, and, if we're lucky, a nice and genuine smile. The hard part for companies is instilling the desire to improve throughout the organization, obtaining the real and serious commitment from management on down to make customer satisfaction the cornerstone of their corporate culture.

And by cornerstone we're not talking about words scrolling across a CEO's teleprompter at the next shareholders' meeting. We're not talking about press releases, sales pitches, ad copy, or any other self-serving corporate-speak that is so pervasive today. We're talking about building a foundation from deep in the soul of the organization, based on the correct belief that customer satisfaction is a critical component to improving the bottom line. If you take nothing else from this book, we hope this message resonates long after you've finished the final chapter. Although we may not answer every question for you, we do intend to make the voice of the customer as loud and clear as possible, beginning with the different ways that customer satisfaction translates into higher sales and profits.

2

LOYALTY: THE COMMON DENOMINATOR FOR IMPROVING CUSTOMER SATISFACTION

We were recently on a Northwest Airlines flight that pulled away from the gate, taxied down the runway, and was just starting to rev its engines for takeoff when the pilot came on the intercom and said we needed to hold on the tarmac to let a thunderstorm pass. And hold we did. Five minutes turned into ten, and ten turned into twenty, all without further explanation from the cockpit. The passengers, already a little restless, became downright grouchy when the sun began to shine and other planes began taxiing around us to take off.

One passenger—we'll call him Fred—began pushing the issue a little further, spouting off to everyone around him that the pilot should either take off now or go back to the gate where he could wait in the bar. Fred threw in just enough obscenities to attract the attention of the flight attendants, who are increasingly cautious these days about unruly passengers.

"Never again," Fred bellowed, "will I ever fly Northwest. I've flown this same damn flight a dozen times this year, but never again. I'll make it a point to fly anyone other than Northwest the next time."

What is the meaning of this anecdote? The obvious answer is that all it takes is one bad moment to send a previously loyal customer scurrying to your competition. While this is correct, it is only correct to a point, because customer loyalty is one of the most complex and misunderstood aspects of consumer behavior. Consider what happened after Fred's outburst almost grounded our plane. Fred's wife intervened and took the wind out of his sails. "Fred, you say the same thing every time we take this flight. And every time you go online and see that Northwest has the cheapest ticket and you book it anyway."

So, the real point of this story is that while customer satisfaction is a critical component of loyalty, it is only one of many factors that determine if a customer will remain loyal or turn tail and run at the first opportunity. Our clients are frequently surprised at how easily someone like Fred will go back to the same brand despite his anger and dissatisfaction and a declared intention to never return.

Take a look at the following chart. Think of the dotted line as Fred, sitting on the airplane, makes statements about how likely he is to ever fly this same airline again. Although we had the common sense not to interrupt Fred to ask him to rate his current experience with Northwest, we're pretty sure that if we had, Fred would have fallen somewhere in the one to four range on a ten-point rating scale. And just like most people in this lowest range, Fred's *intention* to remain loyal to Northwest was just about nil. Our research shows that even those airline passengers who rate their current flight between five and seven are also rather unlikely to say they will fly the same airline again the next time around.

But do consumers follow through with their stated intentions? To answer this we turn to the solid line representing the percent of people who do in fact go on to fly the same airline on their next flight. Note that the slope of the *actual* loyalty line is not as steep as the *intended* loyalty line. This means that despite all the complaining, there is a reasonable chance you may open your doors one

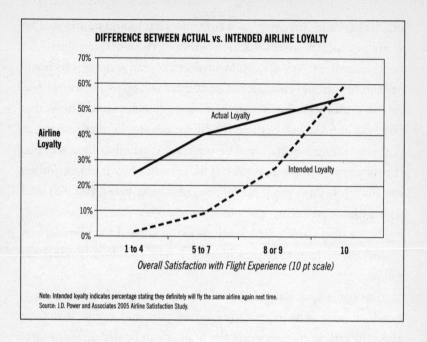

DIFFERENCE BETWEEN ACTUAL vs. INTENDED AIRLINE LOYALTY

Airline Loyalty

Actual Loyalty

Intended Loyalty

70%
60%
50%
40%
30%
20%
10%
0%

1 to 4   5 to 7   8 or 9   10

Overall Satisfaction with Flight Experience (10 pt scale)

Note: Intended loyalty indicates percentage stating they definitely will fly the same airline again next time.
Source: J.D. Power and Associates 2005 Airline Satisfaction Study.

morning and find Fred, wallet in hand, ready to do business with you again.

There are a couple of important lessons to be learned from the difference between intended versus actual loyalty. First, customer satisfaction does in fact impact the likelihood your customers will return, but customer satisfaction is only one of many factors that determine actual loyalty. Second, the impact of satisfaction on loyalty is different for every business. Therefore, you must first understand the interplay between these factors before you can attempt to diagnose just how important customer satisfaction is to your particular business.

A PRACTICAL EXAMPLE OF THE IMPACT OF CUSTOMER SATISFACTION ON LOYALTY

Although it's not our intention to make you relive your old business school lectures, sometimes there's nothing like a hypothetical example to illustrate a point. And to help bring back that old college feeling, let's pretend that yours is a company that manufactures that favorite product of economics professors everywhere: the widget.

Your goal is to sell 400,000 widgets next year, some of which will be sales to your old customers while others will be to an entirely new set of customers. Based on historical demand you know that 500,000 of your old customers will reenter the market looking to buy new widgets next year. The question is whether they will buy them from you or a competitor. If 80 percent of your old customers remain loyal, then you'll be able to reach next year's 400,000 sales goal without attracting a single new customer. Alas, today's widget buyer is a fickle breed, which means you will need to conquest new customers, perhaps to an unachievable level if your loyalty rate drops too low.

Since you have learned the value of listening to your customers, you look back at your customer survey data and realize that these 500,000 customers reentering the market can be divided into three groups based on their level of satisfaction. Group 1, with 150,000 customers, contains the most satisfied—the ones who are completely committed to you and wouldn't leave you under any circumstances. Group 2 has 250,000 customers who are relatively happy with their widget experience but are not emotionally attached to your company. To these customers, a widget is a widget, and it doesn't really matter that much where they buy them. The last group has 100,000 people who have experienced recent service glitches and are basically fed up with everything about you. These are the "Freds" of the world who will search out a competitor to fill their needs.

As you would expect, the *actual* loyalty rate is different for each of the three groups—70 percent for Group 1, 40 percent for Group 2, and 20 percent for Group 3. Simple multiplication shows that 225,000 (or only 45 percent) of your old customers will repurchase your brand of widget this year. Not a bad number, but this means that 275,000 (over half) of your customers will come back to the market, think about it, and *decide to go with a different widget manufacturer.* It also means that to reach your 400,000 customer sales goal, you need to find a way to conquest 175,000 new customers—not such an easy task given the recent global downturn in the demand for widgets. And since it costs considerably more to acquire a new customer than to keep an old one—four or five times more, by many estimates—finding 175,000 new customers will be an expensive proposition.

Since you don't like losing customers to the competition, you initiate a program to improve customer satisfaction and therefore your loyalty rate as a result. You implement a new software program intended to take care of some past service glitches. You make it a policy to accept borderline warranty claims which you previously refused. And you make several other changes that your customers say are needed to make them happy campers.

Now let's fast-forward one year. Your surveys tell you that customer satisfaction has improved, and that once again 500,000 previous customers will be back in the market. The only thing that is different is that this batch of customers is more satisfied than the last group. Instead of 20 percent of your customers falling into the lowest satisfaction bucket, you've reduced the number of disgruntled to 5 percent (or 25,000). Your satisfaction initiatives also increased the size of the fully committed group to 250,000 (up from 150,000 the previous year).

Plug the numbers into the calculator and your loyalty rate improves to 54 percent, which translates into 270,000 sales to existing customers. More important, the increase in loyalty sales means that you need to acquire only 130,000 *new* customers to reach your sales goal—25 percent fewer than the previous year—all because you improved your customer satisfaction. This also translates into significant savings for sales and marketing.

WHEN IT COMES TO LOYALTY, NOT EVERY COMPANY IS CREATED EQUAL

Most people agree that one place to be avoided at all costs is a state's Department of Motor Vehicles. The DMV in most states is a place where renewing a driver's license turns into an obstacle course of long lines and surly employees who seem to delight in making customers miserable. Yet despite the abysmally low customer satisfaction levels of these state agencies, each of us dutifully returns like a salmon swimming upstream every time the expiration date on our license draws near, a fact that gives the DMV a virtual 100 percent loyalty rate.

Why don't we just go somewhere else? The answer, of course, is that there is *nowhere else to go.* The DMV, like other government agencies, is a monopoly, and that brings us to the first law of loyalty: the likelihood that a customer will remain loyal is directly linked to the number of competitors to which your existing customers may defect. The easier it is for your customers to switch to another brand, the more likely they are to do so if you fail to meet their expectations.

This principle isn't affected only by the number of available competitors. Many factors affect the link between satisfaction and loyalty. We refer to these factors as the "cost of switching," and they include:

- Number of competitors
- Frequency of purchase
- Availability of information about alternatives
- Cost of purchase
- Use of "loyalty programs"

The cost of switching is not so much an economic cost as it is the *effort* or *risk* associated with switching to a new or unknown brand. For example, the availability and proximity of competitors impact the effort required to switch. Was your experience at Jack in the Box just so-so? Don't worry, there is always a Taco Bell or McDonald's just around the corner the next time your stomach growls. But if your BMW dealer failed to fix that annoying rattle in your new 330i, you may be annoyed, but you'll probably give them a second chance if going to a different dealer means driving twenty miles out of your way.

Other costs relate to the *risk* of switching. It's risky to switch brands when you don't know anything about the alternatives—as they say, "It's better to dance with the devil you know than the one you don't." Consumers are more likely to stay with a brand, even one that has disappointed them in the past, if they have no way of knowing if the alternatives might be even worse.

This is one way the Internet impacts loyalty. The amount of consumer information now flowing around the planet via the Internet is nothing short of staggering and it is having a dramatic impact on consumer behavior. Now that we have immediate access to ratings of products ranging from toasters to toenail clippers, brand loyalty is on the decline in general. In fact, the Internet is having such an impact on customer behavior that we've dedicated a chapter to the subject later in this book.

The frequency of purchase is another risk related to the cost of switching. If you're going to have to live with a product for only a short time, go ahead, be a daredevil and try something new. What's the worst that can happen? You're stuck with it for a few weeks, at which time you can go back to your old brand. Not so with the purchase of a much longer-lasting product, such as a washing machine or television.

Of course, your inclination to be a daredevil and throw caution to the wind depends on how much that moment of spontaneity will cost you in terms of money—not just time. That's why the price of a product or service also impacts loyalty. For example, maybe you're the type of person who goes down to the vending machines each afternoon for a Snickers bar to get you through the rest of the day. But what if they should add a new bar, one that promises the taste of a caramel-peanut-marshmallow center? Should you buy the new bar or remain loyal to your old standby, the Snickers bar? The risk in shifting your loyalty is minimal because the cost is less than a dollar. If you don't like the new candy, you can just spit it out and buy a Snickers; it's not going to cause you to miss next month's rent payment.

The scenario is different if we are talking about an expensive purchase, such as a car. If you are a longtime Honda owner, you will stop and think twice before buying a new Mazda, even if you love its sporty lines and *zoom zoom* performance. What if after a few months you find yourself longing for your old Honda? It will cost you dearly to trade in your nearly new Mazda, which is precisely why people tend to be more loyal when it comes to expensive product categories.

The final cost of switching is related to companies' use of "loyalty programs." These programs, intended to foster loyalty to a single brand, have been highly successful for a long time. Airline miles, hotel points, and an entire host of similar rewards programs spawn a type of investment account that makes customers think twice before jumping brands. As innovative as these programs have been, however, they remain just one of many factors that determine your customers' cost of switching and therefore their propensity to remain loyal in the face of a less-than-satisfying experience.

To fully understand how important customer satisfaction is to loyalty, you must be clear on where your industry stands in terms of the cost of switching. If you operate a gas station or restaurant or manufacture ice cream, you had better pay close attention to customer satisfaction, because when you analyze the customers' cost of switching against the factors mentioned, it becomes clear that your customers can drop you in a heartbeat with very little effort or risk. However, if you are a public utility or automobile manufacturer, you will probably garner more loyalty than you actually deserve. This is

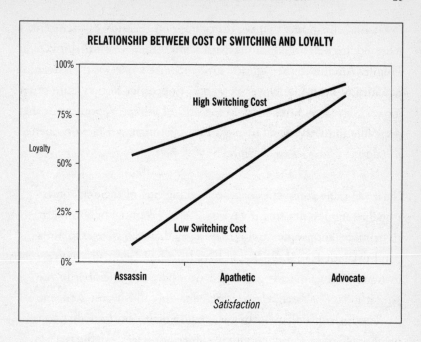

because the cost of switching to a competitor is high, which means your customers may cut you some slack—but only a little.

Even companies that enjoy monopoly status aren't completely immune from the dangers of poor customer service. Just ask your local cable television provider, who, in many parts of the country, receives DMV-level customer satisfaction ratings. For years cable companies had customers over a barrel. The problem was they knew it and acted accordingly. Calls for installation or service went unanswered, weeks passed before a customer could get a service appointment, and a "take it or leave it" attitude had customers literally screaming at their television sets in frustration. But what choice did consumers have? Most areas were served by only one provider, and not many Americans were ready to give up TV. Thus was born an ugly industry stereotype that did little to endear local providers to their customers.

It is at this point that we introduce you to Eddy Hartenstein, a talented engineer who, along with some other forward thinkers at Hughes Aircraft in the eighties, came up with what was then the radical idea of beaming television signals to people's homes from outer space. Hartenstein, who served as CEO of DirecTV, points out that the cable industry's total disregard for customer satisfaction opened the door for satellite television:

> If the cable companies had been taking care of their customers all along, I'm not sure if we would have taken the billion dollar gamble that people would throw away their cable boxes to put a dish on their roof. We might have launched eventually, but certainly not as quickly as we did. You have to remember in the early days of satellite television, not only did it cost someone hundreds of dollars to buy the equipment, [but] satellite cost more to operate each month in subscription fees. So, the fact we launched so quickly, and converted as many cable customers as we have, has a lot to do with the fact that cable companies began to believe they were immune from having to worry about customer satisfaction. That was a big mistake on their part, and one that I go to bed thanking them for every night.

What this illustrates is that even when the cost of switching is high, loyalty is still tied to customer satisfaction. Companies with near-monopoly status are beginning to realize this. Later in the book we discuss Progress Energy and the Salt River Project, two electric utilities that spend considerable effort on customer satisfaction despite the fact their customers currently have no other place to go. Even the California Department of Motor Vehicles has begun looking into the problem because it understands that the benefits of high customer satisfaction extend beyond loyalty, which in their case is guaranteed by their monopoly status.

YOU WOULDN'T HAPPEN TO KNOW A GOOD MECHANIC
YOU COULD RECOMMEND

One of the most commonly held beliefs in business is that the best form of advertising is word of mouth. And there's a reason for that: it's true. Whether it's your neighbor recommending a plumber, or simply telling you about a movie you just have to see, it's a proven fact that direct personal endorsements carry more weight than a traditional television or newspaper advertisement. For example, if someone places a specific brand in their consideration set, they are more likely to buy that brand if their initial consideration resulted from the recommendation of a friend than from any other source.

Just as the impact of satisfaction on loyalty varies by industry, word-of-mouth advertising impacts each industry differently. To determine if word of mouth is "mission critical" to your industry, you must answer the following three questions:

- Does the purchase involve a significant investment?
- Is there sufficient published information available from which consumers are able to make an informed decision on their own?
- How frequently are consumers in the market for that product or service?

Take auto mechanics as an example. As soon as you hear a strange sound emanating from under the hood of your car, you feel that sinking sensation in your stomach and your wallet. Not only might you be facing a potentially expensive repair, there just aren't many published sources of information to tell you which mechanics are good and which ones might be looking to take you to the cleaners. And since most of us can't change our own oil, let alone diagnose a sputtering engine, we go around frantically asking our friends and coworkers if they know of a good, trustworthy mechanic.

The frequency of the purchase cycle is important because not all recommendations come as a result of someone *asking* for advice. If a friend is speaking highly of a good mechanic and you know you have car problems, your ears will perk up and you will quickly put that information to good use. But when another friend lauds his new outdoor barbecue and you are not in the market for such a product, you will likely forget that conversation years later when you decide to buy your own grill. In that case, word of mouth will come into play only if you proactively go out and seek the recommendations of others.

We often hear clients say that people will go out of their way only to tell others about bad experiences, but that satisfied customers remain silent. We've even seen companies use this argument as an excuse for receiving poor satisfaction scores. "Only the angry ones took the time to fill out a survey, so the results don't reflect our true customer base."

The idea that dissatisfied customers are more likely to speak up has, like many commonly held beliefs, some basis in truth but is dangerously misleading when taken as a general principle. Although it is true that dissatisfied customers tend to be a little more vociferous, make no mistake about it—happy customers will also go out of their way to sing the praises of companies that delight them.

Consider our chart (page 29) that shows how many times a new-car buyer tells someone about their dealership experience based on their satisfaction using a one-to-ten rating scale. As you would expect, the number of positive recommendations goes up as satisfaction increases, and negative feedback increases when satisfaction goes down. Since potential customers place so much weight on personal recommendations, it's easy to see why high-satisfaction car dealerships grow their sales at a much faster rate. Remember that graph in chapter 1, the one that plotted each dealer's close rate against its customer satisfaction? Our studies find that the dealers with the highest satisfaction, on average, are much more likely to

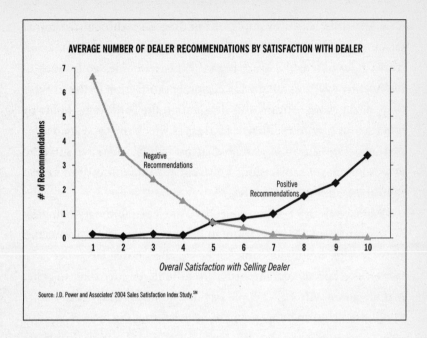

AVERAGE NUMBER OF DEALER RECOMMENDATIONS BY SATISFACTION WITH DEALER

# of Recommendations

Negative Recommendations

Positive Recommendations

Overall Satisfaction with Selling Dealer

Source: J.D. Power and Associates' 2004 Sales Satisfaction Index Study.℠

have a customer walk on the lot because a friend or relative told them it was the place to go to buy a car.

But what about the ones in the middle, whose customers rate their experience as just okay? These customers simply didn't have strong opinions one way or the other. We will talk more about this silent majority—whom we label the *apathetics*—in a later chapter. But for now, it's enough to say that unless you wow them one way or another, either for the good or for the bad, your customers will sit in the trough in the middle of this chart, forever silent about their visit to your place of business.

Loyalty and word-of-mouth advertising are two ways that high-customer-satisfaction companies grow sales and market share. But income statements do not live by unit volume alone. Your bottom line depends on both the number of units you sell and the price you charge for each sale. Once again, however, we find that customer satisfaction plays an important role.

Pulte Homes, which is one of the nation's largest home builders, provides an excellent example of building sales through customer satisfaction. If you haven't heard of Pulte, you may know the company under one of the other brand names its homes go by such as Del Webb or DiVosta. Pulte is a customer satisfaction leader in every sense of the word, earning this designation the hard way—home by home across fifty-four different markets in which they operate. Pulte's customer satisfaction is so high that no matter where we surveyed new-home buyer satisfaction, Pulte either came out on top or was right there among the leaders.

We have always been intrigued by Pulte's extraordinary emphasis on customer satisfaction. If you go back to the previous discussions about loyalty, you might come to the conclusion that customer satisfaction is relatively less important to a home builder than to other manufacturers. After all, people stay in a home for many years, so it's not like old customers are going to be reentering the market anytime soon. And even when they do, home selection is location driven. It's a long shot that Pulte will have a new development in the specific neighborhood a buyer wants to move into. Add to that the recent housing shortage, in which demand outstrips supply, and you would think that all a builder needs to do is avoid creating enemies: sure, it's always nice to have happy customers, but it's not worth the expense of going the extra mile to make them *extra* happy. At least that's what we thought until we began digging deeper into Pulte's numbers.

Pulte acknowledges that home builders cannot rely on repeat customers alone to grow sales. But this doesn't stop Pulte from trying to differentiate itself through customer service, because what Pulte counts on is payoff in word-of-mouth advertising. How big a payoff, you ask? In 1999, about the time that Pulte began organizing itself around customer needs, 20 percent of its sales were influenced by the positive recommendation of another customer. Today that number is 45 percent and continues to grow each year.

Steven Petruska, Pulte's COO, draws some of his inspiration from a classic shampoo commercial by Breck:

The message was simple; if you liked the shampoo you would tell two people, who in turn would tell two people, who would tell two more people, and so on. They really did a good job of driving home the point that if your customers are happy they will bring new customers to you.

I know that right now some of our competitors think we are paying a little too much attention to our customers. They're thinking that the market's hot, and people are going to buy everything you can build anyway. But the market isn't always going to stay this way. Just wait until the tables are turned and it's a buyer's market. Today nearly half our sales are influenced by word of mouth. When the market turns, our customer satisfaction advantage will play an even greater role in our success.

PRICE PREMIUMS

Some companies make the fatal error of believing that if they are an economy brand, or market their product(s) based on price, that customer satisfaction isn't important. We've heard all the arguments: "You get what you pay for. If you want great quality or service, don't be so cheap and buy a higher-end brand."

Hyundai provides a great example of this line of thinking. We'll talk more about Hyundai later in the book, but mention here only that middle management at Hyundai's South Korean headquarters allowed quality snafus to go unresolved out of the misguided notion that American consumers had no right to complain as long as they could purchase a fully loaded Hyundai Excel for less money than a stripped Honda Civic.

The only thing Hyundai managed to prove with this strategy was that there is a threshold of customer satisfaction that every company must meet regardless of how low it prices its products or services. Fail to meet that threshold and the company might as well close up shop. Once that threshold has been met, however, price and customer satisfaction become intertwined in a dance of offsetting forces, a yin and yang that ultimately determines just how many units will be sold.

Don't ever underestimate the intelligence of the American consumer, because he or she is far smarter than we often give credit for. Our research consistently shows that consumers have a good idea about which products are winners and which are dogs. Garner a reputation for providing great customer satisfaction and you can charge a price premium that goes straight to the bottom line. Saddle yourself with a reputation for marginal customer satisfaction and the only way to build market share will be through discounts and other incentives that will wreak havoc on your bottom line.

The key word here is reputation. It doesn't necessarily matter whether a reputation is deserved or not; when it comes to driving purchase behavior through customer satisfaction, perception is reality.

Just consider those venerable midsize sedans, the Chevrolet Malibu and the Toyota Camry. Both models target consumers seeking basic transportation, nothing fancy but always reliable. Both models offer roughly the same size, horsepower, gas mileage, and assortment of basic options. Given their similarity and functional nature, one would think the Malibu and Camry would have both become a commodity within the auto industry, a product to be chosen strictly on the basis of price. Put a $500 rebate on the Malibu and you would assume Toyota would need to react in kind to avoid losing share in a price-driven, commoditized marketplace. This assumption, of course, would be wrong.

The current *real* quality gap between the two models is actually quite small, according to our Initial Quality Study, but two decades of history give the Camry a significantly better *perceived* reputation in the eyes of consumers. To overcome the stigma of its prior sins, General Motors is forced to offer incentives such as zero percent financing and large cash rebates just to keep the Malibu plant running at full capacity. The net result is that customers end up paying about $2,000 less for a Malibu than a comparably equipped Camry.

Consumers aren't shy about spelling out their demand for discounts before they purchase (or even consider) a brand that isn't a customer satisfaction leader. We asked recent Camry and Malibu buyers why they chose their respective models.* More than a third of the Malibu buyers said they based their decision on price or "the deal," compared to less than a fourth of the Camry owners. When you consider that GM sells around a quarter million Malibus every year, that $2,000 price gap means the company loses about $500 million in revenue each year largely because its customer satisfaction does not rise to the level of Toyota's.

The link between price premiums and customer satisfaction certainly isn't limited to automobiles. Consumers across just about every industry have been conditioned to consider product or service reputation every time they contemplate one brand over another. To measure how customer satisfaction impacts hotel pricing, we monitored hotels that compete directly with one another by offering similar facilities and amenities. In almost every case, the hotel with the higher satisfaction score in our annual Guest Satisfaction Study was able to charge more money for a room than the lower-ranked hotel featuring the same level of amenities. In those rare cases where the lower-satisfaction hotel charges more, all we can say is *wait*. Customer satisfaction is a great equalizer, and within a year or two prices will adjust accordingly.

SHARE OF WALLET

In addition to paying more for brands that offer great customer satisfaction, consumers entrust those brands with a greater share of their

*Source: J.D. Power and Associates' 2004 Avoider Study.

wallet. While most of us have a favorite grocery store or restaurant, very few of us are so loyal that we patronize only one establishment exclusively. We generally like to spread our money around, not because we're defecting to another brand, but because we just want to try something different. Let's face it, no matter how much you love the ribs at Tony Roma's, sometimes only a greasy cheeseburger will do.

Share of wallet is most easily understood in an industry where customers simultaneously do business with multiple brands. Most of us have more than one bank account (savings, checking, etc.), and often spread these various accounts across multiple institutions. Look on the counter of your own bathroom and you will probably find health and beauty products from multiple brands. The more satisfied you become with any one brand, however, the more likely you are to begin handing over a greater share of your wallet to that brand.

Consider the relationship that investors have with their online brokers. We divided the major online investment brokerage firms into three groups based on their customer satisfaction scores in our annual study of investor satisfaction. Once we measured customer satisfaction with each broker, we determined what percentage of each investor's trades were placed with each company. Sure enough, the firms with the highest customer satisfaction scores garnered a higher share of their customers' wallets. And although most serious traders won't give 100 percent of their business to any one firm, over time they will shift more and more of their business to the high-satisfaction firms.

Another added bonus of high-satisfaction scores are ancillary sales. Did you just buy a new suit? Tell us how satisfied you were with the sales experience and we'll predict how likely you were to throw in a shirt and a few ties. If your most recent restaurant experience was distinguished by a grizzled waiter and an even grizzlier piece of meat, it's unlikely that you hung around long enough for dessert, let alone a second bottle of wine.

Some business models are predicated upon ancillary purchases.

Luxury hotels, for example, are far more than simply a place to lay your head at night. They are prepared to serve your every need from shopping to dining to recreation. Even at $300 per night for a room, a luxury hotel would go broke if its guests didn't spend money on ancillary services such as room service, health spas, minibars, and laundry service. The likelihood that a hotel guest will use the hotel for these extra services is directly linked to guest satisfaction. Screw up the check-in process, or put a guest in a room that still needs attention, and you can almost guarantee he or she will climb into a taxi to go offsite to dine rather than eat in the hotel restaurant. They will also be less likely to do things such as visit the gift shop or purchase an in-room movie.

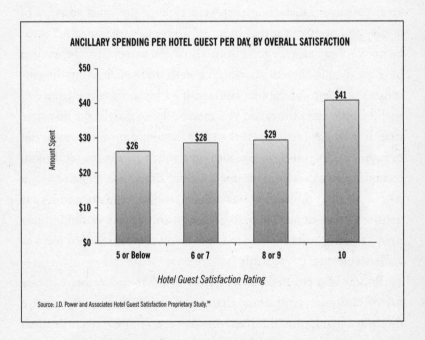

ANCILLARY SPENDING PER HOTEL GUEST PER DAY, BY OVERALL SATISFACTION

Hotel Guest Satisfaction Rating

Source: J.D. Power and Associates Hotel Guest Satisfaction Proprietary Study.℠

MAKING EVERYTHING RUN JUST A LITTLE SMOOTHER

When J.D. Power and Associates began measuring customer satisfaction of public utilities in 1999, there were more than a few eyebrows raised among people who thought that using the term customer satisfaction and public utilities in the same breath was somewhat of an oxymoron: jumbo shrimp, military intelligence, you get the picture. And while it's true that many (all right, most) utilities didn't exactly score among our satisfaction leaders, we did find a few that differentiated themselves from the pack.

Salt River Project, an electric utility located in the heart of the Arizona desert, is one such utility. We asked Mark Bonsall, associate general manager in charge of customer service, why his company pays so much attention to customer satisfaction. After all, happy or not, it isn't as if their customers have anywhere else to turn.

This was evidently a question Bonsall had fielded more than few times, because he immediately articulated quite a few benefits to great customer satisfaction that went beyond the usual suspects of loyalty and positive word of mouth: "To begin with, customer satisfaction is cheap and it's good from a financial perspective. When you have great consumer satisfaction it means that you're fixing the customer's problem on the first contact. It's a lot more cost effective to spend a little extra time, and yes, money, doing it right the first time than it is to have to address the same customer problems over and over again. Do you have any idea how much it costs to send out a technician to a customer's home a second time, or even just have to reopen an old problem in your call center? Well, we do, and it's expensive. We've done the math and it's a simple fact of doing business. Yet, I'm constantly amazed how many companies don't seem to understand this simple truth."

Bonsall also pointed out a number of other, more elusive, benefits of customer satisfaction that are difficult to quantify from a monetary standpoint, but seem to make everything run a little more efficiently just the same. For one, Bonsall equated high customer satisfaction with a form of goodwill capital: "When you run a utility, something will always go wrong; the weather, fires, an auto accident taking our poles. When problems do arise we know we've built up a reserve pool of goodwill that we can call on to keep our customers calm while we fix the problem. If, however, our customers were already dissatisfied with our service, all it would take would be the smallest problem to send them over the edge."

Bonsall, along with many of the other customer-satisfaction leaders, made it a point to discuss the relationship between customer and employee satisfaction, noting that the job of management is much easier when your employees are happy. (We will cover the importance of employee satisfaction in more detail in a later chapter.) Finally, Bonsall explained that as a public utility, Salt River Project is heavily regulated. Bonsall believes that by delivering high levels of customer satisfaction, Salt River Project is able to smooth regulatory interactions in the way it conducts business. Standard & Poor's recently investigated this link and found support for Bonsall's assertion. Their investigation clearly showed that the utilities that scored highest on J.D. Power and Associates' surveys do in fact operate under a more "friendly" regulatory environment, almost as if the various agencies cut them a little slack knowing that in the end these companies will do right by their customers on their own.

The key for Salt River Project, and other companies that top our surveys, is their ability to see the forest *and* the trees, the ability to see the benefits of great customer satisfaction despite the fact there isn't a line item for customer satisfaction on their balance sheet or income statements. The ability to see the big picture, and keep your eyes targeted on the long term, are absolutely essential if a company is to truly build a culture around its customers. And the job of building a consensus around that culture is immensely easier when you are able to articulate just how these changes will help your company grow faster and become more profitable. But comparing the customer satisfaction levels of one company versus another is only part of the story. As we will see in the next chapter, customer satisfaction is complex, and even great companies find it difficult to provide great service throughout the organization.

3

SORRY, BOSS, BUT IT WAS OUT OF MY CONTROL

We would like to introduce you to John, just an average fellow with a wife, two kids, and a golden retriever named Max—all in all a good guy to have a drink with after work or have over for a Sunday barbecue. John manages the local branch office of a national financial services company. Although an easygoing fellow by nature, John has been a little jumpy lately, probably because he is scheduled to meet with the national sales director the following day to go over the quarterly performance of his branch. It's not that John is fearful of losing his job; his branch is still profitable. But, compared to the company's other 120 branches, John's branch is only marginally profitable, and the numbers have declined steadily over the past eighteen months.

So, like everyone who's faced a similar meeting, John spent the week poring over the numbers trying to find a way to explain away his branch's decline. We suppose you could say that too much of John's time was spent searching for a way to cover his ass and make the decline look as if it were due to forces outside his control. And yes, this is time he could have spent to figure out how to turn the ship around, but human nature prevailed and he defensively began looking for excuses.

The problem is that everywhere John looks the numbers are all the same; account retention, revenue per customer, and similar metrics are all down over the past two years, and well below the corporate norms set for each office. There is another number that's down, customer satisfaction, but John doesn't pay much attention to this because it's not a financial metric and therefore not something that management is likely to focus on.

What John needs to be searching for is the *root cause* of his branch's poor performance—those problems that are *driving* the branch's poor performance. And this is exactly why he should be looking at his declining customer satisfaction. Account turnover is only a symptom of underlying problems; reduced customer satisfaction is the cause.

As for John's meeting tomorrow, he's made one fatal miscalculation. While it's true that during previous reviews his superiors didn't pay much attention to customer satisfaction, that policy has changed. Just like many of our clients, John's company has learned that customer satisfaction (or lack thereof) is frequently the deciding difference between top- versus underperforming branches.

ONE POLICY, A HUNDRED DIFFERENT INTERPRETATIONS

We've already seen that customer satisfaction varies by company—some get it, some don't, and some perhaps never will. But even the companies that get it don't get it right all the time, or at least not consistently throughout the organization. No matter how customer-centric a company's culture and policies, those policies are left to individual managers and customer-facing employees to carry out.

Over time each branch develops its own personality, which is why the customer satisfaction of individual branches varies significantly, even among the highest-rated companies. In John's case, he became lax in following up on customer complaints, tending to take the employee's side of any controversy. John also began making exceptions to a few corporate policies—nothing serious, but before long everyone at the branch began to believe that corporate policies were made to be broken, and some employees began ignoring other more fundamental policies that were created to ensure high customer satisfaction.

It didn't take long before customers began to notice the difference and change their behavior accordingly (i.e., defect to competitors). The unfortunate part is that John's company provided him with all the customer data he needed to find the basic problem. From that point all John needed to do was combine a little detective work with a dose of common sense to identify the specific processes that needed attention—something he could have accomplished before his meeting, which, by the way, takes place on the same day the axe falls on his once promising career.

Although J.D. Power and Associates is best known for ranking companies that compete within a given industry, a less well publicized part of our business is measuring the relative satisfaction levels of companies' individual branch locations. Banks, car dealerships, restaurants, and even casinos ask us to determine how well each individual branch or location performs in the eyes of their customers.

Of all the companies for which we measure branch satisfaction, perhaps the most interesting is SCI. Never heard of SCI? We'll give you a hint. SCI, which is short for Service Corporation International, is a company frequently discussed on HBO's hit series *Six Feet Under,* and each year buys more Cadillacs from GM than any single purchaser except the U.S. government. When it comes to the burgeoning death services industry, SCI is the largest provider of funeral, cremation, and cemetery services in North America, operating 400 cemeteries and 1,200 funeral homes throughout the United States. SCI has grown so large that when your time finally arrives, there is a very good chance that SCI will be the last company you ever do business with—or at least the company your loved ones count on to help them celebrate the life you lived.

While the thought of approaching someone who just buried a loved one to get feedback may seem a little out of place, SCI understands that it's better than the alternative of allowing a poorly run funeral home to go on making mistakes. This is because a funeral can be as complicated as a wedding, but unlike a wedding, it must be choreographed on very short notice.

David Warren, SCI's director of communications, tells why his company goes to the expense of capturing the voice of every one of its customers:

> The list of things that can go wrong while planning a funeral is extensive. Our experiences have produced a long list of unfortunate incidences we work hard to prevent. More than once we've watched eulogies stop in midsentence because the speaker could not remember the deceased's name. It's the family's responsibility to make sure the minister knows these details, but we need to make sure our funeral directors don't just leave it at that, but go the extra mile to make sure these details are handled, regardless of whether it's their technical responsibility or not. Collecting feedback about each home is one way we do this. We also listen to each of our branches' customers because customer preferences are different in each part of the country. For example, in towns like Portland and Seattle, two-thirds of our customers opt for cremation, but in the Midwest, cremation accounts for only 15 percent of our business.
>
> But, more than anything else, we gather feedback from each location because customer satisfaction is a great leading indicator of branch performance. We use this feedback to help us determine which of our branches earns the right to carry our Dignity Memorial brand name—all the others must market themselves

under a different name. The other reason we need to measure branch satisfaction is because our expansion plans increasingly rely on franchising. Since we can't control all the day-to-day activities of our franchised homes, we must rely on customer feedback to show us which homes need special attention.

As important as these reasons are, there is yet another reason why more and more companies include customer satisfaction as a key metric for evaluating branch performance. Just as our satisfaction leaders use the customer experience to facilitate growth, time and time again we find that customer satisfaction is closely linked to branch profitability.

LINKING CUSTOMER SATISFACTION TO BRANCH PERFORMANCE

Enterprise Rent-A-Car provides perhaps the best example of turning the results of branch-by-branch research into action. The St. Louis–based giant, with more than 60,000 employees, came from almost nowhere to become the largest rental car company in North America and, arguably, the world. Managing growth is, of course, one of the biggest challenges businesses face today. But managing the type of hypergrowth experienced by Enterprise isn't just challenging, it can be downright terrifying for many companies. Yet, somehow Enterprise defies the odds and seemingly becomes more efficient the larger it becomes.

Enterprise, which consistently comes out on top in J.D. Power and Associates' rental car satisfaction study, manages its growth through a philosophy of providing great autonomy to its individual branch managers. The idea is to be a very large company that feels like a very small company to its customers. Each manager has very specific targets, both in terms of profits and customer satisfaction, but how a manager reaches those targets is left up to the individual.

In this way, the individual branch managers operate as entrepreneurs running their own small businesses.

While autonomy proves to be a great strategy for managing growth, adopting this strategy means that you also adopt its ugly stepsister—inconsistency. The greater the flexibility afforded each branch, the less likely it is that a customer will have the same experience at the Main Street branch as they did at the one on Oak Tree Lane. Of course, the converse is also true. Companies that place all their energy on consistency tend to become rigid, inflexible, and manage to the lowest common denominator of mediocrity.

Consider McDonald's. Although McDonald's and Enterprise are both market leaders, each company approaches the issue of branch autonomy very differently. When it comes to McDonald's, it doesn't matter if you are in Baltimore or Boise; you will plant yourself in the same hard chairs and eat the exact same Big Mac, all served by someone wearing the exact same polyester uniform. Consistent? Yes. But is it satisfying? According to the people who answer our restaurant satisfaction survey, McDonald's is "just OK" at best. Of course, a reputation for consistency can be a very important brand attribute, especially when you find yourself on an unfamiliar stretch of interstate and your stomach begins to grumble. As one road warrior told us about McDonald's, "It ain't great, but at least you always know what you're going to get."

Enterprise takes a very different approach. Rather than standardize every movement an employee makes, it lets the unique talent and personality of each employee shine through, thereby providing each branch with the opportunity for greatness in its own unique way. To make sure all this individual autonomy is herded in the right direction, it continually measures the customer satisfaction of each of its 6,400 branches.

When Enterprise first began measuring satisfaction at individual branches, the results caused concern. Those first surveys revealed a large satisfaction gap across branches. We will discuss in later chapters how Enterprise used this information to narrow the gap, but what we want to focus on here is an important nugget the company found buried in its data—an epiphany that served as the catalyst for transforming Enterprise into one of the nation's true customer satisfaction leaders. It didn't matter where they looked—East Coast, West Coast, or America's heartland—*the branches with the highest customer satisfaction were also the most profitable.* In fact, the branches that ranked in the top third by satisfaction were dramatically more profitable than the branches that ranked in the lowest third.

By measuring the relationship between a branch's customer satisfaction and its financial performance, Enterprise was going where few companies had gone before. The results were clear: narrow the performance gap between branches and overall customer satisfaction will improve. Enterprise began to focus on the special needs of its lowest performing branches while allowing its top performers to continue doing what they do best.

The simplicity of the philosophy embodied in this last sentence is matched only by its importance. In technical business consulting terms, if it ain't broke, don't fix it. By resisting the temptation to micromanage its top-performing branches, Enterprise was able to double its efforts to bring its lagging branches up to snuff.

Enterprise does this by first calculating the customer satisfaction of each branch. After all the surveys are tabulated, a branch may earn a satisfaction score between 1 and 100. In 1996 the gap between the company's highest- and lowest-satisfaction branches was a hefty 48 points, which meant that customers had a vastly different experience depending upon the branch they happened to walk into. By focusing efforts on improving these lower-performing branches, Enterprise narrowed this gap to only 30 points by 2000. Even though the scores of its higher-performing branches remained flat, the significant improvement of the underperforming branches raised the overall corporate satisfaction rating by nearly 10 points, enough to earn the company the top spot in our rental car satisfaction study. What's more important, however, is that when the scores began improving at the low-satisfaction branches, the profitability of these branches rose correspondingly!

You may be saying to yourself that Enterprise makes a nice story but maybe it's just an anomaly. After all, if you look hard enough, can't you always find some statistic somewhere to make your point? Dave Power himself complained early in his career that clients would "torture the data until it confessed," or at least until the data proved the point they had hired him to prove in the first place.

But the Enterprise story isn't an anomaly. Essentially the same scenario plays out every time we analyze branch performance! Take PETCO, the giant pet supplies retailer, as another example. PETCO asked the same question as Enterprise: is there a relationship between the customer satisfaction and financial performance of each of the 700-plus stores? It came to the same conclusion.

PETCO is a company that sets aggressive financial targets for each branch. Call it a stretch goal that only a small number of top-performing branches are likely to meet. Just like Enterprise, PETCO divided their branches into three groups based on customer satisfaction scores. And just like Enterprise, it found that customer satisfaction is a great predictor of individual store performance; the company's high-satisfaction stores nearly met their stretch goals as a group, and a few stores even shattered the mark. But the low-satisfaction stores came up woefully short by reaching only 69 percent of their plan as a group.

The reason for this discrepancy is simple. Customers of the lower-satisfaction stores just aren't as committed to coming to PETCO every time Fido wants a new bone. Fido's parents aren't as likely to be called to action when an employee suggests that Fido might like a new collar to go with that bone. And Fido's parents are also less likely to recommend PETCO when the young couple across the street adopts a little Fido of their own.

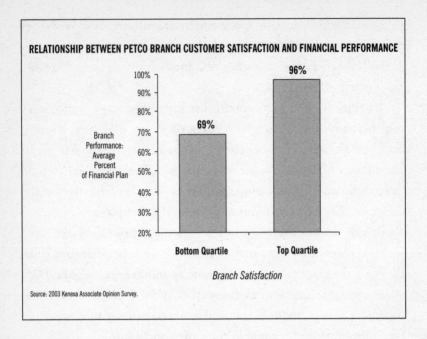

RELATIONSHIP BETWEEN PETCO BRANCH CUSTOMER SATISFACTION AND FINANCIAL PERFORMANCE

Branch Performance: Average Percent of Financial Plan

Bottom Quartile: 69%
Top Quartile: 96%

Branch Satisfaction

Source: 2003 Kenexa Associate Opinion Survey.

And that's not all. PETCO worked with Kenexa, a leader in the field of human resource solutions, to identify the third leg of the tripod. Kenexa surveyed employees at each PETCO branch and found a similar relationship between employee satisfaction and branch profitability. It seems that the branches with the happiest employees also had the highest customer satisfaction, and this winning combination translated into greater branch profitability. We will talk more about the importance of employee satisfaction in a later chapter, but suffice it to say that when it comes to branch satisfaction, you can't have one without the other.

Of course, measuring customer satisfaction is one thing, but knowing how to act upon the results is another. As you read through the rest of the book, we will try to take you through some of the key ingredients we've learned over the years and show you how the companies that top our indexes turn satisfaction measurement into action.

4

THE GOOD, THE BAD, AND THE ADVOCATES

Here is a true story about a simple but profound customer experience. Our guess is that it will sound familiar.

An executive arrived an hour late at his destination airport on a cold and rainy night. After gathering his luggage, he went out to the curbside pickup area to wait for the Hertz rental car bus. While he waited for nearly twenty minutes in the rain, two Avis buses arrived and departed. Eventually, a third Avis bus came by and stopped. The driver looked down at the soaked and bedraggled traveler and asked if he was an Avis customer. When the executive replied that he'd been waiting twenty minutes for the Hertz bus, the Avis driver thought for a moment and then said, "Come on. I'll drop you off at Hertz."

Thanking her profusely, he boarded the bus, sat for a moment, and then asked if Avis had any cars available that night. When she said that they did, he decided to forget his Hertz reservation and told her that he'd go ahead and rent one from Avis. The story doesn't end with that one rental, because the protagonist is one of those people who basically lives on the road. Since that night, not only has he become a regular Avis customer, but he tells that story often and figures that he has converted at least a few people into Avis customers as well.

The Avis bus driver was offering a simple act of kindness on a bleak night. But that one small bit of kindness—which cost Avis nothing, we might add—turned a competitor's seemingly loyal customer into what we call an "advocate" for Avis.

So why do we tell this story? Are we trying to say that you will have a better experience renting from Avis instead of Hertz? Absolutely not. In fact, in our 2004 rental car satisfaction study, Hertz actually ranked second and Avis third. There were a total of nine ranked companies, which means that both Avis and Hertz do a pretty good job of satisfying customers.* The point is that reputations are built by customer advocacy, and advocates are created one customer at a time. At this particular place and time, Avis beat the pants off Hertz to turn this once loyal customer into an Avis customer for life. Of course, at the exact moment this customer was deciding to make the switch to Avis, there was probably some other customer at some other location having just the opposite experience, henceforth decreeing himself a Hertz customer for life. The key for any company is developing more advocates than your competition, because in the world of customer satisfaction, advocates are priceless.

Advocates are customers whose belief has morphed into almost religious zeal about your company, service, or product. They will go out of their way to do business with you again, even if it is less convenient or more costly. Advocates for an airline will take a middle seat, fly at a less convenient time, drive to an out-of-the-way airport, and even pay a premium just to fly their airline of choice. Advocates of a particular restaurant or hotel will offer up inestimable amounts of free and potent advertising by their word-of-mouth recommendations.

*Based on consumers who rented a vehicle from an airport location within six months of the survey date.

Advocates are also immune from your competitors' blatant attempts to take your customers. This is particularly important now that we live in an age in which companies will do almost anything—including paying cash incentives—to get you to switch your allegiance.

Mary Lou Githens, who held the post of senior vice president of customer service for DirecTV, knows this all too well. Githens, whose company earned the top spot in J.D. Power and Associates' Residential Cable/Satellite TV Satisfaction Study two out of the last three years, goes to great length to try to turn its customers into advocates. For Githens, this isn't about being nice; it's about business survival.

As DirecTV's subscriber base has grown, Githens has seen cable operators offer her subscribers up to $700 to switch back to cable. Githens noted that similar attempts to "buy love" in other industries, such as the credit card and cell phone businesses, made it feel like the only thing these companies were doing was "exchanging hostages."

DirecTV's best defense against these aggressive conquest promotions is to make sure that its customers are so happy with their service that they won't even listen to the promotions being offered up to return to cable. In a world where all companies do is pay people to switch back and forth, nobody wins—except perhaps those consumers who laugh all the way to the bank.

Over the years, we've come to realize that when Dave Power named his first big study the "Customer Satisfaction Index," he may have unintentionally sold the idea too short. This is because we realize that the power of advocacy means so much more than mere satisfaction. In fact, in our work with clients, we've divided the world of customers into three clear categories: advocates, apathetics, and assassins.

While advocates will openly and actively promote your product or service, assassins will go out of their way to trash your product or service and subvert your business (don't ever underestimate the wrath of a customer scorned or mistreated). In the vast middle are the simply satisfied. If this book is successful, it will demonstrate how you can turn your simply satisfied customers into advocates.

Here is how we define each group:

Advocates

- In order to create an advocate, a company must go beyond the expected level of service and quality to create a truly memorable customer experience.

- Advocates are fiercely loyal to a brand, refusing to switch even in the face of aggressive promotions from competitors.

- Advocates will suffer inconveniences to purchase your product over the competition's, and may be willing to pay a premium for the privilege.

- Advocates proselytize. They tell anyone who will listen—and even some who won't—about their experiences and become your best salespeople.

Apathetics (the Merely Satisfied)

- Customers are apathetic when you just meet their basic expectations. This is why satisfaction is sometimes defined as an absence of problems.

- Though they tend to remain loyal, merely satisfied apathetics will not endure any inconvenience or make a special effort to use your product or service, or be willing to pay a price premium.

- Apathetics are susceptible to a competitor's advances. Offering frequent flyer miles, better interest rates, significant rebates, or free upgrades is often enough to create switchers.

- Apathetics keep their mouths shut and tend not to speak about their customer experiences, good or bad.

Assassins

- An assassin is created when you fail to meet the basic expectations set forth by consumers in your industry—or fail to properly rectify a problem once it has occurred.

- Assassins actively seek out your competition, defecting even if they have to pay more or suffer inconveniences to switch to a competitor.

- Assassins are vocal and go out of their way to poison your brand by trying to convince others not to do business with you. Our research suggests that assassins are 50 percent more likely to tell someone about a bad experience than an advocate is to tell someone about a great experience.

Assassins can react differently depending upon their individual personalities. Some will react aggressively while others will be more passive. Jeremy Dorosin is the prototypical example of the former.

In 1999 Dorosin walked into his local Starbucks and purchased a $200 espresso machine. The box looked like it might have been opened and then taped shut, but a store employee assured him that the machine was brand new. Since it was the last one in the store, Dorosin bought it, took it home, tried to make a cup of espresso, and promptly discovered that parts were missing and other parts were visibly rusted. When he tried to return it to Starbucks, they refused to take it back. Dorosin complained to Starbucks' regional office in San Francisco and was again rebuffed.

After getting no satisfaction from the company's headquarters in Seattle, Dorosin didn't go away silently. He pulled out his checkbook and spent thousands of dollars of his own money to purchase a series of ads in *The Wall Street Journal* asking, "Had any problems at Starbucks Coffee? You're not alone. Interested? Let's talk."

The media picked up the story and Dorosin began to appear on national television shows like *Hard Copy* to tell his tale of coffee-making woe. Starbucks tried to make amends by sending him a new espresso machine, but Dorosin said it was too little, too late. He responded by demanding not only that Starbucks publicly apologize in *The Wall Street Journal,* but that they also fund a center for runaway children in San Francisco. Needless to say, Starbucks refused to give in to Dorosin's excessive demands, so Dorosin started his own Web site, *Starbucked.com,* as a clearinghouse for disgruntled Starbucks customers. Dorosin's Web site remains active to this day.

Dorosin's extreme behavior makes for a great story, but he is the exception to the rule, at least in the sense that few corporate assassins will spend thousands of dollars of their own money just to complete their corporate hit. But even the most casual assassin will make some effort to convince those within their traditional sphere of influence to not do business with you.

In years past that sphere was traditionally limited to neighbors, coworkers, and the odd soul one might run into at a party. Today, however, all assassins can have a global reach thanks to the Internet. And we're not talking about extremists like Dorosin who create their own Web sites, but everyday people who post their opinions on Internet bulletin boards—which, our research finds, are being used increasingly by consumers to plug in to the collective experience of the populace in an effort to help them make better buying decisions.

Whereas Jeremy Dorosin may go down in the Assassin Hall of Fame, Andrew Burch represents the majority of assassins who fly beneath the radar to cause injury without their targets even being aware they are under attack. Burch is a pretty typical guy who had been a longtime Sears customer in Sacramento, California. So it should come as no surprise that, when he needed a new vacuum cleaner, he drove to Sears and walked out with a high-end Hoover vacuum that his salesman had recommended.

Unfortunately, this particular Hoover stopped hoovering after just two months. When Burch brought it back to the store, he was directed to a Sears service center at another location across town. Being a patient guy, Burch made the drive to the service center, where he was told the machine would be repaired in a week. Burch was satisfied. But one week stretched into two, then three, then four. Required parts were back-ordered and no one could tell him how long it would actually take to get his vacuum back.

Burch would have been happy if Sears had provided him with a loaner vacuum to use over the holiday season. But Sears had ended its loaner program two years earlier. Burch went back to his original Sears store and asked for a refund or an exchange. Instead, he was told that the Sears policy book dictated that the store could take no action until the vacuum had been in the service center for *sixty straight days*. If the vacuum wasn't fixed by then, Burch could come back into the store and he would be taken care of at that time.

From the perspective of the staff at Sears, this was a textbook case of how to handle an angry customer. Burch listened to what the reps had to say and took the news without creating a scene. Most important, Sears did not have to incur any costs to placate Mr. Burch.

Unlike Dorosin, Burch did not create an activist Web site or spend his own money taking out inflammatory ads. What he did do, however, was purchase a new Sony digital video recorder to tape the birth of his new son . . . from Best Buy. You see, Andrew Burch has pledged to never shop at Sears again. He has relayed his story to countless friends and coworkers. He tells them that he could have bought his vacuum cleaner for less money at another retail store but he went to Sears because he believed that Sears was an organization that stood behind its customer—classic advocacy behavior. But, because of its mishandling of this one transaction, Sears not only managed to lose an advocate, it created an assassin in the process.

So who is the more dangerous assassin, Jeremy Dorosin or Andrew Burch? That's a little like asking which smells worse, limburger cheese or a skunk; both types of assassins are deadly to corporate profits. But at least with an aggressive assassin like Jeremy Dorosin you know what you are getting from the beginning. Passive assassins like Burch pose a more significant danger, not only because they are greater in number, but because when they walk away, you don't even realize you have just suffered a fatal hit.

The case of Andrew Burch provides an important lesson: companies need to reevaluate their goals when dealing with angry customers and ask themselves what constitutes a "win" on the part of the customer-facing employee.

For most companies, a "win" is defined as:

1. terminating an angry encounter as quickly as possible,
2. avoiding a public scene,
3. accomplishing points one and two without incurring a monetary cost.

The problem with this line of reasoning is that it provides short-term relief without contemplating the possibility of (or costs associated with) creating an assassin. And much like the proverbial elephant, assassins never forget.

TELL US A STORY

We recently asked people across the county to tell us if they ever had an experience with a company that was so good (or so bad) that it forever changed their opinion about that business or, more important, their buying behavior. Andrew Burch's story about Sears is an example, and we will continue to draw upon these stories throughout the book. Of course, there is always a danger lurking when you use anecdotal stories to make your point. Just because someone weaves an assassin's tale about Sears does not necessarily mean that Sears is a low-satisfaction company. These stories are nothing more than a recounting by a single customer of a single encounter that, although important to them, does not necessarily reflect the experiences of that company's broader base of customers.

So why do we share these stories, some of which may reflect badly on otherwise great companies? We share the details of these individual customer experiences to bring color and context to what would otherwise be a cold world of data and statistics.

Nevertheless, when we looked at the themes contained within these stories in aggregate, we uncovered a few broader truths that carry over to the market in general. For example, although a single assassin story does not mean that a company is bad, we did find a remarkable relationship between a company's likelihood to have an assassin's story written about it and that company's likelihood to score in the bottom half of our satisfaction studies. Of all the companies for which a customer shared an assassin's story, nearly two-thirds scored in the bottom half of that company's respective J.D. Power and Associates' industry study.* However, of all the companies featured in an advocacy story, only a third scored in the bottom half.

So while it's true that no company should get too worked up over any one disgruntled customer, neither should it disregard an assassin out of hand. Where there's smoke, there's fire. And for every customer who speaks directly to you in the form of a complaint, there are countless others who, like Andrew Burch, walk quietly out your door but speak loudly to others.

Another interesting finding that emerged from these stories as a group was that a customer once scorned can be like an elephant that never forgets. When it came to the horror stories of good businesses gone bad, we expected to hear from assassins who were seething from a recent bad experience that still burned fresh in their mind. After all, time heals all wounds, right? So you can imagine our sur-

*Based only on stories written about companies that J.D. Power and Associates ranks as part of a syndicated research study.

prise when we began hearing from people who still harbored bad feelings about incidents that occurred twenty or even thirty years ago—to the point where, in their mind, the company in question basically had come to represent evil itself. Whereas a spat with a spouse may be forgotten after a good night's sleep, it seems that a bad customer experience takes much longer to heal.

One man passionately described in great detail every new car he'd purchased since a Dodge dealer let him down in the 1960s, stopping to make the point that each of these new purchases was *not* a Dodge because of what this dealer did. Without prompting, he ended his story by posing a question: "So how much money do you think that one dealer cost Dodge?" Although we didn't have an answer, we are pretty confident that this dealership never knew the ramifications of its actions—all the Chevrolets and Hondas that this onetime customer purchased in subsequent years because it failed to avail itself of the opportunity to satisfy his needs when it had the chance.

We will discuss the best ways to handle angry customers in a later chapter. In truth, the bigger challenge that most companies face today is moving their apathetic customers into the advocate column. This is because in most industries the number of apathetics outnumber assassins at least five to one, which means you can get more bang for your satisfaction buck by identifying cost-effective methods for turning your merely satisfied apathetic customers into advocates.

THE PLIGHT OF THE APATHETIC

Any discussion about customer satisfaction requires that we acknowledge the intangibles—the psychology of customer behavior that transcends surveys and defies conventional wisdom. The "random acts of kindness" as evidenced in the Avis story may be enough to move one customer to switch rental car companies while a different customer might have taken the ride to Hertz, offered a hearty thanks, and never been seen at an Avis counter again.

Even though people's behavior can be erratic and unexpected, the numbers tend not to lie. Great companies don't worry about Freudian neuroses or individual quirks. They decide to implement a high level of service, quality, and performance as part of their very culture and assume that the payoff will be huge.

Of course, the transition of customers from apathetic to the ranks of advocacy is not an uncomplicated task for most companies. Desire to be among the best is certainly a first step, but the reality of moving up the satisfaction hierarchy requires a cultural change at the heart of an organization and a willingness to spend the money and the time to make it happen. Most companies get as far as the lip-service level, but moving from average to superior is a more difficult assignment. We will go into more detail about the role of corporate culture in chapter 8.

Jim Collins opened his best-selling book *Good to Great* proclaiming that "Good is the enemy of great." Although he was not referring specifically to customer satisfaction, these six simple words are just as appropriate in describing its essence. Because for many people customer satisfaction means little more than the absence of problems, companies that never experience the Jeremy Dorosins of the world find it easy to get complacent. They do not feel the potential of greatness calling out for them to drive their apathetic customers toward advocacy.

One needs only to think of real-life examples to understand the difference between apathy and advocacy. You go out to a new upscale restaurant. You are greeted promptly and seated after only a few minutes' wait. Your server, although somewhat mechanical in his delivery, recites the evening's specials and takes your order. Your meals are delivered in a timely manner, and the taste is about what you've come to expect of other similarly priced restaurants—nothing more, nothing less. Twice during the meal your server walks by and quickly asks if everything is okay. The second time he comes by, you ask for your check. No desserts are offered, which is fine by you because you're watching your weight. Overall, you're satisfied with the experience.

Now fast-forward to the next day when a coworker asks you how you liked the new restaurant. Based on this experience, you respond, "It was fine." This quick three-word response is typical of the merely satisfied apathetic. You don't take the time to sing the praises of either the food or the service. In fact, you wouldn't have even discussed your experience in the first place if you hadn't been directly asked.

When it comes to the question of whether you would go back to this restaurant again, although you're not opposed to returning, it probably isn't going to be the first place that jumps to mind next Saturday night. And if you later find yourself calling this restaurant to make a 7:00 dinner reservation and are told that they can seat you only at 6:00 or 8:00, you'll probably respond, "No thanks, I'll try to get a 7:00 reservation somewhere else." This is because apathetic customers will continue to do business with you only on their terms, not yours.

It doesn't matter what business you are in—this scenario can be easily changed to demonstrate the differences between your apathetic customers and your advocates. Consider the next time you board a flight for a business trip. The plane pulls away from the gate only a few minutes late and takes off without incident. The flight attendants—who are pleasant if not overly enthusiastic—serve you a box lunch consisting of some cheese, a cookie, and a halfway edible sandwich. Upon arrival, your bags actually make it out to the carousel, and you set off for the rental counter having survived yet another cross-country trip. For most business travelers today, this would constitute a successful experience. After all, the flight wasn't canceled or delayed two hours, and the bags didn't end up in some other city.

Unfortunately, working only to *minimize* problems seems to be par for the course in the airline industry. This explains why if it weren't for the fact that airlines try to buy our loyalty through frequent flyer programs, most of us couldn't care less which airline we fly.

Into that scenario insert JetBlue, an upstart airline that has made a huge impact in a short time. Under CEO David Neeleman, JetBlue started with a fleet of brand new planes and installed wider leather seats with more legroom and a live DirecTV screen on the back of each seat. Most important, Neeleman instituted a culture built on friendliness and quality service. He insisted on strict hiring standards and instilled a passion among employees to do things the right way.

"We started from day one with the premise that we wanted to bring humanity back to air travel," Neeleman says. "We knew if people liked the experience of air travel more, if the whole experience with interacting with our company was better, then we could levitate above a commodity business. We could get people to say, 'Gee, even though you fly to Kennedy Airport and I'd rather fly to LaGuardia, I'll drive out there just because you're a better company.'" Simply stated, Neeleman set out from the beginning to create an airline built on advocacy, not just satisfaction.

Since its initial flights in 2000, JetBlue has become the envy of the industry. JetBlue dominated J.D. Power and Associates' most recent study on airline passenger satisfaction, statistically beating traditional legacy carriers like United and American by incredible margins.

But, as we stress throughout this book, satisfaction is worthless unless it translates into favorable business outcomes. To that end our studies show that, compared to other airlines, JetBlue has an unprecedented number of advocates who do in fact go out of their way to fly the airline. Just as CEO Neeleman predicted, JetBlue advocates will drive to a less convenient airport or fly at a less convenient time to fly this airline instead of a competitor. You might be saying to yourself that people are making these sacrifices because JetBlue offers lower prices. While price certainly has something to do with Jet-Blue's success, we find business travelers willing to go out of their way to fly JetBlue for its service, saying the cost of the ticket is relatively less important to their decision. Perhaps this is why, in an industry characterized by massive losses and Chapter 11 filings, Jet-Blue had sixteen consecutive profitable quarters as of late 2004.

It becomes obvious that just keeping your customers merely satisfied in today's competitive environment is akin to running in place or sliding backward. By meeting but not exceeding the basic levels of customer service and quality, a company is leaving itself vulnerable to attack from just about every angle, including price. Apathetic customers are certainly willing to stay loyal to your brand, but they are unlikely to endure an inconvenience or pay a premium to do so. And they are open to new marketing messages and entreaties from competitors. Given a better price, they are far more likely to shrug and say, "I'll give it a try." And at the end of the day, they are *not* standing next to the copy machine extolling the virtues of your product or service.

IS IT WORTH IT?

It may seem intuitive that a company should do whatever it takes and spend whatever it costs to move beyond basic customer satisfaction and provide the best possible customer service. In fact, after reading the past few pages, you might think that our position would be that nothing but the best will do. But, in an environment characterized by technological breakthroughs and dynamic changes in all manner of customer interactions, companies must balance the costs versus benefits of customer satisfaction. In one of those unfortunate concessions to business reality, we must admit that it is not always economically advisable to strive to be the best. As it turns out, sometimes just being good is good enough.

For example, consider a national service company with a large call center that currently tracks an average wait time of ninety seconds before a caller is connected to a live person. The company's research shows that customers are satisfied (albeit not ecstatic) if calls are picked up within two minutes but get increasingly cranky beyond that point. And if they're still listening to Muzak after five minutes, heaven help the poor representative who finally picks up the call, because their inner assassin has probably bubbled up in much the same way that mild-mannered Bruce Banner turns into the Incredible Hulk.

The director of the call center approaches the COO with a proposal to shorten the average wait time from ninety seconds down to thirty. Her plan calls for increasing the call center staff by half in conjunction with installing new telephone routing equipment, all of which will increase the call center's annual operating budget by 35 percent. Should the company invest the money?

After crunching the numbers, the company determined that the payoff for reduced waiting times did not justify the cost—even though the shorter wait time would indeed improve satisfaction. Research showed that the reduced time moved customers further along the satisfaction curve but failed to lift them into the zone of advocacy. On the other end of the spectrum, because callers were at least acceptably satisfied with the current ninety-second wait, very few customers were forced into the assassin range. And since the research showed that overall satisfaction with the call center was driven more by the *way* the representative handled the call rather than the time it took to pick up the call, the cost of reducing times would not have a significant impact on loyalty, word of mouth, or any other behaviors that impact profitability.

This brings us to an interesting point about satisfaction: there is relatively less change in behavior associated with improving satisfaction in the middle of the satisfaction curve than there is on either end. This concept is best illustrated graphically.

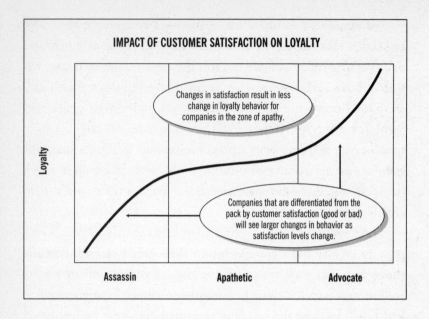

Recall that in chapter 2 we showed two examples of the relationship between satisfaction and loyalty; the loyalty line was steeper for industries with a low cost of switching. In practice, we typically find that the loyalty line is really more of a curve. The curve is flatter in the middle (home of the apathetics), but becomes steeper on each end where the line either rises into the advocacy range or drops down into the realm of assassins.

The chart here illustrates the typical satisfaction-versus-loyalty curve. The flattening in the middle of the curve reflects the fact that unless a company is able to truly separate itself from the middle of the pack, small increases in satisfaction within the simply satisfied range will yield a relatively smaller impact on behavior. Although customers will be more satisfied if an operator comes on the line in thirty seconds instead of ninety, this isn't the type of reduction that is likely to induce them to go out and spread the word, go out of their way to use the company again, or undertake any of the other behaviors associated with advocacy. But if the phone is picked up by a live customer service representative before the second ring, and that person has both the authority and ability to quickly resolve the problem, that may be enough to tip the scale into the advocacy range. Then again, make them sit on hold for five minutes, and you're liable to have an angry assassin on your hands.

It is critical—and we mean absolutely *critical*—that companies learn to look at how customer behavior will be altered by changes in products, processes, or policies. We call this "analyzing the ROI of CSI," and it holds the key to making customer satisfaction work for you.

ROI of CSI (in other words, the return on investment to any customer satisfaction initiative) is analogous to how economists analyze supply and demand to determine optimal pricing strategies: What is the optimal wait time for a customer in a call center, the optimal grade of leather for a car seat, the optimal content of an airline meal (or, as some airlines are beginning to ask, is the cost of a meal really justified in the first place)?

In the eyes of the customer, best is always better than good—air travelers would always prefer prime rib over lasagna, which in turn is preferred over a cold sandwich, which of course is better than nothing at all. Providing the best, however, just isn't always economically feasible. Not every company can be The Ritz-Carlton; someone has to be the Holiday Inn, and someone even needs to be Motel 6. You just need to balance the financial benefits of any action against the cost.

Just because you're Motel 6 doesn't mean that you shouldn't spend money to improve customer satisfaction. You may find that providing coffee and donuts in the morning is cheap compared to the resulting increase in satisfaction, but that installing down comforters in every room is not. The analysis required to properly make these decisions isn't that difficult; it just requires looking at things a different way:

1. Determine how a change will impact the way your customers *feel* about your products or services (measured in terms of customer satisfaction).

2. Determine how the resulting change in customer satisfaction will impact how your customers *behave* (loyalty, word of mouth, willingness to pay price premiums, etc.).

This is important, because customer satisfaction is completely meaningless unless it translates into profit-generating behavior on the part of customers. The mistake we see companies make time and again is that they balance the cost of an initiative against the technical benefit—reduced waiting in the call center—instead of measuring the cost against the increase in customer satisfaction (and ultimately how increased satisfaction will impact profits). The problem is that some benefits, while appearing to be objectively significant, may have only a limited effect on satisfaction and behavior. Until a company really thinks through the cost versus benefit of increased customer satisfaction, the race to implement new technologies or add staff may be a waste of capital.

You may be asking yourself, Why all the talk about the need to turn apathy into advocacy if the cost to do so outweighs the benefits? The answer is that companies need to be aware of the possibility that they could be wasting their satisfaction dollars. The reality is that most businesses underestimate the value of improving customer satisfaction and are therefore more likely to make the mistake of *not* implementing an improvement initiative. This frequently occurs because they fail to see the long-term benefit of increased satisfaction.

Great companies spawn advocates. Great companies look beyond their next quarterly profit report. And as we will see in the next chapter, great companies understand all the different ways they touch their customers so they can maximize their return individually across each touchpoint.

5

DIFFERENT COMPANIES, DIFFERENT TOUCHPOINTS

It might be difficult to compare the fortunes of a plumber, a major Japanese automaker, and a U.S. office supplies retailer, but Mike Diamond Plumbing, Toyota Motor Company, and Staples have one very important point in common: each has demonstrated an in-depth knowledge of the various ways its business touches customers and has used that knowledge to maximize both their sales and customer satisfaction. For our purposes here, each company offers up dramatic examples of how the three major categories of businesses—service providers, product manufacturers, and retailers—touch their customers in a unique way.

THE SERVICE PROVIDERS

To understand and frame the cases and the data that we will provide throughout this book, it is important to note that customer satisfaction is not a giant blanket that fits snugly over every company and every industry. Service providers, for example, must satisfy their customers across three very distinct interactions:

- Objective quality of the service performed
- Subjective experience of how the service is performed
- Process by which the service is acquired

This same basic framework holds true for every service, from doctors to carpet cleaners to restaurants.

When evaluating customer satisfaction with a service provider, it is critical to differentiate between the tangible *quality* of the service provided and satisfaction with *how* the service was provided. In the case of doctors, this can be thought of as the distinction between the *medical outcome* and the doctor's *bedside manner*. Or, when evaluating a restaurant, it's the difference between how the meal *tastes* versus the *service* provided by the staff.

Mike Diamond's story illustrates what can happen when an insightful business owner figures out how to win customers by rethinking what service actually means. In so doing, this young, entrepreneurial plumber was able to grow his business from a single truck to what is now the largest residential plumbing contracting company in Los Angeles.

When Diamond started his business at age nineteen, he was a typical small-time plumber with a set of tools and a desire to make a living at something he was good at. But Diamond became frustrated that his good work did not translate into increased business. That's when he first began to realize that there were two distinct elements in a customer's experience with a plumber. The first was the plumber's technical ability to fix the problem and the second was how a plumber interacts with customers. He knew that just about every good plumber had the technical skills needed to fix a leaky pipe, so obviously an unclogged drain was not going to be the foundation for his future.

Then, he had an epiphany. If all good plumbers could fix a leak, there had to be a different, perhaps more important, differentiator. He thought about how plumbers had come to be perceived in society. Diamond recalled watching *Saturday Night Live* on TV and see-ing Dan Aykroyd bring the audience to tears showing off his "plumber's smile" as he crawled beneath a sink. He noticed that this portrayal wasn't just on *Saturday Night Live*—plumbers tended to be shown as ill-groomed Neanderthals whenever they appeared in a movie or television show. This realization of how society viewed plumbers spelled opportunity for Diamond. If people assumed all plumbers possessed the same technical skills, a plumber's appearance and behavior in a customer's home might offer a significant compet-itive advantage.

Diamond, who now employs more than one hundred plumbers, initiated a "Smell Good" campaign for his company more than twenty years ago. When his plumbers check in with their supervisors each morning, they must be clean-shaven, well-groomed, and show-ered or they don't go out that day. Some don't like the regimen and quit. But most have flourished, as has Diamond's business.

Here's what he had to say about satisfaction in the service sector:

When we were just a small plumbing company running a cou-ple trucks, I used to sit up at night and ask myself what I needed to do to grow my business. You have no idea how frustrating it is to do the perfect job fixing a leak or a toilet and receive a mostly indifferent response. People expect plumbers to be able to fix leaks. And they're right. When it comes to technical com-petence you can pretty much throw a dart at the phone book and find someone who can fix the majority of your plumbing problems.

So I took a step back and began really listening to my cus-tomers to see what a plumber needed to do to get that "wow" re-action, the type of experience that would get them to tell their neighbors about us. What we found was that people really no-ticed how service techs look when they come to their door. We've all heard the cliché about plumbers and butt cracks. People were frustrated that a lot of service technicians looked like they just walked through a sewer—or worse, smelled like they just walked through a sewer. So the home owner is standing there thinking, "Great, now I'm stuck here with this guy for the next two hours."

This is why we started our "Smell Good" campaign. We advertise that a Mike Diamond plumber will show up on time and smell good, or your service call is free. And we mean it. All our plumbers wear clean white shirts. They put on cloth booties before they enter your home and bring their own red carpet to place down in the home so they don't track in dirt. They also bring their own towels to clean up afterwards. If our managers detect an odor in the morning when the plumbers arrive for their assignments, they send them home for a shower.

The response has been astounding. We've become the largest residential plumbing contractor in Los Angeles, with more than 100 plumbers. We not only have high levels of repeat business but we're now at the point where customer referrals are our single biggest source of new business. And we found another benefit we hadn't expected. The best plumbers in town now call us looking for a job because here they get a sense of pride they can't get with any other plumbing contractor. The key to this growth is that we listened to our customers and began to measure ourselves like they did: fixing the leak was the least important part of the service.

Does this mean that for service providers, "how" you perform your service is more important than the "quality" of the service performed? Absolutely not. Diamond found that because the technical proficiency of most plumbers is similar, the "how" provided the key to customer satisfaction, not to mention profitability. If we lived in a world where there was only a fifty-fifty chance that a plumber could fix a leak, the quality of the work performed would be the key to a plumber's success.

Pulte Homes came to a similar conclusion, the realization of which formed the basis of a fundamental operational restructuring. A dozen years ago Pulte handled customers' technical issues in pretty much the same way as every other home builder did. When a customer called in with a leaky faucet or loose floorboard, the call went out to the trade in question. This meant that a plumber or finish carpenter who had spent the last six hours deep within the bowels of a new home construction was called off the job to come to the customer's new home to handle the repair. This seemingly simple solution set a number of problems in motion. First, the technician in question was just that, a technician. And worse yet, a technician who spends most of his time with other technicians, not customers. As such he may not have the personality to be the best customer service representative. Add to this the stress of being called off his regular job—and the missed deadlines that go with it—and you don't have the best recipe for building advocates. And finally, just as Mike Diamond found, home owners don't like tradespeople traipsing through their homes looking like they'd just spent the day out on a construction site.

Pulte resolved these issues by creating an entire army of customer relations professionals whose sole job is to work with customers' livability issues. According to Pulte, their job is as much about providing the softer side of customer service as it is about wielding a hammer or a wrench. They are required to keep themselves clean, and are hired as much on their personality as anything else. The results speak for themselves, not only in great survey scores for customer service, but in the tremendous amount of goodwill that drives Pulte's brand.

Restaurants provide another example of this same issue. On one hand there's the "quality" (of the food—taste, freshness, etc.), and on the other hand you have the "how" (defined by the friendliness and attentiveness of the staff). J.D. Power and Associates recently conducted a study on dining satisfaction, covering restaurants from fast food to fine dining, and one thing always held true: people were, and are, more forgiving of poor service than of poor food quality. Don't get us wrong—if a restaurant screws up in either area, customer satisfaction quickly heads south. But over time we begin to forgive that waiter who forgot to bring us that second glass of wine or left us waiting for our check. Serve one bad steak, however, and don't hold your breath waiting for that customer to return.

Given how much of our lives are spent in service encounters—from air travel to hospital visits to hotels to restaurants to rental cars and beyond—this is a particularly fertile environment for finding a competitive advantage. It often feels like the world has devolved into a giant complaint department—people at water coolers and cocktail parties one-upping each other with horror stories of service encounters gone wrong. As we shall see, the opportunities to shine are everywhere, and sometimes these opportunities cost little or nothing to implement. The payback can be enormous and highly profitable. And yet, once again, we are overwhelmed with what seems to be a steady stream of failures on the part of service providers to grasp the essence of why customer satisfaction matters, let alone how to get good at it.

THE PRODUCT MANUFACTURERS

For product manufacturers, the touchpoints are somewhat different. We've identified two primary and two secondary touchpoints in which a customer must be satisfied when it comes to a product:

Primary Touchpoints
- Product execution (features, performance, design, etc.)
- Product quality (a product's ability to continue to operate defect-free over time)

Secondary Touchpoints
- Sales experience
- Service experience

Execution and quality are considered primary touchpoints because they apply to every manufacturer regardless of whether it produces luggage or lawn furniture. The sales experience is considered a secondary touchpoint because most products are purchased through retailers that have no connection to the manufacturer. The service touchpoint applies even less frequently because most products are simply used until they wear out—the duration of which is measured in terms of quality—and as such are not even subject to "service."

In those cases in which a manufacturer is involved in the sales or service of a product, these two secondary touchpoints become important elements in our overall satisfaction with a product. Consider an automobile manufacturer that is involved in all four touchpoints: it not only builds the car but is involved in both its sales and service through a network of franchised dealerships. The ability to excel across all of these touchpoints determines overall customer satisfaction. Few have mastered that art, however. Lexus became an instant industry legend by grabbing top positions in each of these categories almost from day one. Because Lexus excels across every touchpoint, it has the highest overall ownership satisfaction of all brands. For just about everyone else, the quest to excel in every category has proved to be more elusive.

Toyota, for example, wrote the book on automotive quality (indeed, they spawned Lexus!). Any way you slice it, from transmissions to turn signals, Toyotas, more than just about any other brand, will continue to operate defect-free over time, just the same as they did the day they rolled out of the factory. But just because a Toyota has great quality doesn't mean that you are going to stop and stare every time a Camry or Corolla passes by. Toyota's quality also doesn't mean their cars are particularly powerful, or that the seats are any more comfortable, or that the air conditioner blows any colder. These attributes all relate to the product's execution, which is something for which Toyota is ranked only average.

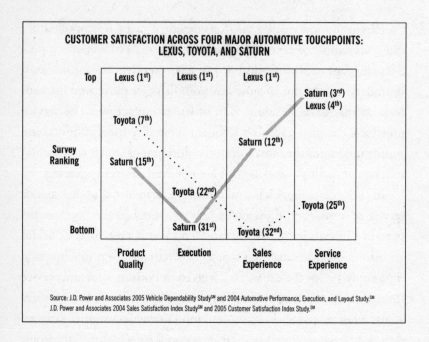

CUSTOMER SATISFACTION ACROSS FOUR MAJOR AUTOMOTIVE TOUCHPOINTS: LEXUS, TOYOTA, AND SATURN

Source: J.D. Power and Associates 2005 Vehicle Dependability Study℠ and 2004 Automotive Performance, Execution, and Layout Study.℠ J.D. Power and Associates 2004 Sales Satisfaction Index Study℠ and 2005 Customer Satisfaction Index Study.℠

Which is more important to *total ownership satisfaction*—quality or execution? When it comes to cars, that depends on who's doing the owning. For the typical midsize car buyer whose biggest concern is getting from point A to point B, quality and reliability tend to trump execution attributes such as styling or performance. That's why the Toyota Camry is the best-selling car in the United States and commands a price premium of thousands of dollars over some other midsize cars that offer the same levels of style, comfort, and performance. But, for someone buying a sporty vehicle, the satisfaction equation may be very different. And as we point out many times throughout this book, you won't be able to make customer satisfaction work to your advantage until you understand which of your touchpoints are most important to your customers.

There is a side to the Toyota story that most people are not aware of. As Toyota's reputation for product satisfaction grew during the late 1970s and 1980s, its dealers found themselves in the enviable position of having greater demand than supply. Unfortunately, this classic economic equation led to increasing arrogance on the part of Toyota salespeople. Consumers told us that Toyota salespeople were beginning to display an attitude of, "Hey, buddy, if you don't want the car, I've got a list of people who do." Despite the haughty attitude, many consumers wanted a Toyota more than they cared about poor sales treatment—and Toyota sales soared as a result.

Although demand for Toyotas continues to grow every year, increased production has evened the supply and demand equation significantly, and customers are therefore less willing to put up with arrogant salespeople. On top of that, much of the competition has begun to catch up and manufacturers such as Hyundai and Chevrolet, among others, now offer vehicles that are much more comparable in terms of quality than they were in years past.

Consider this statistic: Out of thirty-seven automobile brands sold in the United States, Toyota ranks thirty-third in sales satisfaction, according to our surveys. In 2004, roughly three million people walked into Toyota showrooms to shop for a vehicle, but half ended up walking out to purchase a competitor's car or truck.

We looked into this carefully. Why, we wondered, did more than a million people decide *not* to buy a Toyota after initially considering it? It certainly wasn't because they thought Toyota had inferior product quality. Some, we found, weren't willing to pay the price—remember that a Toyota Camry sells for about $2,000 more than a comparable Chevy Malibu. But price isn't the end of the story because Toyota can easily manage prices through rebates and incentives. Of course, some shoppers chose to buy something else because they weren't captivated by Toyota's execution. But, when you stop and think about it, the Fords and Hondas that compete with Toyota's bread-and-butter models aren't really that much more exciting.

What Toyota really has to worry about is that 15 percent of Toyota shoppers decided to buy something else because they *didn't like the way they were treated by the dealer or its salespeople*. Imagine what this means. Toyota spends hundreds of millions of dollars in product development and quality control, and one in six shoppers tell the entire brand to take a hike just because they run into a salesperson who doesn't know what he or she is doing.

We're not suggesting that Toyota has the only dealers that frustrate buyers. All of the manufacturers' dealers do now and then. It's just that Toyota loses more customers due to dealer treatment than its competitors. And after years of gaining market share on the shoulders of product quality, Toyota now realizes that future growth will depend on providing a sales experience that matches the quality of its vehicles. Just as the strength of a chain is determined by its weakest link, product manufacturers find it difficult to rise above their weakest touchpoint. Knowing Toyota's track record of accomplishing anything it sets its mind to, we fully expect that it won't take long before Toyota shoppers notice an improvement.

THE RETAILERS

When it comes to retailing, carmakers such as Toyota are in the unusual position of setting up their own retail distribution through their own independent dealer network. The dealer becomes the face of Toyota such that a bad experience shopping for a Toyota reflects poorly not only on the dealership but on the entire Toyota brand.

The auto distribution system is clearly the exception to the rule. While there are a few other products that are sold through factory-direct channels (Gateway Computers, KB Homes, etc.), most of the millions upon millions of products on the market today are sold through independent retail outlets over which their manufacturers have little or no control. More important, this means that when it comes to overall ownership satisfaction, the sales experience from the perspective of the consumer is separate and apart from the product experience.

If you buy a pair of Bass shoes from Nordstrom and the shoes begin to fall apart in a month, you won't storm out vowing never to set foot in a Nordstrom again. Instead, your anger is directed at Bass, and given Nordstrom's reputation for handling product returns in a manner that always favors the customer, you are likely to come away from your sales experience feeling even better about Nordstrom, and will most likely simply purchase a brand other than Bass next time around.

The separation of the sales and product experience cuts both ways. If you walk into Circuit City to look at a high definition Sony television you've been dreaming about and encounter an uninformed salesperson, it's unlikely that this experience is going to make you decide to buy a Toshiba instead. You still want the Sony, it's just that you'll have to find another retailer to buy it from.

We therefore need to look at the customer touchpoints of retailers differently than those of product manufacturers. This is important, because both the role and significance of retailers has grown significantly. It wasn't that long ago that you simply trotted down to the local family-owned market on the corner to do your shopping whether you needed just a carton of milk or you were stocking up for a Thanksgiving feast. Or, if it was a hammer you were after, you went down the street to see Joe at Joe's Hardware.

Today, however, we live in an era of unprecedented choice, where big box retailers—selling groceries, hardware, or just about anything else—have all but replaced the local family-owned retailers that previously dotted our neighborhoods. But man does not survive by big box alone. Filling the gap are various niche retailers to service our needs. Convenience stores such as 7-Eleven and Circle K are there for when you need to quickly pick up just a few items and don't have time to venture into the aisles of a big box supermarket. On the other end of the spectrum are online retailers that simultaneously offer the convenience of shopping from home while searching an inventory so large that it would be the envy of any big box retailer no matter how large.

Faced with all these choices, we need to ask ourselves two important questions:

1. How do consumers decide at which retailer to shop?
2. What are the retailing touchpoints that drive satisfaction?

When choosing a retailer, every consumer evaluates four key factors before coming to a decision:

- Location
- Selection
- Price
- Shopping experience

We're not saying that people will sit down and consciously analyze each of these four factors before deciding where to go to buy a pair of shoes, only that these four factors are balanced in our minds as we decide where to shop. And as with most things in life, these four factors often require a trade-off—for example, the convenience of a 7-Eleven versus the price and selection of a giant supermarket.

The first three factors are easy to define; in fact, they are completely quantifiable: store X is five miles from home, charges $50 for the new Nike running shoes, and carries four other brands of running shoes from which to choose. The fourth factor—the shopping experience—is more difficult to define; let alone quantify. Yet the shopping experience—or your expectation of what you believe the shopping experience will be like—can be the most critical factor in choosing which store to shop in. This is especially true where competing retailers are similar in terms of pricing and inventory.

To complicate matters further, the shopping experience is itself broken down into three individual touchpoints:

- Ambiance of the physical facility (cleanliness, displays, etc.)
- Interpersonal experience (courtesy, availability of help, etc.)
- Store policies (returns, exchanges, hours, etc.)

It is from within these three touchpoints that our customer satisfaction with a retailer is primarily defined. It should be noted that price, inventory, and location play a significant role in deciding which retailers to visit, but have relatively less impact on customer satisfaction.

Staples provides an excellent example of a retailer that understands the interplay between these factors. When Staples first opened its doors in 1986, it was the first big box retailer dedicated to office supplies. Until then small businesses and consumers shopped for pencils and paper in much the same way our grandparents shopped for groceries—at a small, often family-owned business that carried a limited selection. But if you needed a calculator, or what would have been called an adding machine in those days, you had to go to an entirely different store dedicated to business machines.

By applying the big-box concept to office supplies, Staples became a true one-stop shopping source. Whether you were shopping for a $2 pencil sharpener or the latest all-in-one printer/fax combo, Staples had what you needed, and probably carried three or four different brands.

The target market was huge. Not only did Staples attract individual consumers shopping for their home offices, it became the preferred supplier of businesses of all sizes. In an effort to continue to fuel its growth, Staples looked at the four reasons people choose a retailer and understood that its inventory was the key touchpoint that differentiated it from the crowd. To drive the point home, Staples adopted the tagline, "Yeah, We've Got That."

By the mid-1990s Staples' annual sales topped the $3 billion mark and it looked like the sky was the limit for this darling of Wall Street. Unfortunately, as we approached the end of the decade, two things began to happen. First, Staples was no longer the only game in town. By that time two other big-box office supply retailers (OfficeMax and Office Depot) had opened their doors; as a result, Staples lost a bit of its differentiation in the marketplace. Another problem was the end of the Internet boom, which sparked a recession that hit the office supplies business particularly hard.

Sales of technology, office furniture, and other higher-priced capital goods in Staples' inventory slowed down. Same-store sales declined for the first time in 2001, and Staples founder and chairman, Tom Stemberg, along with new CEO Ron Sargent, decided it was time to go to the source—their customers—to find out what could be done.

"The thing we heard loud and clear was that service has got to improve if you're really going to differentiate yourself in this industry," Sargent said.

Sargent understood that without the pricing and inventory advantage it used to hold, Staples' future success depended on attracting customers based on the shopping experience touchpoint. Staples began actively soliciting feedback from customers and found that it needed to make changes across two components of the shopping experience touchpoint: its facilities and customer service (the interpersonal experience).

Customers pointed out that Staples stores, with their warehouse-like environment, had become dated. A little too "'80s," as one customer put it. Simply stated, they wanted Staples to be easier to shop. As one Wall Street analyst put it, "It's one thing to be able to say you carry every brand under the sun, but what good does it do if you can't find it when you get there?"

Staples did two things to make their physical stores easier to shop. First, like many companies that hit a wall, they went back to their roots—back to the small-business customers from which they grew. They walked the aisles and were shocked to see how far their business had strayed. Everywhere they looked, traditional business products competed for shelf space with Britney Spears backpacks and other clearly nonbusiness products that were better suited to Kmart than the nation's office supplies leader. In response, they cut 800 consumer items out of inventory. Second, they modified their facilities by softening the warehouse feel and putting out bigger and more readable signage.

Next they turned their attention to the interpersonal side of the shopping experience. They wanted their salespeople to play a more active role by possessing the requisite knowledge to help small-business owners make informed purchase decisions. This required significant amounts of training in addition to a new philosophy of how associates interacted with customers. If a customer asked where the pens were kept, associates were no longer supposed to simply point them to aisle three; they were to personally walk them over and remain with them to help make their selection. Finally, they looked at their store policies to make sure they had the best return policies in the business.

The changes paid off. Sales jumped 11 percent between 2003 and 2004 while operating income soared by 26 percent. Earnings per share grew by 27 percent in 2003 and another 25 percent in 2004 as the $14 billion giant regained its top position in the marketplace.

For CEO Sargent, there is no doubt about the source of the turnaround. "It's basically just asking customers, 'What's important to you?' and then executing on it." And to anchor their newfound focus on an easy shopping experience, they changed their tagline from "Yeah, We've Got That" to "Staples, That Was Easy."

The formula, of course, will be different for every retailer. What works for Staples may not work for Home Depot. The important thing to remember is that whether you are a retailer, product manufacturer, or service provider, the journey to higher profitability through customer satisfaction can't begin until you understand all the different ways your company touches its customers.

TURNING KNOWLEDGE INTO ACTION

As we've pointed out, there is no single path to customer satisfaction. Companies that score the highest in our satisfaction studies first look at the specific ways they touch their customers and then act accordingly. Is the most important touchpoint the person who answers the phone in the call center? Is it the salesperson out on the floor? Is it simply the quality of the work performed? The winners, we have learned, find the right targets by listening to their customers, evaluating each touchpoint, and deciding which will have the greatest impact on customer satisfaction—in other words, which will ultimately determine buying behavior. And once they find their target, they don't hesitate to muster their resources, take aim, and fire.

As we move this discussion forward in the book, we will see how the best companies learn how to find the target and where to aim. We will bring our thirty-five years of hitting these very targets to each chapter and hopefully provide a blueprint for action. As we will repeat often, customer satisfaction isn't achieved sitting back and passively wishing and hoping. It must become corporate oxygen, part of the air that a culture breathes. We learned this a long time ago, and our years of work have only reinforced our conviction, that listening to the voice of the customer is the key marker on a path to long-term success.

6

TOO MUCH OF A GOOD THING

Nothing succeeds like success. If that old saying were true, the Atlanta Braves ought to have the most satisfied customers, not only in baseball, but in all of business. Instead, the Atlanta Braves may be asking themselves if it's possible to be too successful. Since 1991, the Braves have won an unprecedented fourteen consecutive division titles, and played in five World Series. You'd think that filling seats for a team with Atlanta's track record ought to be a cinch.

But it seems that the Braves' winning ways have made their fans complacent and, dare we say it, even bored. Despite the team's remarkable run on the diamond, attendance has dropped steadily during the past decade. From 1997, when the Braves averaged more than 42,000 fans at each game, customers have been disappearing at an alarming clip. In the 2004 season, average attendance dwindled to less than 30,000 per game, which ranked Atlanta tenth out of sixteen National League teams—dismal for a team with its scope of achievement.

What makes the 31 percent drop in overall attendance over the past seven years more baffling is that the team continues to perform brilliantly on the field. The 2004 squad seemed destined for a dreary season, perhaps a last-place finish. But against the odds, the Braves won the division yet again, and their manager, Bobby Cox, was named manager of the year. Such heroics ought to draw throngs of eager fans; instead, the only thing the Braves achieved was yet another year of fan apathy. After fourteen straight years of winning the division title, it seems that it will take something even better—in other words, something unexpected—to energize its fans.

In contrast, consider the Boston Red Sox, who up until 2004 hadn't won the World Series since 1918. During the intervening eighty-six years, the team's fortunes were a mixture of frustrating futility and abject heartbreak. Red Sox fans had earned the adjective "long-suffering," and the litany of on-the-field and off-the-field disappointments had reached legendary proportions.

To make matters worse, these frustrations took place in the oldest stadium in baseball. Fenway Park, which was built in 1912, tortures fans with amenities such as nonexistent parking, wooden seats, legroom barely adequate for small children, and structural supports that obstruct the view of the field. Larry Cancro, senior vice president of Fenway Affairs, says, "If you ever watch a Red Sox game on TV and wonder why the fans are always standing, one of the reasons is that Fenway isn't always the most comfortable place to sit for three hours."

Combine this with the fact that the Red Sox have steadily increased ticket prices to the point that they are now the highest in the game, and you would expect that the Red Sox would be the team with the eroding fan base. But this hasn't been the case, as attendance to Red Sox games has grown each of the last five years. Even after a heartrending loss to the hated New York Yankees in game 7 of the American League Championship Series in 2003, the team achieved the impossible in 2004, selling out every single ticket for every game of the season, an average capacity of more than 100 percent.

At the root of Atlanta's attendance problems and Boston's attendance bonanza lies one of the key ingredients of customer satisfaction: expectations. When the Braves' historic run of success first began, the team's winning ways produced a significant "Wow" factor that translated into tickets sales. But over the years, winning division titles became expected and no longer produced the kind of excitement that drives fans to the stadium.

Compare this to Red Sox fans who never enter a season *expecting* their team will win the division let alone a World Series. Even when their team is three runs up with two outs in the ninth inning, Red Sox fans always sense that disaster is just around the corner waiting to strike. They even have a name for it—the *Curse of the Bambino*—so named because they believed the baseball gods were punishing the Red Sox for having traded Babe Ruth to the Yankees in 1920.

Even though the Red Sox never won their division title during 1999–2004, they have steadily improved to the point that they are at least a competitive second-place finisher to their hated rivals, the New York Yankees. And improvement is the key, because it meant that each year the Red Sox were *exceeding the expectations* of their fans. So, when the Red Sox beat the Yankees in 2004 to have the opportunity to win their first World Series in eighty-six years, excitement went off the charts. At a time when the Atlanta Braves were literally giving away playoff tickets, the clamor for World Series tickets in Boston was so intense that people used innovative methods, such as the Internet, to try to get a ticket to a game. On craigslist. org, a popular buy, sell, and barter Web site about which we will talk more in later chapters, rabid Red Sox fans offered everything from free dental work and old cars to various forms of "companionship" for a ticket to a game. One man even offered a pair of seats for any woman willing to have his baby—and the scary part is that we're not sure he was joking:

Second row, on the field, home plate seats to see Game 6 in Boston. All you gotta do is give birth to a child for me. (Males, have your wife do it.) My wife is unable to have a child and I have been looking forward to having a child my whole life. So if it's a deal, let me know.

In this eternal hope—now finally rewarded—was a crucial ingredient of customer satisfaction. As long as Red Sox ownership put a competitive team on the field, a team with at least a reasonable chance of winning the World Series, customer expectations were met. Indeed, now that those expectations have been exceeded in the glory of victory, many wonder what will happen to those very expectations and how they will impact ticket sales in years to come.

THE POWER OF EXPECTATIONS

In any analysis, customer expectations play a huge role in customer satisfaction. And without question, customer expectations now are higher than at any time in the postindustrial era. With an unprecedented amount of choice in consumer goods and services, and with the remarkable improvements in quality and design, customers of most businesses expect perfection or something close to perfection all the time. The options delivered by advances in technology and science have heightened expectations and lowered tolerance for failure in just about every industry. Globalization has spread these expectations to every corner of the planet. Customers in Shanghai will soon be as demanding as those in New York or Paris.

Simply put, our *satisfaction* with a product or service is a function of two separate factors:

1. Our expectations going into a business encounter
2. The actual experience itself

The fact that expectations play such an important role in determining customer satisfaction carries numerous important ramifications for businesses:

- Consumers have learned to continually expect more, which means that customer satisfaction is a moving target. Standing still is not an option. A company must improve or be passed.

- Consumers have heightened expectations for each touchpoint we mentioned in the previous chapter. It is not enough to improve product quality; companies must also offer exciting new features and better service.

- Today's "wow" factor is tomorrow's standard equipment. A company can gain a short-term bump in customer satisfaction and sales by introducing a new service or product feature, but soon enough the competition will introduce the same or better. Thus, the new breakthrough product or service quickly becomes a baseline expectation.

High expectations have become a fact of the marketplace. Even low expectations are high. Dropped cell phone calls, a common trait of cell phone usage just a couple of years ago, are no longer tolerable. Snail-like modem connections to the Internet are fast going out of vogue. Highways littered with broken-down cars with steam pouring out from under the hood are a distant memory. Now it's better lightbulbs, better shoes, better screening for illnesses, better quality produce in the supermarket, better digital cameras, better, better, best.

The higher the expectations, the higher the bar is set for meeting or exceeding them. A stay at a Four Seasons Hotel is accompanied by a Louis Vuitton suitcase full of expectations. One surly bellhop or piece of burnt toast on a breakfast tray could fracture the experience. But if expectations are low, the satisfaction bar is correspondingly low, and companies have a great opportunity to exceed expectations to produce advocates. An extra-friendly desk clerk at a Marriott or Hilton can turn a nomadic business traveler into a regular customer, or, as we discussed before, the kind act of a simple bus driver can create an Avis customer for life.

The psychology underlying expectations is simple: You go to the cineplex to see the latest installment of *Star Wars* but it is sold out. Instead of going home, you buy tickets to *Sideways,* a movie you've never heard of. "What the heck," you say to yourself, "I'm already at the theater." Having no preconceived expectations, you are surprised and delighted by what is a relatively unknown independent film. Had you seen *Star Wars,* however, you would have enjoyed the movie, but the actual experience may not have lived up to the hype and buildup. News stories of fans waiting in line for weeks to see the first screening, and television talk shows featuring interviews of everyone from George Lucas to Chewbacca, only serve to build expectations to a level that is difficult to meet, let alone exceed. This explains why so many supposed blockbusters leave audiences feeling a little disappointed.

In a society in which we are barraged by marketing messages coming at us from every conceivable medium, customer expectations are tightly wound around an unprecedented flow of information. It is tougher than ever to surprise anyone but still possible to delight people if you can match expectations with experience. For adept companies with the aim of a superior marksman, hitting the moving target of customer satisfaction has become part of the fabric of the enterprise.

HOW TO HIT A MOVING TARGET

Achieving customer satisfaction isn't a sprint or a marathon. Both those metaphors presume there is a finish line and a chance to enjoy the victory at the end of a race. Rather, it is a continuous challenge without an end. Business cycles spin relentlessly and yesterday's losers become tomorrow's winners. Customer expectations in this day and age keep rising and companies that cannot keep up and stay ahead of the curve face serious problems, if not extinction.

No company understands this more than Lexus. Lexus is one of those rare companies that excels at everything it does, from design to manufacturing to sales and to service. Since its creation as a luxury brand by Toyota in 1989, Lexus has been at the top, at one time or another, of just about every automotive satisfaction study that J.D. Power and Associates has conducted:

- 2004—first place in initial quality
- 2004—first place in long-term vehicle dependability
- 2004—first place in sales satisfaction (tie with Jaguar)
- 2003—first place in dealer satisfaction

Lexus's continued success is no accident. Since the August 1983 meeting in Japan when Toyota chairman Eiji Toyoda approved the plan to get into the luxury car market, Lexus has kept a laser eye on the mission. "It is time to build a car that is better than the best in the world," Toyoda said that day. It was an audacious move for a company whose brand was synonymous with low-cost vehicles. The German automakers publicly sneered at the idea of a luxury vehicle emanating from Japan. The world would never buy it, they arrogantly believed.

Indeed, when Lexus introduced its first model, the LS 400, in 1989, it was designed specifically to compete with the BMW 7 Series and the Mercedes S-Class. Lexus even took the bold step of publicly unveiling their new car for the first time in Germany, right on the Autobahn and, more important, right in the face of the competition. And compete it has. Over the past four years, Lexus has outsold every luxury brand including both BMW and Mercedes-Benz to become the best-selling luxury automaker in U.S. history.

As great as sales have been, the most remarkable thing about Lexus is the way it has used customer satisfaction to build its brand. In our more than three decades of measuring customer satisfaction, no company has had such consistent levels of excellence across every touchpoint. Lexus accomplishes this monumental feat by viscerally understanding the critical relationship between manufacturer, dealership, and customer. Denny Clements, who previously served as the head of Lexus in the United States, explains that in order to create advocates, Lexus must not only produce the best products, but must also provide a superior customer experience at the dealership. "We can control the product and the marketing," Clements says. "But the dealer has to control the customer experience."

Of course, the downside is that by setting the bar that high, Lexus finds itself in the same position as the Atlanta Braves, constantly searching for new ways to "wow" its hyperdemanding customer base.

Clements points out that successful carmakers must worry about two deadly sins: complacency and arrogance, and that Lexus is only able to stay on top by fostering a culture of "total paranoia." Clements says that successful companies can't get caught up in their own accolades—believing their own press releases, if you will. "We act like we're a lap behind all the time," he says. Clements uses J.D. Power and Associates' CSI study as a dealer report card. As great as Lexus is, it finished only fourth in the 2003 CSI study of service satisfaction, behind Acura, Infiniti, and Saturn. The company instituted a number of service initiatives throughout the year aimed at getting back to the top in 2004.

"The day the 2004 results were released, my assistant came into my office and announced that we had improved a full seven points in the CSI survey," Clements recalls. "And that is a big improvement, let me tell you. I asked him if those seven points were enough to get us back to the top. He shook his head and said that not only didn't we go back to the top, we dropped to fifth place. I couldn't believe it! We improved by seven points and actually dropped a ranking place. That's why you can't rest as a company. Customers just expect better service each year. Trust me when I say that the kind of experience Lexus provides its customers today is light-years ahead of anything that *any* car company provided twenty years ago. Yet today we're in fifth place."

THEY DON'T MAKE 'EM LIKE THEY USED TO . . . THANK GOODNESS

The idea that product quality was better in the "good old days" is a myth. We measure quality across a myriad of industries and we can state unequivocally that product quality is on the rise. In the automotive sector, where we've conducted our Initial Quality Study (IQS) since 1986, the number of problems reported by owners during the first ninety days decreases every year.

"People don't realize just how much better cars are built today than they were just 20 years ago," J.D. Power III says. "I can say with confidence that from a quality standpoint, the worst vehicles being sold today are as good as the best vehicles that were sold in 1980."

Think about it. It is rare nowadays to see a car stranded on the side of the highway. If you do, it's usually for a flat tire. And for people in the Snow Belt, where road salt and corrosion used to turn car bodies into Swiss cheese, those days are gone as well. According to federal government statistics, the average vehicle on the road today is nine years old, but in 1977 the average age was only a little over six years. The reason for this increase is simple: car companies build them better today than at any time in the past, and there is no reason to believe vehicle quality won't continue to improve in the future.

This kind of improvement isn't limited to cars. The days of planned obsolescence, if not over, are dwindling. Products from washing machines to desktop computers are being built to last longer than ever. Improved electronics, tighter manufacturing tolerances, and new materials such as titanium and carbon fiber all have contributed to a longer product life cycle. Quality and defect-reducing programs such as TQM (total quality management) and Six Sigma have set new standards for products leaving the factory.

What does this mean for current and future generations of customers? Without a doubt, the answer is higher expectations. Consumers don't care about *why* things last longer; they just want the product to work properly and efficiently right out of the box and keep working that way for years to come.

One way to address higher product expectations is by incorporating new features and benefits. In our energized consumer culture, fortunes and market share can be had by introducing jazzy and exciting features. The advances come so fast it is difficult to track them all. And like the Atlanta Braves' curse of winning, the downside of rapid innovation seems to be rapid boredom setting in.

Do you remember the first camera that was introduced that actually focused itself? It made quite a splash the first year out. But how long did it take before customers expected every camera to include this capability? The list of product innovations that quickly went from "wow" to "Is that all you've got?" goes on and on.

As we write this book, there are numerous product innovations that are just beginning to gain traction in the marketplace that may become basic expectations by the time the first printing goes out of date. Automobile manufacturers are just beginning to offer DVD video players in their vehicles; how long will it be before they become as common as air conditioning or electric windows? How soon will it be before the majority of American homes have flat-screen high definition televisions installed in their living rooms? Will there come a day when we wouldn't consider boarding an airline that didn't offer live DirecTV in every seat à la JetBlue?

When we posed this question to Mary Lou Githens, DirecTV's vice president of customer service, she quickly replied, "I certainly hope so." JetBlue's seatback television offering, with thirty-six channels of live satellite television, is setting off sparks in the airline industry. Our studies show that the television service is a key factor in JetBlue's high customer satisfaction rankings, and once someone has experienced this unexpected bonus, passengers are reluctant to fly airlines that offer just a single in-flight movie. As Ms. Githens points out, when it comes to televisions in homes, DirecTV competes with cable but it isn't likely that the cable companies are going to find a way to tether themselves to an airplane.

We have long been a "new and improved" culture. The era of "whiter whites" and "better tasting" has morphed into a new era of heightened expectations and minuscule attention spans. But, as in Newtonian physics, every action has an equal and opposite reaction. For all the positive response to innovation and change, there is a price to be paid, and service provider expectations illustrate the conundrum in a powerful way.

CAN I GET SOME SERVICE AROUND HERE?

Raising product quality is a function of innovation and technological breakthroughs. But improving customer service is often more a matter of what a company is *willing* to do, as opposed to product innovations that are limited by what a company is *able* to do.

Most people will agree that we live in an aggravation-based society, and everyone has an endless supply of service-based horror stories. Amid this sea of disgruntled customers is opportunity. Companies that effectively address the service quandary can position themselves to reap a significant competitive advantage. Often, service improvements are right there under a company's nose waiting to be identified by a resourceful manager or executive. But identifying an opportunity is only half the battle, because companies may be wary of initiating any program that will raise customer expectations.

Given the countless success stories in the service sector, from Lexus offering free loaner cars to service customers to Enterprise Rent-A-Car offering to pick up customers at their homes, it is hard to imagine companies refraining from implementing a great new idea. Yet every time a company adds a new service, it runs the risk of having competitors follow suit. This not only negates the competitive advantage that the company enjoyed for the short run, it raises the cost basis for the entire industry in the process. If a new service ends up as nothing more than an added capital expense, it can mean a short-term gain but a long-term burden. The price wars among the major airlines are a case in point. Travelers may flock to buy cheaper tickets when one airline drops its price, but the others must follow suit immediately and, as has been proven in recent years, the entire industry suffers.

Or consider the automotive rebate. Until 1975, there was no such thing as a car rebate. But that year, a floundering Chrysler Corporation and its rock-star leader Lee Iacocca offered a $200 rebate to provide incentive for buyers to give Chrysler a serious look. The Super Bowl ad, which featured pitchman Joe Garagiola barking out, "Buy a Car, Get a Check," set off a firestorm in the industry.

The ploy worked well—for a short time. But then human nature kicked in and before you knew it people no longer viewed the rebate as a sales incentive; they came to *expect* it. Not only did the rebate lose much of its positive impact on sales, it made it nearly impossible for Chrysler to take it away. At the same time, competitors began to offer rebates of their own. In a 1980 speech, Iacocca himself expressed regret at introducing the concept, claiming it was the equivalent of getting buyers hooked on drugs.

But the genie was out of the bottle. Rebates were here to stay. And after the tragic events of 9/11, General Motors took the concept to another level. Fearing that a powerful recession would pummel car sales, GM offered a previously unheard-of zero-percent financing for up to five full years. Ford and Chrysler immediately followed suit.

The results were staggering. The month of October 2001 was by far the largest single month in automotive sales history! But it didn't take long for people to get over the "wow" factor. The carmakers were stuck and had nowhere to go, except perhaps to offer negative financing and actually pay people to buy a car.

With tongue in cheek, one analyst said, "It was like it was déjà vu all over again"—meaning that, just like Chrysler's rebates of the '70s, the post-9/11 zero-percent financing gave a huge short-term lift to sales but left carmakers with an expense that they couldn't take away.

Today, between rebates and low-interest financing, auto manufacturers spend nearly $3,000 per car on incentives, which is effectively killing profitability. And worse, the incentives are relatively ineffective at increasing sales at the industry level. Experts believe that all incentives do is spread market share around and that roughly the same number of vehicles would be sold if all the incentives were eliminated.

Does this mean that service companies should forgo offering new services that they know would improve customer satisfaction? Not at all. Innovation is a cornerstone of great customer service. What it does mean is that successful companies must evaluate the potential return on investment for any service offering that will impact customer satisfaction before implementing it.

Specifically, companies must ask themselves:

- How much will the new service cost our company?
- How much will the new service increase customer satisfaction, and if it does, will the resulting increase in customer satisfaction translate into increased sales?
- Will the competition follow our lead, and if so, how long will we keep our competitive advantage?
- If the competition does follow, will the new service: (1) justify higher prices across the industry, or (2) create opportunities to win customers from other industries?

The answers may vary from one company or one industry to the next. But we have consistently noted in our studies that the award recipients are the ones that tend to take risks and push the customer satisfaction envelope.

For example, consider Washington Mutual Bank, the giant Seattle-based financial institution. With $268 billion in assets and earnings of nearly $4 billion in 2003, WaMu, as it is known, is the nation's sixth largest bank. What's more impressive is the fact that shareholder value has grown at the compound rate of over 20 percent in the 22 years since the company went public.

In an industry that was never known for being particularly responsive to consumer needs, banks were seen as cold, arrogant, and decidedly indifferent to customer satisfaction. The term "banker's hours" refers to a time when banks were open only from 10 A.M. to 3 P.M. on weekdays, ignoring the fact that these hours could not have been worse for customers. Without an alternative, customers were forced to accommodate the banks rather than vice versa.

The advent of automated teller machines, the loosening of federal banking regulations, and the sudden increase in competition changed everything. Faced with competition from other more customer-focused financial institutions, banks were forced to rethink their strategies to survive. Most banks now have Saturday hours and stay open after 5 P.M. on weekdays. They have ramped up their marketing and advertising in an effort to hold on to or woo back customers. Although banks for the most part have improved their services enough to systematically avoid becoming production facilities for assassins, banks as an industry are still well behind the learning curve when it comes to customer satisfaction.

Washington Mutual stands out from the crowd and is of particular interest in this chapter because it used the low expectations people have of banks to its advantage. CEO Kerry Killinger points out that Washington Mutual decided two decades ago to focus on the individual investor rather than on the large corporate clients or the high-end wealthy individuals that most banks build their business around. Killinger understood that to most people the terms "bank" and "customer service" are an oxymoron that should never be used together in the same sentence. Like Southwest Airlines or Wal-Mart, Washington Mutual could target a vast mass market for the typical, underserved consumer and build its market share by exceeding consumers' perennially low expectations. By capitalizing on these low expectations, Killinger believed he could turn this huge, largely ignored population into loyal, lifetime customers. According to our studies, the plan worked stunningly. Washington Mutual comes out at or near the top in customer satisfaction in banking in nearly every market we've measured.

To accomplish this, WaMu literally rethought how people interact with banks. Since no bank had previously taken a customer-friendly approach, WaMu decided to look outside the banking industry for guidance, ultimately positioning itself more like a traditional retailer rather than simply as a place where people stored their money.

One of the first things WaMu did is offer free checking for smaller investors, something that was unheard of at the time. You could almost hear the collective groan from competing bankers who were aghast that this upstart would raise the bar on customer expectations.

WaMu's actions provide the classic example of a new customer service initiative. The opportunity to provide free checking was always there; it didn't require the kind of technological breakthrough needed to be able to watch television while cruising at 40,000 feet. All it took was the belief that doing right by the customer would pay dividends in the end. No bank wanted to be the one to let this particular genie out of the bottle. WaMu reasoned that the loss of these checking fees would be worth it because: (1) people would switch to WaMu because of free checking, and (2) competing banks would be slow to follow because of their historical indifference to small investors.

The gamble paid off. WaMu's market share soared and, just as they had predicted, the competition was slow to follow. And when it did, many did so only half-heartedly with free checking programs that turned out not to be all that free after all. Even today research shows that WaMu is the first bank that comes to mind when people think of free checking.

Free checking was only the beginning. WaMu made customer service a foundation for its business strategy. The bank radically redesigned its branches, turning the usual cold and stodgy environment into an inviting and welcoming retail outlet. At its newest branches customers are greeted by a concierge who directs them to the right teller window or loan officer. Since many customers come in with their children, WaMu set up a children's area replete with Nintendo games. The décor is warmer and more friendly, and consumer financial products, from books to software, are available for purchase.

"We tried to develop an experience that was more fun, more interesting, a little quirky," Killinger says. "We wanted them to view us as trying to help them with more solutions, as being on their side rather than jamming the wrong product down their throats or trying to extract extra fees out of them." The bottom line: WaMu wants to change people's *expectations* of what it means to do business with a bank.

Although WaMu's competitors may have been slow to react, they certainly aren't stupid. They have seen WaMu's success, and some, Bank of America in particular, are migrating toward WaMu's softer and gentler approach to consumer banking. As this occurs, WaMu may in fact achieve its goal of changing consumers' banking expectations. But, as a wise man once said, "Be careful what you wish for." Once consumers come to expect the WaMu experience, services that once wowed and delighted them could become nothing more than baseline expectations which, if left unmet, could become the breeding ground for a new generation of assassins.

Raising expectations also means that WaMu will need to find

new ways to push the envelope to once again differentiate itself from the crowd. This is precisely why customer satisfaction is a moving target that never sits still for any company. As we will see in the next chapter, managing customer expectations also means that there is a fine line between promises and overpromising.

7

PROMISES, PROMISES

One surefire way to send your customer satisfaction scores plummeting is to overpromise and underdeliver. In a society overwhelmed by ceaseless marketing messages and unremitting hype, consumers have become wary of unfulfilled promises that dash their expectations. Companies have learned this lesson in various hard ways.

Progress Energy, for example, is a $9 billion energy giant based in Raleigh, North Carolina. Until a few years ago, Progress, like most utilities, believed that the only thing customers wanted was a promise of uninterrupted service, regardless of the circumstances. But over time Progress learned that people accept that technical problems can and will occur, and when they do, more than anything else they want a realistic forecast of when the problem will be fixed. What makes customers angry are promises that aren't kept.

With 2.9 million customers in the Carolinas and northern Florida, Progress faces one of the more difficult customer satisfaction challenges in the utility industry. Its core customer population lies right in the heart of hurricane alley, and when hurricane season kicks in in late summer, hearts beat a lot faster at Progress headquarters. During the fall of 2004, an unprecedented four hurricanes ripped through Progress's territory. Emergency crews had hardly removed their boots from one storm before another hit with equal or more savagery. The storms combined to kill 154 people, level more than 25,000 homes, and cause more than $42 billion worth of damage in Florida alone. The hurricanes caused nearly $400 million in damage to Progress's equipment, making them by far the most expensive storms in the utility's history.

Hurricanes inevitably mean widespread power outages—hundreds of thousands of homes at a time—and there is nothing like a customer waiting for days or weeks for the power to come back on to really test the mettle of a company (or the patience of its customers). Yet despite these challenges, Progress Energy has emerged as one of the few utilities that consistently comes out near the top in our satisfaction studies.

Among the reasons for its success is that Progress learned to take the time to listen to customer expectations. "You need to listen carefully to what your customers are telling you," says Fred Day, president and CEO of Progress Energy Carolinas. "And we haven't always done that as well as we do now. We sometimes thought that we knew more about what the customers wanted than they did." More than anything, customers didn't want empty promises; they wanted reliable information, specifically about when they could expect power to be restored after an outage.

Day says the company's philosophy is pragmatic. You need to improve customer relations every year. "You're either going to get better or you're going to get worse," Day says. And one key aspect that Progress has improved is not creating unrealistic expectations for its customers.

"We had the perception for many years that when the lights went out, our job was to do everything humanly possible to get the power back on as quickly and safely as possible," Day says. "It seemed intuitive, but what the customer was really saying was 'Hold on a minute. I want you to get the lights back on. But more immediately I want you to take a few minutes and figure out what you've got to do and tell me how long it's going to be before you can get them back on. Give me your best guess so I can make appropriate plans.'"

In other words, customers were more upset waiting in the dark, both literally and figuratively, without a clue as to when the power would be restored. The frustration of waiting was made worse by the lack of information. Passengers on airplanes sitting interminably on the runway have a similar response. If the pilot takes the time to explain the reason for a delay and how long it might last, passengers tend to be far more accepting.

For Progress, the act of listening to its customers on this issue was a huge learning experience. "Over the last three or four years we have focused a lot of time and resources on addressing this customer expectation," Day explains. "We said that we would provide estimated restoration times to customers when their lights are out no matter what it might take. Because that's what they were telling us over and over again that they wanted."

For example, after each major storm, customers can call a toll-free number, or if they still have the ability to connect to the Internet, they can check the Progress Web site for the specific date that power will be restored in their area—true expected dates, not just pie-in-the-sky dates given out to pacify customers at that moment.

You might be asking yourself why a company that essentially holds a monopoly over its service area would care so much about customer satisfaction. After all, if customers don't like doing business with Progress they can't just go over to the phone book and pick a different electric company. When it comes to loyalty, a typical ROI of CSI analysis shows that no matter where someone is on the satisfaction curve, they are going to keep doing business with Progress. The only way to avoid dealing with Progress is to move—or turn Amish. Yet, despite their stranglehold on the market, Progress's commitment to customer satisfaction is so unrelenting that it is one of only very few utility companies that consistently stand out in our satisfaction studies. Remember, any utility company can talk about its customer focus in an interview, but in the case of Progress, this talk is backed up by years of objective, quantifiable satisfaction leadership.

Progress's decision to focus on customer satisfaction is based on its deep-rooted belief that satisfying customers is far more important than just keeping customers from defecting to a competitor. Day believes utilities need to understand that it is crucial to be perceived by customers, employees, shareholders, and regulators as a company that does its absolute best for customers. Proof of high customer satisfaction not only helps its stock price, but it gives the company more credibility when asking regulators for key decisions that impact the company. And even more important, unhappy customers cost money. "Doing a great job for our customers, day in and day out, is one of the best long-term financial strategies we can have," Day insists.

BUT WAIT, IF YOU BUY NOW . . .

After years of studying broken promises, we have identified three questions that companies can ask to isolate the root cause of broken commitments. The answers to these questions indicate whether a company has a process, training, or cultural issue on its hands.

- Was the commitment or promise sanctioned by the company, or was it made by an individual employee acting without authority?
- Was the promise made with the good faith belief that it would be fulfilled to the complete satisfaction of the customer, or was it made knowing the end result would not fulfill customer expectations?

- Was the commitment made to a prospective customer during the sales process, or was it made to an existing customer?

Let's begin by looking at the extreme example of "bait and switch" advertising, in which a company offers a great deal on a car, a sofa, or a vacation package, but once the customer is lured in, she is told that product is sold out and is then pressured into buying something else at a higher price. Answering the three questions reveals the following: First, since the promise is made as part of corporate advertising, it is by definition sanctioned by the company. Assuming that the company's *intent* was to sell the customer something other than the advertised item, the promise was made with the knowledge that it would not be fulfilled—or, in layman's terms, it was a lie. Finally, the promise is made to a prospective customer in an effort to make a sale rather than to placate an existing customer.

Thanks to stronger legislative enforcement, blatant corporate-sponsored misrepresentations during the sales process are becoming less common. Instead, companies are more likely to rely on tactics in which claims are technically accurate but couched in such a way that customers may initially be led to believe they are getting something more.

The free-checking wave that emanated from the banking industry is another classic example. Consumers quickly became cynical when they realized that "free checking" offers were laden with disclaimers, contingencies, and hidden fees that rendered the accounts anything but free.

Cell phone plans whose advertised rate is only good for the first three months, automobile lease rates that require large down payments and carry severe mileage penalties, round-trip airfare advertised for $49 but available only on a handful of seats, and credit card companies using the fine print to bury the fact that they can raise the interest rate at any time—these all are common examples that represent a gamble on the part of the offering company that the additional traffic generated by the potentially misleading claims will outweigh the resulting loss in customer satisfaction.

Advertising, by its very nature, attempts to portray a company's wares in the best light possible, and the difference between good versus misleading advertising can be a very fine line. Each company must decide for itself when it crosses that line. As to where that line sits, we can provide one important rule. Do your customers become aware of the true nature of your claims *before* they sign on the dotted line?

It's one thing to lure potential customers into the store who don't realize that the special rate is good only for the first three months if they are made aware of this important limitation before they sign. It's quite another if they sign without realizing the true nature of what they've purchased, for nothing will make someone boil over faster than the feeling that they've been had.

To honestly evaluate how your company performs, ask yourself two important questions: (1) Are fixed processes in place to ensure that customers truly understand what they are getting before they buy, and (2) Are those processes there just to provide legal protection or are you honestly making a good-faith attempt to provide customers with all the information they need upfront to allow them to make informed buying decisions?

Perhaps you're thinking, "If we make a point of bringing up every limitation, we run the risk of losing the sale." All we can say is that, in our years of tracking satisfaction, we've seen that full and honest disclosure during the sales process (both in spirit and in fact) is one of the fundamental features that characterize companies with high customer satisfaction scores. High-scoring companies refuse to mortgage their future and their reputations for a short-term bump in sales. These companies are very clear that short-term profits are meaningless if they come at the expense of a hard-earned spotless reputation. This is one of the key reasons that companies with high customer satisfaction scores gain market share over time. Remember, it is the tortoise and not the hare that wins the race in the end.

DON'T BE SEDUCED INTO TAKING THE EASY WAY OUT

Broken promises are not limited to the sales department. Just ask anyone who has waited in vain for a service technician to arrive at their house. The following true story is one to which we can all relate:

> We'd been having intermittent reception problems on our TV for about two weeks. I'd been putting off calling the cable company until it went out and my wife missed the final episode of *Sex in the City*. Let me tell you, I caught hell for that one. I called Adelphia Cable the next day, and was told that it would be two weeks before they could get someone out to my house. Didn't have a choice, so I took the appointment. Guy showed up on time and worked for an hour trying to fix the problem. He says he needs another tool that isn't on the truck, and would it be OK if he comes back first thing in the morning. Well, I wasn't happy about having to take another morning off, but the guy seemed like he was really trying, and I definitely needed the TV fixed. So I take the next day off, but guess what, the guy is a no-show. I call the customer service number and the woman on the other end tells me—rather indifferently, I might add—that drivers aren't allowed to set their own appointments and that I'll have to wait another two weeks for a follow-up appointment. That did it. I hung up and immediately called DirecTV. They set an appointment to come out in two days. And the best part is I received a call from the home office telling me that the service technician would be fifteen minutes late. I don't even consider fifteen minutes to be late. That's what I call great customer service!

Because of one missed appointment—and a lack of empathy in rectifying the problem—a longtime Adelphia customer became a new DirecTV subscriber. In a postscript to this story, the customer indicates he is now paying more for DirecTV than he ever did with Adelphia and is happy to do it, we might add.

Unfortunately for companies, this is not an isolated story. When people told us their consumer horror stories—the ones that led them to never do business with a company again—we discovered that the genesis of many assassin stories lay in the leftover bad feeling from a broken commitment or an unfulfilled promise that left the customer hanging and feeling helpless—that they had nowhere to turn.

Perhaps the most common broken promise of all is the one that is made with the intention—or at least the *hope*—that it will be fulfilled. We call these "best-case scenario (BCS) promises." Promises such as these are likely to be kept, provided of course that the supply train arrives on time, all the needed tools are on the truck, ordered parts are in stock, nobody calls in sick, address labels are filled out correctly, and all the planets fall into perfect alignment. In other words, best-case scenario promises are *likely to be broken*.

Companies need to learn how to avoid making best-case scenario promises. To do this, they first need to address the reasons that BCS promises occur in the first place:

- The desire to avoid conflict by telling the customer what she wants to hear, and
- Overly complex or inefficient processes that increase the likelihood that something will go wrong, thereby causing a commitment to be broken.

When an employee takes the easy way out by telling a customer what she wants to hear, the statements may be the result of a personal desire to avoid conflict or to follow corporate policy on handling a given situation. Let's face it, when confronted with an angry customer who wants to know if her order will arrive by Tuesday, or if someone will look into the problem and promptly get back to her, there is always that little voice urging us to just say whatever the customer wants to hear . . . to just get her off your back and let somebody else worry about the consequences later. The urge to commit to what the customer wants to hear is particularly strong if there is at least a *chance* it will actually happen.

Even when employees want to give full and honest disclosure, sometimes they are prevented from doing so by company policies that put more weight on placating the customer at that moment than on running the risk of upsetting them by fully disclosing bad news all at once.

Commercial aviation is one of those industries where the temptation to make BCS promises is high. Running an airline is fraught with problems that are essentially unsolvable, yet our research shows that the airlines that treat their customers to a steady flow of information and candor fare the best. Given that bad weather and unexpected mechanical problems are more than simply inconveniences but are serious safety issues, the airlines work under tough conditions. Continental Airlines is a company that learned the hard way the danger of making BCS promises.

In 1994 Continental Airlines was by any measure a company on the brink of disaster. Continental not only scored at the bottom of J.D. Power and Associates' airline passenger satisfaction study, it placed dead last in government statistics for on-time arrival and customer complaints of lost baggage. Given these less-than-impressive numbers, it should come as no surprise that the airline was also in bankruptcy.

That year Continental hired a new CEO, Gordon Bethune, who pledged to turn the airline around. This promise turned out to be an understatement as Continental managed to go from the bottom to near the top in both the J.D. Power and Associates and government rankings in just one year. Continental's turnaround can be attributed to numerous factors, but high among them was the airline's firm commitment to *not* creating misleading expectations for its customers.

Bethune points out that one of the worst—yet most frequent—mistakes airlines make is keeping customers in the dark regarding delays. A common scenario takes place at the gate. Passengers are told there will be a delay, often without explanation. They are urged to stay around the boarding area because the delay might be short and if they need to board, it will be done quickly.

Larry Kellner, the current CEO of Continental, and Bethune's handpicked successor, says, "What makes customers angry is when they are told not to leave the gate area because the flight is likely to board in ten minutes. The same announcement is made eighteen times over a three-hour period and people are now hungry, tired, and frustrated. We focus hard on avoiding that."

Given that the gate personnel probably have no idea when the plane will actually board, Kellner wants his people to make every effort to tell passengers the truth. In this case, Kellner wants his passengers to be told, "If you leave the gate area, don't be gone for more than ten or fifteen minutes, because as soon as the problem is resolved, we're going to board. But we don't want you to sit on a cramped plane for long stretches when it is more comfortable here inside where you can get something to eat or use the restroom."

Much like the customers of Progress Energy, airline passengers understand that problems may occur, and all they want is to be kept informed and dealt with honestly. Kellner compares this to getting a shot from your doctor. "Statistics show that if you tell the patient in great detail about the procedure beforehand—they call it good bedside manner—the patient will be much more relaxed about the whole thing than if they have no idea what's coming next," Kellner says. "It's how we work with our passengers so they know what to expect, and then you deliver on those expectations. When something doesn't quite work out, you tell them why it doesn't work out. When you don't know, you tell them you don't know."

And not only is honest communication with customers one of the most effective means to satisfying them, it costs essentially nothing to implement. You'll find this a recurring theme throughout this book.

IT DOESN'T COST ANYTHING TO BUILD A SAFETY NET

Avoiding best-case scenario (BCS) promises are probably the easiest customer satisfaction fix in this book—just don't do it! Train your people to be conservative in their commitments. If you can deliver in a week but it will take two weeks if anything goes wrong, don't put yourself out on a limb by giving the shorter estimate. You are just asking for that limb to break right out from under you. As Larry Kellner said, when you don't know something, tell the customer you don't know.

The facts are simple. If you tell a customer it will take seven days to do something and you get it done in seven, your customer satisfaction will be higher than if you had told the customer it will take five days but it actually takes you six. Even though you actually get the job done one day sooner (six instead of seven), customer satisfaction is lower because you missed your commitment by a day.

If there was ever an industry ripe for broken promises, it's home building. As anyone who has purchased a new home will attest, the promised move-in date is like a house of cards. Push back this promised date just a few days and the world begins to implode upon itself. Home builders understand this, and our research shows that most try very hard to keep to their committed schedule. But, as important as this promised date is, the move-in date is also a commitment that is subject to the whims of everything from the weather to material suppliers operating halfway across the country.

Keeping customer commitments is another area in which Pulte Homes excels, according to our data. We asked Steven Petruska, Pulte's COO, if there was any method to their success. Petruska didn't even need to stop and think about an answer; this was obviously something Pulte had spent time working on. Just as other leaders have suggested, the first key is communication. Pulte doesn't just provide home buyers a date and then disappear from the face of the earth. They've established a series of seven predetermined meetings in which a company representative sits down with customers to go over every element of the construction process.

Petruska notes, "If it's looking like there might be a glitch, we want to communicate this to our customers as soon as possible. We let them know exactly what the problem is from the start. People are a lot more forgiving than we sometimes give them credit for. You just need to avoid the temptation to stick your head in the sand and pretend the problem is going to go away on its own. This only delays the inevitable. You may be able to avoid an uncomfortable conversation today, but it's going to be a heck of a lot more uncomfortable if you wait until you have no choice but to notify your customer."

Petruska also says that Pulte works hard convincing salespeople that it's all right to say no. Research shows that the root cause of most broken promises is telling a customer what they want to hear and then hoping to find a way to make it come true. Petruska says that, compared to its competitors, Pulte is much more willing to tell a customer something can't be done, even at the risk of losing a sale: "I'd much rather have a prospective client walk out the door today because I told them the truth than sell them a home and have them go out bad-mouthing us in the neighborhood because we couldn't do something we should have known we couldn't do all along. We use our reputation to drive business. That's why we place so much emphasis on [the J.D. Power] surveys."

Another way to help insure that commitments are met is for everyone to know the economic implications of screwing up. Remember Mike Diamond, our Smell Good plumber from chapter 1? It is part of Diamond's customer commitment that if his plumber doesn't show up on time, the service call is free. Diamond points out that this means both the schedulers and the plumbers themselves know that a promise to be there at a certain time is just that, a promise, and not just a target they should aim for.

Diamond's point is well taken. Even if a broken promise doesn't cost the company a direct economic penalty, every employee should act as if it does.

TRIPPED UP BY INEFFECTIVE PROCESSES

As the old adage says, "A chain is only as strong as its weakest link." This means that the likelihood that a commitment will be broken is directly proportional to the number of employees required to fulfill that commitment. At most companies it is unlikely that the person making the promise is the same person who is responsible for fulfilling the promise. The net result is an increasing number of unhappy customers running around in circles as the buck is passed from one department to another.

As companies grow larger, many times through massive consolidation, and more and more business is conducted remotely through phone centers and the Internet, the opportunity for mistakes grows exponentially.

Here is a common scenario: a customer, already frustrated by a missed deadline or broken promise, descends into the ninth level of consumer hell trying to get the problem rectified. A call to the company becomes a series of interminable waits on hold finally interrupted by an actual human who passes the buck and claims that they are not responsible. Each torturous stop along the route is met with an employee who knows nothing about this customer's problem, and whether the employee is sympathetic or not, the customer is left feeling helpless.

Jasmeet Singh, a cell phone subscriber from Denver, tells his story:

I subscribed to AT&T Wireless last September. I got my cell phone shortly after arriving in the United States a year earlier. Because I did not yet have sufficient credit to start the service, I had to pay a $400 deposit which was refundable only at the end of the contract. I purchased the service online and received a picture phone from the AT&T Wireless online store. The price was supposed to be $29 along with my subscription. But when I received the phone, it was defective and I called AT&T customer service for help. I waited on hold for 30 minutes and was told they would send me a new phone but I would first have to pay another $214 for it, but not to worry because I would get a refund in two months. So rather than the $29 I thought I was expected to pay up front, I've now paid out $614 for the service plan and the phone! I received the new phone and it worked fine. But they never sent me the shipping labels I needed to return the broken phone which I needed to do to get my refund. I called again, was put on another long hold, and was once again promised that the labels would arrive in a week. They didn't and I called again and was given incorrect information yet again. In all, it took six months for me to finally receive credit for the phone. All I can say is I am now anxiously waiting for my contract to end so I can discontinue my service with AT&T.

Going back to our original three questions, we see that AT&T's promise to refund Jasmeet's $214 was: (1) made after he had already signed up for the plan, (2) an accurate description of what should occur under the company's policy, and (3) a pledge that the operator honestly believed that the company would fulfill. This means that AT&T's broken promise to Jasmeet was the most innocent in nature, but also the most common.

Although we are not privy to the exact internal processes involved in providing Jasmeet his refund, we are fairly confident that the operator who made the commitment to Jasmeet played no further role in the process once she got the ball rolling by typing some basic information into her computer. Jasmeet, and millions like him, hang up the phone, basically taking it on faith that a company will execute a complex chain of events that must be properly choreographed before the situation is handled. This creates angst on the part of the customer, which significantly lowers satisfaction, leading to the training ground of corporate assassins.

We can safely assume that everyone reading this book has a similar story if not many similar stories. The good news is that if your commitments are being broken because of inefficient processes, then your problem is quite fixable. The bad news is that far too many companies do not address the problem until their reputations have been severely damaged.

One of the best ways for consumer-driven companies to address the problem is to minimize the number of stops a problem must make before it is resolved. The best scenario is to empower your employees to handle problems on their own. But absent this ideal, there are still numerous actions companies can take to ease this customer angst.

With the call center becoming a flash point in our modern economy, it is instructive to think about how a company ought to run its own such facility. Recent controversy over the mass exporting of call-center operations, especially by high-tech companies, to overseas locations such as India dramatizes the issue. Is carving costs out of the operation more valuable than providing high-quality service?

Staples, the $14 billion office supplies giant, is one of only a few companies to be officially recognized for excellence under J.D. Power and Associates' Call Center Certification Program. What really got our attention was not only the care with which Staples hires and trains its call center personnel, but its philosophy about getting customers what they need in a timely and efficient manner.

For example, like many other call centers, Staples used to monitor call times and give specific time maximums that each call should not exceed—the goal being to push as many calls through the system each hour by getting people off the phone as quickly as possible. According to Doug Woodard, vice president of customer service, Staples did away with that guideline years ago. "We did away with that because we incent our employees on behavior," Woodard says. "We specifically tell all our associates that the right length of a call is whatever the amount of time your customer needs."

In fact, Staples call center employees are trained to "read the need" and listen for what the customer really wants. While one customer might like friendly banter, another might want to place the order and get back to work quickly. Staples also routes calls based on customer needs to employees with appropriate skills. Menus are kept short, simple, and clear, and if a customer has a problem, a live person must never be more than single button away.

Is there a payoff for this philosophy? Absolutely. Staples credits much of its growth to its call center operations, which have become more than just an avenue for problem resolution, but a key to customer retention and incremental sales. In terms of ROI of CSI, the sales and profits that accrue from spending more time with each customer are greater than the incremental cost of employing a greater number (and higher caliber) of call center employees.

DÉJÀ VU—ALL OVER AGAIN

In the old days (i.e., before the advent of the information age), we waited impatiently for a live person to answer the phone, and even though it may have taken a transfer or two, we usually found ourselves speaking to someone who could handle our problem soup to nuts. Now that we have superior tools and technology at our disposal, it isn't clear that we are receiving any more efficient service.

One of Jasmeet Singh's biggest frustrations with AT&T was that every time he called back he was connected to somebody different. This forced him to relive his problem again and again from the beginning. Ideally, a customer should be able to reach the same employee who made the initial promise.

The impact of being able to reach the same individual should not be underestimated. Customers want to feel as if there is a real person with a real name who will act as their personal champion when it comes to getting their problems resolved.

J.D. Power and Associates recently conducted a study to see if people would prefer buying vehicles direct from automobile manufacturers instead of negotiating with their local dealership. For the purposes of this study, the participants were told that buying direct meant that they would need to wait over a month to take delivery, but that they could save up to $3,000 by cutting the dealer out of the process.

We were surprised at how many people said that they would rather stick with the car dealer, even if it meant giving up the savings associated with buying factory direct. But what really surprised us was the reason. It wasn't the fact that they had to wait to take delivery from the factory. Instead, people wanted to know that if they had a problem, there was one person they could go to in order to seek satisfaction. As one man told us, "I want to be able to look up at the dealer's sign and see the name of the person to find if I feel the need to put my hands around somebody's neck. You just can't do that when you're dealing with some big factory in Detroit."

Even if it's not feasible to route calls to the same operator, account representatives should have access to complete and up-to-date information about a specific order or encounter. This at least minimizes the need for customers to rehash old ground, and allows the account representative to begin showing empathy right from the beginning. Of course, the best way to reduce the number of broken promises is to minimize the number of people required to handle the problem and to assign one person with the responsibility to see the problem through to resolution. We will talk more about empowering your employees in chapter 12.

ROAD TO REDEMPTION

Living up to customer expectations is based on a complex set of variables that most companies struggle to turn into a coherent strategy. We have not been able to put a specific price tag on the cost of a broken promise, but it may well be priceless.

Promises can be specific, isolated incidents or they can be implied over time. In one of the more remarkable admissions in corporate history, General Motors unveiled an advertising campaign in 2003 that essentially admitted that the giant automaker had let its customers down by losing sight of quality over a long period of time. The campaign, called "The Road to Redemption," acknowledged that GM had let quality slip and that it was now committed to making good on those promises of the past.

Based on our data, General Motors has in fact turned the corner and is now heading in the right direction. "We were working together to figure if there was anything we could do to demonstrate to customers how much quality had improved at General Motors," says Gary Cowger, president of GM North America. "Somebody threw out the idea, 'Why don't we basically fess up to the fact that we did let people down and we need to come back and try again. Because we can deliver on the promise.'"

Such contrition from one of the world's biggest companies was both startling and refreshing. A promise broken and then made good can be even more powerful than a promise never broken at all. But the ability to follow through on commitments and fulfill expectations is one of the cornerstones of customer satisfaction and a requirement for turning your simply satisfied apathetics into advocates. As we shall see in the next chapter, making good on these promises must start at the top.

8

SENDING A MESSAGE FROM THE TOP

The year was 1987 and the domestic automakers had finally re-signed themselves to the fact that the Japanese were here to stay. What began as a trend in California and was perceived as consumers' knee-jerk response to the gasoline shortages of the '70s had taken root across the country. To the domestic automakers' dismay, even after gas prices stabilized, cars such as the Honda Civic and Toyota Corolla continued to gain share not only on the West Coast, but also in small Midwestern towns that traditionally bought American.

Although the loss of share was daunting, the domestic automakers believed their problem was self-limiting. "Okay," they thought, "Americans may have fallen in love with small economy cars from Japan, but the Japanese will never be able to sell a large car in this country." And this was a comforting thought, because small cars were a loss leader for domestic automakers. Their real profits came from the larger, option-laden vehicles, which they felt were immune from Japanese attack. And so the executives from the Big Three went to bed at night content that although they may be losing the battle for small cars, they would still win the war for corporate profits and market dominance in the end.

Halfway across the globe, executives at the European automakers were even less concerned about America's growing acceptance of Japanese vehicles. After all, with the exception of Volkswagen, the Europeans didn't even sell small cars in America. They didn't even sell large cars, for that matter. They sold *luxury* vehicles. And a luxury vehicle isn't just defined by its size; it exists because of its brand cachet—something that no Japanese automaker could deliver, or so they thought.

So you can only imagine the reaction on both sides of the pond when, on August 24, 1987, Toyota announced the unthinkable. It would create Lexus, an entirely new division dedicated to building and selling what they said would be the best luxury vehicles in the world. You could almost hear the laughter filtering down from corporate towers in Detroit and Stuttgart, "An office worker may pay $10,000 for a Toyota to get back and forth to work, but there is no way a doctor or a lawyer is going to plunk down $40,000 for a Toyota, even if you give it a fancy name like Lexus."

Toyota was undaunted. It set out to redefine luxury beyond the traditional attributes of leather trim and a powerful engine. To Lexus, luxury would be defined by the total ownership experience, including a defect-free vehicle coupled with great dealer service.

Development progressed quickly, and in September 1989 Lexus delivered its first vehicles into the waiting hands of customers. Its flagship vehicle, the LS 400, carried a list price of just under $40,000. By comparison, a fully loaded Mercedes S-Type sold for nearly twice that amount. That's okay, Mercedes thought; Lexus needs that price advantage to make up for the stigma of driving a glorified Toyota.

The cars sold well initially, but a few months into the program the one thing happened that Lexus feared most, and that executives at competing car companies secretly dreamed: the cars began to experience a problem. We're not talking about a stuck-on-the-freeway type of problem, but just a little crack in the armor that Lexus knew could snowball into a deluge of bad press for a company trying to establish itself under the eye of a microscope. It seems that two customers in different parts of the country complained about a glitch in their cruise control.

Lexus faced a decision. After all, it was only two cars, and thankfully this particular cruise control glitch didn't pose a safety issue. It could quietly fix those two cars and wait to see whether others surfaced with similar problems. Or it could issue a recall and let the world know that Lexus engineers were human after all. To those we interviewed for this book, the decision was simple. Since Lexus was counting on its dealers to deliver a level of service head and shoulders above that of any other automotive brand, Lexus needed to take the high road and set an example, one that is still talked about among automotive insiders today.

So, just a few months out of the gate, Lexus recalled every LS 400 it had sold. They made this decision knowing full well that competitors like Mercedes, BMW, and GM were just waiting for the company to stumble, ready to pounce on every miscue. They could almost hear the cheering from Stuttgart and Detroit at the misfortune of this early recall. They knew competitors would use the recall to proclaim that Japanese automakers need to learn their place, stick to selling small economy cars, and let the more established manufacturers cater to the world's automotive elite.

But remember, Lexus set out from the beginning to redefine the meaning of luxury. They realized that this recall provided them with an opportunity to really show the world that they were dealing with an entirely new kind of car company, a company that didn't just talk customer satisfaction, it lived it. So, when Lexus owners received their recall notices, they were in for a surprise. The notices not only included a detailed apology letter, but owners were advised that their dealer would come to their homes, pick up the car, and leave them a loaner car free of charge while the repair was made. Every car was returned to the owner washed, detailed, and with a full tank of gas.

There was even a gift sitting on the driver's seat as thanks for their patience.

And when a customer lived beyond the normal range of a Lexus dealership, the company's field personnel took it upon themselves to drive to the home, break out their tools, and fix the problem right there in the customer's own garage. In at least one case this meant getting on a plane and flying a technician to Alaska to fix a customer's car, because Lexus didn't yet have any dealers outside the continental United States.

For all practical purposes, we believe this recall marked the day that Lexus was truly born, and not the day it sold its first car. This is because the recall was the day that Lexus showed the world what it really meant to be customer-focused.

PUTTING TEETH IN THE PLATITUDES

Lexus's story is important because it provides one of those rare examples in which a company eschews an inexpensive short-term solution to a problem in favor of a more costly but permanent fix. When Lexus recalled every LS 400 it had sold, it told the world it wasn't just saying it planned to be the best; it lived it, and backed up the claim from the top all the way down to the technicians who drove out to customers' homes. Remember, Lexus was in no way legally, or even morally, obligated to issue this recall. They did it simply because they felt it was in the best interest of their customers.

Let's face it. Every company says that customer satisfaction is a paramount goal. Countless CEOs begin their speeches or their annual report letters by declaring: "We've built our company around the philosophy that we will do absolutely everything possible to satisfy our customers." If you feel as if you've heard all of this before, you have. Corporate America has embraced the verbiage as a mantra over the past decade.

In truth, talk is cheap, particularly when it comes to customer satisfaction, a concept that companies and their advertising agencies increasingly believe is on sale to the highest bidder. Claims of love affairs with customers have become such common chatter in business that most employees, managers, and customers themselves don't even hear it anymore. We intend to be more than a bit exclusionary in our discussion. We want to talk about the companies that really mean it!

The leaders, like Lexus, have made the commitment that goes beyond conversation, below the surface, and into the actual daily mechanics of doing business. Other leaders, such as Enterprise Rent-A-Car, are magnanimous enough to admit they weren't always so customer-focused. Enterprise freely acknowledges that a decade ago many people within the organization were just paying lip service to customer satisfaction but no one was doing anything to improve it. And just like Lexus, Enterprise decided to set an example from the top, decreeing that henceforth no manager would be eligible for promotion if their group's customer satisfaction score fell below the corporate average. All it took was for a few otherwise capable managers to be passed over before everyone got the message that the focus on customer satisfaction was anything but a passing phase. To emphasize the point, Enterprise redesigned its operating reports so that a manager's ESQi (Enterprise's internal customer satisfaction index) score was prominently displayed right up there alongside operating profit and fleet growth.

It wasn't easy, but everyone got the message. Employees even coined a term for that period when someone wasn't eligible for promotion: they called it being in ESQi jail, and that is probably an accurate description of what it must have felt like for these individuals. Enterprise points out that they lost a few high-potential managers who were frustrated at being passed over. But, as they say, the proof is in the pudding. Never before had low-performing branches worked harder to improve customer satisfaction; and as the ESQi of the underperforming branches improved, so did their profitability. And that's the key: customer satisfaction is nothing more than a tool to a more profitable business, not an end in and of itself.

For companies such as Lexus and Enterprise, the commitment to creating customers who are advocates is more than words in a mission statement; it is part of the fabric of the entire organization. These companies implement and adhere to policies that back up the words with action. They don't hesitate to spend resources today knowing that it may be years before that investment is fully recouped on the strength of loyal, satisfied customers. The difference is real and stark.

In the quest for turning the merely satisfied into advocates, the winners understand a few critical truths:

- Customer satisfaction must become an integral part of the corporate culture.
- Companies can't just mouth the words, they have to sing the song . . . loudly.
- Employees must understand that the customer satisfaction push is not just a passing phase; it is here to stay.
- Financial as well as strategic decisions must be made based on generating long-term customer satisfaction, even at the expense of short-term profits.
- The customer satisfaction commitment flows like a waterfall from the top.

The single biggest reason that customer satisfaction initiatives fail at most companies is the fact that employees do not believe that management is fully committed to the concept. Employees say to one another, "Just go about your job the same old way and in a few months management will forget all about customer satisfaction and move on to something else." The unfortunate fact is that at many companies this is exactly what happens.

The problem is exacerbated when employees see management acting in ways that are inconsistent with their claims about customer satisfaction. Rewarding top salespeople who achieve their numbers through questionable tactics, delaying needed repairs to facilities, tightening up on return policies . . . the list goes on and on. Consider Lexus. Its recall didn't just send a message to potential customers that Lexus was a different kind of company; it sent an equally powerful message to dealers and field personnel who deliver the interpersonal touchpoints. When dealers see the level of commitment that Lexus pays toward long-term customer satisfaction, their employees respond in kind, which helps explain why Lexus has been in the top five in the Sales Satisfaction Index Study for thirteen out of the fifteen years the company has been in business. At Enterprise, when employees see the almost fanatical attention that senior executives give to customer satisfaction, they immediately understand where their own priorities must lie.

If we've learned anything over the years, it is that before a company can become effectively focused on customer satisfaction, the message must be communicated in both word and deed from the senior leadership. Just talking a good game will not get it done. What separates the leaders of the companies that top our studies is that they don't just talk the talk, they *walk the walk*. They let everybody at the company know, from the board of directors on down to lowest-paid entry-level employee, that customer satisfaction is not just a buzzword, it is a commitment that the company takes very seriously.

NERD VALUES

It is a basic truth in creating loyal relationships that companies starting out with a long-term view of their customer base will finish higher in our studies. This isn't to suggest that turnarounds are impossible. Market forces sometimes outweigh even the best customer satisfaction efforts. As we saw with Enterprise, even a giant corporation can turn the ship around to use customer satisfaction as a beacon for its strategic vision. But for those who, like Lexus, fashion a customer-focused strategy from the outset, the path from satisfaction to advocacy is generally a smoother ride. And sometimes lessons emerge in the most unusual places, especially in the volatile technology sector during the past decade.

In the midst of the Internet bubble of the late 1990s, for example, a self-described nerd named Craig Newmark managed to build a remarkable Web-based company named craigslist. Starting in the mid-nineties as a way to help his friends get the word out about various community events in San Francisco, craigslist.org has grown into a profitable online bulletin board which boasts as many Web page hits per month as Amazon.com. The listings, for everything from jobs to apartment rentals to exercise machines sitting in the corner collecting dust, are displayed in simple text without even a hint of glitz or hype. The focus is on providing real-time community access. Need a last-minute date to your cousin's wedding, or a partner to play a little tennis with after lunch? Just pop over to craigslist.org and you're on your way. Although the site was originally created to focus on San Francisco, craigslist now operates in 170 cities in the United States and overseas, with users in other locales literally begging Newmark to come to their towns. Take a look for yourself; you will find the site at www.craigslist.org.

Perhaps the most interesting aspect of craigslist is how its beginning stands in stark contrast to other Internet start-ups during the late 1990s. You remember—the days when it seemed like all you needed was a PowerPoint presentation and an idea for a product or service that could be sold online and you could walk away with millions in seed money from an overheated venture capital community.

We still talk about the day we invited twenty-two-year-old Brian Stafford to speak at our International Automotive Roundtable. Stafford, despite his youth, had convinced venture capitalists to bankroll him a cool $200 million to launch carOrder.com, a new type of online car buying site. Stafford's little start-up had so much money dropped into its lap that his salespeople were known to hand out complete sets of graphite-shafted Callaway golf clubs emblazoned with the company logo as business cards. We watched as young Mr. Stafford stood before hundreds of the nation's most battle-tested car dealers and lectured about New Age marketing and paradigm shifts, stating confidently that the industry in which they had grown up was about to change. His company would make money with everything the customer did—research, shop, buy, you name it. He spoke eloquently beyond his years about his company, his distribution model, and just about everything *except* whether customers really wanted or needed the services he had to offer. As we watched, it became obvious that Stafford's "build it and they will come" philosophy did not incorporate "a listen to your customers" aspect.

While Stafford was suggesting to these third-generation car dealers that their children might want to consider a career outside the family business, Craig Newmark stayed far away from the hype and turbulence. He spent his evenings quietly verifying the customer information to make sure that his site was accurate and up to date. Newmark kept his operations small and simple. Unlike Stafford and thousands like him who flocked to San Francisco's digital gold rush, Newmark did not start his Web site with the goal of making billions of dollars. He simply listened to people who felt the need for a clearinghouse of real-time community information. He was among those rare Internet visionaries who saw the medium as a vast limitless community to be served rather than as a golden goose to be exploited. Craigslist makes its profits by charging employers and apartment owners in selected cities to advertise their listings. The rest is free, as in absolutely no charge to either the buyer or the seller.

What makes craigslist such a popular phenomenon is that while companies like carOrder.com burned through cash on a one-way rocket ride to insolvency, Newmark never lost focus on his customers. He always kept his eyes on the long term, believing that by providing people what they want, even without banner advertisements and cross-sell promotions, he would always be able to make enough money to satisfy his modest needs.

As the popularity of craigslist soared, Newmark continually refused offers to run banner advertising on the site or take his nascent venture public, believing that neither was in the best interest of his customers. When asked if he is surprised at his company's current success, the iconoclastic Newmark is adamant that he simply doesn't believe the laudatory magazine and newspaper pieces craigslist has generated. "I don't want to believe it because I want to stay hungry," Newmark says. "People get complacent about success and they sometimes forget to stay in touch with customers. I'm not going to do that."

When it was clear to all observers that craigslist was one of the information age's true Internet success stories, Craig Newmark did something that opened the eyes of quite a few pundits. Craig Newmark simply walked into the office one day and announced to his core group of employees, who idolized his vision, that he was stepping down as CEO to take a position in the quality control department. "I deposed myself as CEO in a rather vicious corporate takeover that I mounted against myself," he says. "Now I am staff, not management, and I report to the customer service manager."

Newmark felt this new position—investigating customer complaints about apartment owners in New York placing misleading listings on the site—played a much more important role in determining the experience of his customers than his role as CEO. Left unchecked, the misleading nature of these advertisements would undermine the consumer confidence he had worked so hard to garner. The job of CEO now rests with Jim Buckmaster, someone who Newmark believes will take craigslist into the future while still carrying out the ideals he fought to instill.

Now we're not suggesting that Michael Eisner should have stepped down years ago to don a Mickey Mouse costume or that Bill Gates should hand over the reins so that he can focus on writing code, but we are saying that businesses can learn a lot from craigslist's almost myopic focus on putting customer needs ahead of short-term profits. According to Newmark, "I call it 'nerd value,' which is to do something where you'll earn a comfortable living for yourself and beyond that, it's most gratifying to change the world a little bit."

While executives at giant, publicly held corporations don't have the luxury to think about their companies in such an altruistic light, swinging the pendulum back just a little in the direction of Newmark would help many companies balance their scales so that all their energy isn't focused on the next quarter's profit reports. There must be a balance between the long and the short term, and focusing on customer needs is one of the best ways to ensure your company will be around in the long term. Just ask the executives of the Big Three who refused to invest in small-car technology for decades because they didn't want to give up the short-term profits associated with the chrome-laden behemoths that lined their coffers during the 1960s.

THE LONG AND THE SHORT OF IT

We don't need to conduct a scientific market research study to know what will happen if you show a group of kindergarteners a big sugar cookie and ask if they would rather have that cookie right now or wait until next week when you will give them two cookies. Despite the fact that you are offering a staggering 100 percent return in just a week's time, every kid in that class is going to reach for that cookie in your hand. Why? The answer is simple. *Fun with Dick and Jane* forgot to include a chapter on calculating present value.

Switch the scenario so that you are now the owner of a retail clothing store with a choice between two different ways to handle a customer who is trying to return a dress she just purchased but soiled when a car in your parking lot splashed mud on it as she walked to her vehicle. Choice one is to refuse to take back the dress, thereby keeping the profits from the sale. Choice two is to take back the dress, knowing that even after cleaning you will need to place it on the discount rack, where you will be lucky to sell it for half what you originally paid the manufacturer.

Which alternative should you choose? There's no question that choice number two will give you the most satisfied customer. But, as we've said throughout this book, it's not just about customer satisfaction but weighing the benefits of customer satisfaction against the cost—the ROI of CSI. You know that if you don't take back the dress you keep a profit of $50 but may lose this customer for life. If you take back the dress, you not only lose the $50 profit on the sale but will incur a $10 cleaning charge and an additional $25 loss when you resell the dress off the discount rack. This means that taking the dress back will cost you $85 in profits *today,* a loss that you are not legally obligated to incur.

To truly maximize your profit *on this particular customer,* you must consider more than the impact on profits today, but also how this customer's behavior toward your store will change depending upon which alternative you choose. Unfortunately, to know this about this specific customer you need a crystal ball, which for the purposes of this hypothetical customer we just happen to have. If you don't take back the dress, the calculation is simple: this customer will never do business with you again. If you take back the dress, she accelerates her purchases to the point that she's generating $200 in profit per year. She also tells her friend about the experience, and as a direct result of this recommendation, her friend becomes a loyal customer as well. We don't even need to add up the numbers. If you knew that this would be the outcome you would take back the dress without a moment's hesitation. The long-term benefit far exceeds the short-term loss.

But, like most examples in a book, real life isn't that simple. The main problem is that there aren't any magic crystal balls that tell us how each individual customer will react. What we do have is a plethora of data that tell us how customers, on average, will behave based on given levels of customer satisfaction (recall chapter 2, which linked satisfaction to business outcomes). By combining these data with a dose of good old-fashioned common sense, businesses can balance tactical versus strategic decision making. And, as we've mentioned before, too many businesses take on the persona of those kindergarten children who pass up future rewards in order to take a bite out of that sugar cookie today.

Recall that in preparation for this book we invited people from across the country to tell us about their own consumer experiences that were either so good or so bad that it forever changed not only their opinion of but their behavior toward a company. We broke these stories into two groups: those who became advocates and those who became assassins. Once they were divided in this way, our analysts pored through the stories to unearth the root cause of what each company had done to drive that customer into either camp. What we found was that this often boiled down to a moment of truth when a company was faced with the decision of whether to (1) incur a cost (or forgo a revenue opportunity) in order to build long-term customer relationships, or (2) maximize the short-term profit potential of a transaction at the expense of customer satisfaction.

Considering the myriad of activities that encompass all the reasons someone becomes an advocate or assassin, it was surprising even to us how often the outcome hinged on these choices between long-term versus short-term thinking. More than a fourth of the advocacy stories had at their heart an experience in which an employee took a long-term approach to a problem, regardless of the fact that it cost the company money to do so. Our storytellers appreciated the sacrifice and rewarded each company accordingly. Conversely, 11 percent of all assassin stories were rooted in a short-sided view in which a company refused to incur even a minimal cost to make things right. This is important, because it was not the fact that there was an underlying problem that drove the customer over the edge (product breakdown, missing reservation, etc.), it was the company's refusal to share in the cost to make things right.

TOP FIVE ROOT CAUSES BEHIND ADVOCACY AND ASSASSIN STORIES

Advocacy Story		Assassin Story	
Above-and-beyond service	47%	Poor product quality	20%
Long-term act (short-term loss)	27%	Unwilling (or takes too long) to fix	19%
Courteous/empathetic	18%	Disinterested service	17%
Great product quality	11%	Rude	16%
Low price	9%	Short-term thinking	11%

Source: J.D. Power and Associates request for consumer stories (2004).

Consider the plight of a longtime American Airlines customer who decided to try the airline's Web site to trade in his frequent flyer miles for a pair of tickets that he and his wife could use to escape the Boston winter for a trip out west. Although he found the site to be confusing, he muddled through it and completed the transaction online, or so he believed.

As the trip approached, our traveler began sorting through his e-mail to find the electronic confirmation from American. It wasn't there. Surely the airline must have sent something he could bring to the airport to verify his reservation. He called the airline, and the reservation agent told him that there was no confirmation because the customer had apparently not completed all the forms online. He had to complete the transaction by a certain date, but when he failed to do so, the reservation was voided.

Not to worry, said the helpful agent. She checked the flight and there would be no problem rebooking two seats on the same flight. He thanked her profusely and told her to reserve the seats. The gratitude ended, however, when she told him the airline needed him to pay an additional $50 penalty because the flight was now less than twenty days away.

"Wait a minute," the customer said. "Why should I pay a $50 penalty when I tried to buy the tickets before the deadline?" The agent, being a veteran of such situations, knew how to hold her ground, and suggested he talk to her supervisor. He did, and told the supervisor, "I've been an American customer for nearly twenty-five years. You guys are the ones trying to push everyone to your Web site, and now I'm the one getting penalized because the site is confusing. Come on, this is the first time I tried to use your site. Surely you can waive this charge under the circumstances."

Nice try, but the answer was still "no." The supervisor kicked the matter upstairs yet again by getting someone from the IT department on the line to explain what had happened.

When the IT supervisor got on the line, he had no problem finding the electronic record of the customer's first attempt to purchase the ticket. "You reserved the ticket but you never hit the purchase key," the supervisor said brusquely. The unspoken implication was, "This was your fault because of your own stupidity." The customer couldn't believe it. Rather than resolving the problem, these two managers focused their efforts on proving that he, the customer, was in the wrong.

By now the customer had lost his patience and laid his cards on the table, "So what you are saying is that you've found the records showing that I wanted to buy this ticket before the deadline, and that my long association as an American customer doesn't mean anything to you? You realize that you will lose a valuable customer here over $50?" The two supervisors stood firm and got what they wanted from the beginning. The customer paid the surcharge, thereby putting an extra $50 into American Airlines' bank account.

The postscript to the story is that the customer immediately called his travel agent and told her that he would no longer fly American as long as there was any other airline available to make the flight. He went back to the airline's Web site one last time to send an e-mail to the customer service department explaining what had transpired. Within a few days, he received an apology and a promise of a travel voucher for, you guessed it, $50.

"Too little, too late," the customer thought. In its attempt to earn an extra fifty bucks—which it ultimately gave back to the customer in the end—the airline lost a once-loyal customer and set off an assassin who would repeat the tale many times, one of which was to us.

It may not always make sense to let your lowest-level employees approve a cost-related benefit for a customer—though we will point out in a later chapter that empowering customer-facing employees is a powerful and effective tool. But companies must have a mechanism in place to kick such encounters upstairs quickly for resolution. The alternative is exactly what happened here. The company eventually ponies up the refund, the service, and an apology, but ends up with an assassin anyway—the worst of all worlds.

Although some customers will in time forget about a bad experience, others attach no expiration date on a bad experience. In fact, we are sometimes amazed by customers who, like elephants, never forget.

For example, General Motors has struggled mightily to overcome the negative karma it created in the late 1970s and 1980s when its design and quality levels plummeted. Many buyers will simply not consider a GM car, despite the company's great strides in quality and customer satisfaction improvements in recent years.

Frank Burrows is still angry about the Pontiac Trans Am he purchased in 1977! Listen to his story:

To me, no company ever dropped the ball like Pontiac did almost 30 years ago. I had purchased my dream car at the time, a black Pontiac Trans Am 6.6-liter with the T-Top and gold bird on the hood. This was back in the days when the warranty lasted only 12 months or 12,000 miles.

My car had only 7,000 miles on it but I had owned it for 13 months when I began to hear strange sounds coming from the rear end. I took it to my dealer and the mechanic said, "There's another one." It seems that Pontiac had inadvertently used a lubricant that wasn't rated to handle the temperatures generated in the Trans Am positraction rear end and many were failing. Since this was a known error on the factory's part, you'd think GM would pay for the repair, especially since my car had been driven a mere 7,000 miles. Guess again. I had to shell out $500, which was a lot of money to me in 1977. I was so angry that I wrote numerous letters to GM, none of which were ever answered. *Needless to say, I've never bought another GM product since then, and never will.* Given that I've bought eleven cars in the years since then, how much did that decision cost GM?

Lord only knows how much easier GM's Road to Redemption campaign would have been, or if it would have even been needed at all, if the company had done a better job of taking care of customers like Mr. Burrows regardless of whether the warranty had just expired. It also doesn't matter whether the cause of the problem is exactly as Burrows states—Pontiac installing the wrong grade of lubricant. What matters is that from the perspective of the customer, *perception is reality.* And in GM's case, these negative perceptions continue to linger to the point that millions of people each year actively refuse to consider a General Motors vehicle because of quality concerns, despite the reality that the GM of today makes some of the finest automobiles in the world. The lesson is simple: a penny saved today may cost you dearly down the road.

Scottrade, a leading online brokerage firm, provides an excellent example of long-term thinking when it faced steep declines in its equity trading business following the collapse of the Internet bubble in 2001. Business for all trading companies plummeted as much as 70 percent as investors, shaken by dramatic declines in their portfolios, simply stopped trading altogether. While competitors instituted new fees to try to make up for this short-term loss in revenues, Scottrade's founder and CEO, Rodger Riney, steadfastly refused to follow suit. The most lucrative of these new fees was what the industry called inactivity fees, which were a way for the trading companies to make money off their customers even when they weren't out there trading and generating commissions.

Riney resisted the urge to institute the inactivity fees despite the fact that they were guaranteed to raise short-term profits:

We had just gone through some of the most wonderful, profitable years in brokerage history—1998, 1999, and early 2000. We were blessed with more business than we deserved. We did very well and our customers were active, good customers. They gave us a lot of business and profitability. And when the market started down, many of our customers took a pretty major drubbing in the bear market. So we just didn't feel that it would be right to institute inactivity fees against those same customers who had just given us such great business during the good times. We couldn't say to these same people, "Well, you haven't done anything for me during the last three months so I'm going to assess you a fee to keep your account active with us." It just wasn't the fair thing to do to our customers.

The interesting part is that, much like Craig Newmark, Riney made this decision based on what he felt was the right thing to do for his customers. He did not make the decision out of the belief that it would benefit his bottom line in the long run—but it did.

Just as Newmark and other satisfaction leaders have found out, when doing right for your customers forces you to miss a short-term profit opportunity, you are likely to find yourself rewarded in the end.

Word quickly spread, and customers began flocking to Scottrade. Even during the worst of the recession, the company remained profitable, and as the recession ended and the economy picked up, Scottrade found itself with more new business than it knew what to do with. And, in case you didn't know, Scottrade has won J.D. Power and Associates' customer satisfaction award for online brokers for five years in a row, making it truly one of the best of the best companies to do business with.

Scottrade's refusal to charge inactivity fees is an example of only one type of long-term thinking. This occurs when management expresses its desire to care more about long-term customer satisfaction than short-term profits in the form of corporate policies and regulations. These policies apply equally to every customer, giving the company the opportunity to shamelessly tout its customer-centric policies to the world. When, like Scottrade, a policy differentiates a company from the competition, that policy will help define who a company is in the eyes of consumers.

The other form of long-term thinking cannot be dictated by management. This is because situations arise that are not directly covered by the rules. In such situations employees dealing with customers (and their immediate supervisors) must make decisions on the fly. The choice of whether to allow the return of a dress that is soiled before the customer even reaches the car is a situation that won't be found in any employee handbook and is therefore left to the best judgment of the individual employee. Or, as in Frank Burrows's case, the decision not to cover the cost of his repairs may have been the decision of a single individual in GM's service chain. Of course, Mr. Burrows may have been tripped up by a corporate decision handed down in the form of a memo stating that GM would not be responsible for any Trans Am rear ends' failing warranty—we don't know. What we do know is that your employees need to be prepared to make these types of decisions on their own, and on the fly.

So how do your employees choose between an immediate profit or long-term customer satisfaction? They make these decisions based on the example set by senior management, which brings us back full circle to the beginning of the chapter. When an employee at Lexus, Enterprise, or Scottrade is faced with such a decision, she knows how management feels about building customer commitment, and will always make the decision that is in the best long-term interest of the company.

Management can also help by providing written guidelines that help calibrate its position on the long- versus short-term scale. Nordstrom, the department store chain famous for its exemplary customer service, directly communicates its position in the employee handbook. According to Robert Spector, author of *The Nordstrom Way*, the company handbook provides a list of rules for customer behavior. "Rule No. 1: Use your good judgment in all situations. Rule No. 2: There will be no additional rules."

The balancing act between long- versus short-term thinking isn't limited to retailers and service providers. Manufacturers face these decisions every day. Should we spend the money to tighten tolerances so that our new super-deluxe transmission will last 200,000 miles instead of 150,000—even though the warranty expires at 50,000? Why spend the money? The customer won't know the difference on a test drive, and most will have traded their car for something else long before the transmission fails. But what if the additional 50,000 miles of transmission life helps give the brand a reputation for quality and durability? What if this reputation drives people to buy your brand over the competition? What if this reputation increases your resale value by 10 percent? It all comes down to which you care more about: the money you make today, or the money you make one, two, or even ten years down the line when your investment in long-term thinking really begins to pay dividends.

Like everything else in life, the winners find a way to balance short-term profitability against the benefits of long-term customer satisfaction. There is usually a method for identifying what will constitute a win in any given situation—for both the company and the customer. Getting the customer to go away quietly for the least amount of cost is not a winning strategy. But giving away the store over and over again is not a sustainable formula either.

In the next chapter we will explore the two primary components of customer satisfaction in greater detail—those elements that you as a leader control, and those that are controlled by your frontline employees who actually touch your customers every day. We often say that customer satisfaction is driven as much from the bottom up as it is from the top down. Fail to strike a balance between the two and it is your customer who will feel the squeeze between these two competing forces.

9

HITTING THE JACKPOT

Have you ever heard of the town of Jackpot, Nevada? If not, don't feel bad, because you are not alone. Jackpot is a tiny hamlet nestled in the high plains of Nevada just south of the Idaho border along Highway 93. While Las Vegas, its distant cousin to the south, is the glitzy, glamorous gaming capital of the world, Jackpot is a remote gambler's oasis, home to a small handful of casinos that draw most of their trade from people in Boise and Twin Falls, Idaho. Las Vegas regulars, if they thought about Jackpot at all, would label it, "the middle of nowhere."

But for the 1,500 residents of Jackpot, gambling is not only the town's lifeline and economic foundation, it is the reason Jackpot exists. And at the center of it all stands Cactus Petes with five restaurants and 26,000 square feet of casino space. Cactus Petes is not only Jackpot's largest casino, it is the birthplace of its parent company, Ameristar Casinos.

Compared to other companies in the gaming industry, Ameristar is rather unique. Although its corporate headquarters overlook the neon lights of the Las Vegas Strip, Ameristar does not even operate a casino in Las Vegas, nor for that matter in any of the other traditional gambling meccas such as Atlantic City or Reno. Instead, Ameristar's gaming properties are located in and around smaller cities, like St. Charles, Missouri, Vicksburg, Mississippi, and Council Bluffs, Iowa. Unlike Caesars Palace, the MGM Grand, or the Bellagio, which attract tourists from around the globe, Ameristar casinos depend largely on a cadre of regional repeat customers.

The fact that the town of Jackpot continues to even exist is nothing short of a minor miracle. Jackpot is so remote that even its local Idaho customers must drive anywhere from one to three hours down a deserted two-lane road just to get there—a road that is so dark and desolate that it looks like it was special-ordered by Hollywood to serve as the set for an alien abduction movie. It's the kind of place we recall from our childhood, where the boogeyman lived just around the next corner.

Adding to the town's challenge is the fact that Jackpot is no longer the only game in town. Recent changes in the law mean that several Indian gaming facilities have opened in Idaho, literally in the backyard of much of Jackpot's traditional customer base. At the same time, big Las Vegas–style casinos in Reno are aggressively marketing to Idaho's gambling population by offering discounted travel packages that include airfare and hotel accommodations; it is actually quicker for a Boise resident to fly to Reno than to drive to Jackpot.

With so many of the chips stacking up against it, you might think that the folks at Ameristar would be thinking about folding their hand and preparing for the day when Cactus Petes closes its doors for the last time, written off as just another victim of changing times. But if this is what Ameristar is thinking, it's holding its cards close to the vest, because you would never know it by its actions. In fact, just the opposite is true. For starters, in 1990 Ameristar built a new sixteen-story four-star hotel—the tallest building in Nevada outside of Las Vegas and Reno—to handle what turns out to be an *increasing* number of guests coming to Cactus Petes.

How does Cactus Petes continue to thrive when, pardon the expression, all the chips are stacked against it? According to the property's management, the secret to Cactus Petes success is providing an atmosphere that is so outwardly friendly that no one would ever confuse the experience with a traditional Vegas-style casino. It is a level of service so friendly that it not only is visible on the surveys that Ameristar conducts every month but is immediately apparent to anyone who walks through the door.

Ameristar understands that many images come to mind when people think about casinos, but "friendly" typically isn't one of them. The impression that most casinos are somewhat cold and calculating is well-deserved. This is because no industry in the country is more process-driven than the casino industry. Everything that happens in a casino happens for a reason. Ironic as it sounds, when it comes to the gaming industry, nothing is left to chance but is instead the result of carefully orchestrated process engineering designed to maximize profits in every conceivable way.

Take a simple game of blackjack. Between the floor managers, electronic player loyalty cards, and the ever-present eye-in-the-sky, casinos measure everything that happens at one of their blackjack tables 24 hours a day, 7 days a week, 365 days a year. And many of these observations are designed to maximize the number of hands that can be dealt at a given table each hour.

This quest for speed has led to numerous process refinements to this age-old game. Instead of using a single deck of cards, most casinos deal from a "shoe" containing six or eight decks that can last half an hour before needing to be reshuffled. When shuffling is required, mechanical shuffling machines are there to speed the process along. Even the cards themselves have been designed for efficiency, with a tiny electronic sensor implanted in each card to automatically tell a dealer when she has blackjack, thereby eliminating the need to bend down to sneak a peak at her "hole" card.

Another way to maximize the number of hands that can be dealt each hour is to speed up the pace of play of the patrons sitting at the table. Dealers are taught to keep the game moving as quickly as possible, dealing cards, counting up players' hands, and exchanging money at a near-superhuman pace. Players are forced to keep up with the action and there is little conversation or personal interaction with the dealer, who often appears more like an automaton than a person. Speak only when spoken to—that's the process that dealers are supposed to follow at the big Las Vegas casinos. A quick smile, a courteous "thank you," and a pat on the table for good luck is about all a player should expect at many of the Las Vegas Strip casinos. Anything that slows down the pace of play is discouraged, which is one of the reasons Las Vegas casinos instill a process that limits all extraneous conversation.

Ameristar is just as numbers-driven as any Las Vegas casino, but it turned the problem around by looking at the numbers from a different angle. What if our dealers were encouraged to engage in friendly banter with their players? Sure, this might slow down the pace of play, but what if the friendly atmosphere at the table drove people to sit at the table a little longer—bet a little higher, perhaps?

For this reason Ameristar breaks the mold and encourages its dealers at Cactus Petes—and across the Ameristar brand—to engage their customers, to get to know customers by their first names, and to create an atmosphere akin to a popular neighborhood bar.

"We want our customers to say, 'Boy, I like Bob the dealer and we're going to have a good time when we're playing blackjack,'" says Paul Eagleton, chief marketing officer for Ameristar. "We have a relationship with a group of our customers that is similar to what you see on *Cheers*. When it feels like that, they want to bring their friends."

Don't worry that a hand may take a few seconds longer to complete; go ahead and ask them about their dinner that night, or who they think is going to win the Super Bowl. The payoff is higher customer satisfaction, and this is more important than being able to squeeze out a couple more hands each hour.

THE BLACKJACK EXPERIMENT

By encouraging dealers to interact with customers, the blackjack tables at Cactus Petes become a Petri dish for testing a key principle that underlies all customer experiences—that customers' ultimate level of satisfaction results from the combination of two factors:

- The processes imposed by management, and
- The personal interaction that takes place between employees and customers.

This simple principle, which is the logical extension of the touchpoint discussion in chapter 5, holds true for any customer encounter. Management can do everything within its power to establish processes designed to maximize efficiency and customer satisfaction, but all its efforts will evaporate like a mirage in the desert if a customer encounters a rude employee charged with carrying out those processes. Of course, the converse is also true. Even the best employee, regardless of his or her personality, will find it difficult to salvage a customer experience sabotaged by poor processes.

Consider your company's telephone operator. It is management's job to make sure its operator is armed with a list of employee extension numbers that is accurate and up to date—a process. It is completely up to the operator, however, to exhibit a warm and friendly personality that makes callers feel welcome. If either component breaks down, the result is a dissatisfied customer. For the restaurant owner, it won't matter if Wolfgang Puck or Emeril Lagasse are personally cooking the meals in the kitchen. All it takes is one churlish waitress, fresh from a fight with her boyfriend, to send customer satisfaction down the drain.

At Cactus Petes we wanted to see if we could calculate the present value of an engaging, gregarious dealer versus a somber, nononsense Las Vegas–style dealer. The test was simple: Cactus Petes designated two blackjack tables for the experiment that would take place over forty-eight hours. One table was staffed exclusively with outgoing, friendly dealers who would engage players in affable conversation. We called this *the interactive table.*

The other table, dubbed *the business table,* was staffed by polite but generally less communicative dealers. These dealers were instructed not to speak unless spoken to. Though they could answer players' questions, they would not initiate or encourage conversation. They would deal the cards with the goal of playing as many hands as possible during any given hour.

The interactive table may not have been able to deal as many hands per hour, but it definitely delivered more smiles per hour. The gregarious dealers kept the atmosphere loose and enjoyable, with conversations starting not just between players and dealers but among players themselves. It really did feel like the bar at *Cheers.* We watched time and again as someone would lose their last chip, start to walk away, but stop themselves by reaching into their wallet to buy more chips. It was as if the players had become emotionally invested in the table and the relationships that had been built over the course of playing.

It was therefore no surprise that when the final hand was dealt and we counted up the money, the interactive table dropped 13 percent more player cash into the casino's coffers than the business table. Think what this means: 13 percent more revenues *today* just because of a smile and a little friendly conversation. And this doesn't even begin to count what will certainly be even more revenue the casino will realize in the future because of the loyalty and advocacy that the interactive table's atmosphere fostered.

PROCESS VS. PERSONALITY: A TALE OF TWO HOTELS

Perhaps the best example of the role of process vs. personality comes from a tale of two hotel chains that take very different paths in winning over customers. Starwood's Westin Hotel chain and Fairmont Hotels & Resorts are two companies that consistently perform well in our guest satisfaction surveys. Each hotel faces unique challenges, which is why each approaches the issue of customer satisfaction differently.

A few years ago Westin was what would best be described as a middle of the pack performer. Although most guests were satisfied, they didn't rise to the level of advocacy. This meant that every time someone checked out of the hotel, management was left hoping against hope that customer would somehow find their way back to a Westin the next time they traveled.

What Westin needed was a *passion point*—something to serve as the focal point that would turn its simply satisfied guests into advocates. Something that would make business travelers issue standing orders to their travel agents to always book their room at a Westin whenever feasible. Westin took a very process-oriented approach to finding its passion point and began asking where its guests spent most of their time. The answer, of course, was in bed. And with this simple realization, the *Heavenly Bed* was born.

If you haven't stayed at a Westin recently, the marketing tagline tells you everything you need to know about the Heavenly Bed: "You're invited to mingle with some of the world's finest linens, a few thousand feathers and a custom-designed pillow-top mattress at the ultimate slumber party." And if you really sleep soundly, Westin will even sell you a Heavenly Bed for about $1,500, an offer that a surprising number of guests have taken Westin up on.

How much difference can a bed make? In our survey of upscale hotels, Westin received such high marks for the comfort of its beds that this one attribute almost single-handedly drove overall guest satisfaction. For the purpose of this chapter, the key point is that the Heavenly Bed is rooted in a decision by management—which we define as a process because the success or failure of the bed is independent of the personal interactions between its customers and employees.

Fairmont takes a different approach to making a stay at one of its hotels a memorable experience. Unlike other luxury hotel chains, such as the Four Seasons and The Ritz-Carlton, that are blessed with modern, purpose-built properties designed around the needs of to-day's traveler, Fairmont is known for operating older historic prop-erties. Although Fairmont properties such as the Savoy in London or the Copley Plaza in Boston literally ooze character from every pore, they also lack many of the modern amenities that most travelers take for granted—especially those forking out over $300 a night for a room. Smallish bedrooms, even smaller bathrooms, and the absence of central heating and air conditioning may be par for the course for early turn-of-the-century construction, but they give Fairmont a real challenge when it tries to match the guest satisfaction of its com-petitors.

Although Fairmont may suffer from process envy, like Cactus Petes it tries to balance the book on satisfaction by overperforming on the people/personality side of the equation. Chris Cahill, Fair-mont's president and COO, believes so strongly in the people side of the equation that he's even created processes for personality. Fair-mont adheres to what is known to insiders as the 10/5 rule. When-ever an employee—any employee—comes within ten feet of a guest, that employee is required to visually acknowledge the guest's pres-ence through eye contact, a smile, or a nod. Should that distance narrow to five feet, the employee must issue a verbal greeting. While it may sound cold and calculating to hear it described, in practice the policy helps to make every guest feel welcome.

Another way that Cahill tries to maximize the personal side of the equation is a simple instruction: whenever an employee interacts with a guest, she must stop and ask herself one question—What could I do to make this moment, no matter how routine, a memo-rable experience for this customer? He even formalized the program with a name, "Turning Moments into Memories," and went as far as naming a memory makers manager to propagate the concept across the entire chain.

"It's about trying to understand what you can do for that guest at that moment," Cahill explained. "Usually, it's the small things that make the difference, not the big things."

To illustrate his point, Cahill references unsolicited letters Fairmont received from guests describing a positive encounter with a Fairmont employee. One of Cahill's favorites wasn't even from a Fairmont customer, but from a man staying at a competing hotel across the street. Having learned that his hotel stopped offering room service after midnight, he called the Fairmont to place a food order. Not only was the Fairmont kitchen still open, it offered to walk across the street and bring the order right to the man's room in the competing hotel. Although we didn't check, we are pretty sure that this man chose to stay at Fairmont the next time he was in town.

SHOULD YOU CHARGE EXTRA FOR SMILING?

In chapter 2, we pointed out that few companies actually attempt to provide the best service possible. Instead, most companies provide only the best service they believe they can afford. And because most companies underestimate the return on their customer satisfaction investment, the tendency is to perform *less* service than is financially optimal. A company that sells itself short in this manner is just begging for customer satisfaction problems.

Corporate strategists take it for granted that only the highest-end luxury-level brands really go all out for customer service. For example, we now have so-called *six*-star hotels, replete with personal butlers, private swimming pools, chauffeurs, and furnishings fit for royalty. Critics write off the high customer satisfaction scores of ultra-luxury brands, arguing that their satisfaction is bought and paid for through these lavish amenities that no mortal brand could ever hope to offer.

Although this argument is accurate to a point, it is also dangerously shortsighted. The accurate part is that there *is* a direct correlation between customer satisfaction and price. Unless a company blatantly wastes its money, the more it spends on customer processes, the more satisfied its customers will be. A few of the more common ways that companies can buy love through processes include:

- increasing the number of employees available to serve each customer (shorter lines, more individualized attention, etc.)
- upgrading the ambiance of facilities (luxury appointments, fresh paint, etc.)
- higher-quality products (upgraded materials, tighter production tolerances, etc.)
- additional features (voice-activated dialing on cell phones, etc.)

Consider the cost of furnishing a hotel room after the construction crew packs up, leaving behind four bare walls and a cement floor. A top luxury hotel such as the Four Seasons might spend $60,000 to furnish a guest room, while an economy chain like Motel 6 might spend only around $10,000 per room. Mid-priced brands such as Hampton Inns or Courtyard by Marriott will spend somewhere in between. It doesn't take a rocket scientist to realize that nicer furnishings (a process) will make customers feel better about their experience (satisfaction), which translates into a willingness to pay higher room rates (behavior). The chart on page 147 illustrates this relationship by plotting the customer satisfaction of each major hotel brand against the average price of a room.

If we amortize the $50,000 difference between the cost of furnishing the luxury versus the economy room over three years, we come up with a difference of about $50 a night—an amount that is far less than the actual price difference between these two classes of lodging. The cost of furnishing a room, however, is only one of the processes that separate the two.

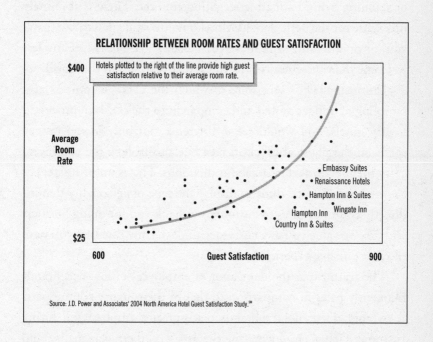

RELATIONSHIP BETWEEN ROOM RATES AND GUEST SATISFACTION

Hotels plotted to the right of the line provide high guest satisfaction relative to their average room rate.

$400

Average Room Rate

$25

600   Guest Satisfaction   900

Embassy Suites
Renaissance Hotels
Hampton Inn & Suites
Hampton Inn   Wingate Inn
Country Inn & Suites

Source: J.D. Power and Associates' 2004 North America Hotel Guest Satisfaction Study.℠

A top luxury hotel may have one staff member on duty for every three guest rooms while a budget motel may have only one staff member for twenty or thirty rooms. The luxury hotel will have a lifeguard at the pool watching out for the safety of guests, while the budget motel not only doesn't have a lifeguard, it probably doesn't even have a pool!

You get the picture. No matter where you turn in a hotel you will find examples of process decisions that determine the level of customer experience, and each of these processes comes with a price tag. So the answer is yes, luxury brands that spend more on their customers have a significant customer satisfaction advantage that justifies their higher prices.

But remember, processes make up only half the equation. The

personality of the employees carrying out those processes makes up the other half, and *personality is free.* So what if the clerks who hand out room keys at Motel 6 aren't wearing matching navy silk blazers or standing behind a marble reception counter? There is absolutely no excuse for the desk clerk at Motel 6 not to smile, fail to say thank you, or do anything whatsoever that makes her guests feel any less welcome than the guests of the finest luxury hotels in the world.

Unfortunately, if you were to watch the check-in process at a sampling of budget motels and compare it to the check-in process at luxury hotels, you would see a difference not only in the money spent on the physical check-in area but also in how the employees carry themselves as they go about their jobs. This is unfortunate, because it doesn't cost a dime to display the type of personality that indirectly communicates to customers a thank you for doing business with us, we value you as a customer, and we truly care that you have the best possible experience.

The reason that the demeanor of employees of low-end brands frequently pales in comparison to that of their luxury counterparts is twofold. First, luxury brands place greater emphasis on hiring customer-facing employees on the basis of their personality and communication skills. They also have a greater pool of talent from which to find those people-oriented employees. Second, and perhaps most important, luxury brands make it clear to employees that *how* they go about their job is just as important—if not more important—than their technical skills.

We will talk more about the hiring process in the next chapter. Our concern here is the poor-stepchild mentality that often permeates the culture of lower-priced brands until everyone at the company begins to believe it's acceptable to provide second-rate service. Management becomes complacent, which trickles down to the employees, and before you know it those employees might as well be wearing signs around their necks saying, "Hey, buddy, don't look at me, you get what you pay for."

Do your own ROI of CSI analysis. If your company competes in the lower- to mid-priced segments of your industry, you're probably making the right decision by *not* investing in many of the luxury processes enjoyed by your upper-tier competitors. Or you may find untapped process opportunities where you can provide great perceived benefit for relatively little cost; JetBlue's decision to install leather seating is a classic example.

However, just as Hyundai discovered, being the low-cost provider does not justify poor products or service. Even if you don't offer complimentary champagne while your customers wait for their personal shoppers, there is nothing stopping you from having the friendliest, most engaged employees in the industry.

Just look at the companies that serve as the customer satisfaction leaders in this book. Most of these companies are, by and large, decidedly nonluxury brands. Some even compete in the lowest-priced tiers of their respective industries. Their success in delivering best-in-class customer satisfaction is simple. It begins at the top with a culture that lets everyone at the company know that customer satisfaction is more than a buzzword. It moves on to processes by targeting those areas that will have the most positive impact on customers. And finally, it's driven home by employees who understand that although they don't work for the Four Seasons or Neiman Marcus, there is no reason they can't treat their customers as if they did. As we will see in the next chapter, great employees who can deliver this level of service don't just line up at your door. Hiring the right people, training them, and empowering them to do the right thing are a key part of the blueprint for creating customer advocates.

10

THE SUPERHERO WHO DRESSED
AS A JANITOR

It is one thing to go around saying you always hire the best people for the job, but it is quite another to actually prove the theory. For Bill Mossontte, the owner of Mission Hills Bowl, a popular bowling center near Los Angeles, his theory about hiring was tested during a recent Southern California Bowling Proprietors' Association meeting, where once a year the members open up their books to compare key financial metrics. Says Mossontte:

We were sitting around comparing everything from how often we cleaned the lanes to the cost of a bottle of vodka. Mission Hills Bowl is pretty profitable, so I was feeling kind of smug as we went through the numbers. And then—*boom*—I saw it. It was like somebody had misplaced a decimal or something.

My per employee labor cost was completely out of whack. I expected it to be a little high. After all, I've always paid whatever it takes to hire the best people, but this was ridiculous!

All the way home I began wondering if maybe the big corporate bowling centers like AMF and Brunswick had it right. Maybe I was wasting money paying people more than twice the minimum wage just to sharpen pencils and hand out bowling shoes.

The next morning I called Tracy Murphy, my general manager, into my office and told her I wasn't sure it made sense to continue paying people like this anymore. Tracy didn't even hesitate. She said, "Bill, the only reason we are making these kinds of profits is *because* of your employees." And to emphasize the point she just pointed right up there on the wall to that picture of Super Danny.

Dan Joyce—or Super Danny, as he is affectionately known by hundreds of Mission's regular bowlers—is typical of Mossontte's employees. And even though his official job title is porter—which means that his day is spent stocking restrooms and cleaning up after birthday parties—Dan Joyce is paid more than the assistant managers at some bowling alleys.

So why pay someone twice the market rate to make sure the restrooms are clean? Mossontte explains that he doesn't pay Joyce because he is especially good at taking out the trash, but because he has the rare ability to bring smiles to customers' faces as he goes about his job. The following is just one of the many Super Danny stories that Mossontte told us:

I'm in the bar one night and a bowler who I'd never met walked up to me and said he wanted to talk to me about one of my employees. I'm thinking, "This doesn't sound good," but he tells me that this was his first time at Mission, and while he was taking his bowling balls out of the trunk—these days most good bowlers bring three or four balls with them—one of my people recognized he wasn't a regular and came over to welcome him to Mission.

Turns out that Danny was cleaning up the parking lot and saw this guy that he didn't recognize, so he figured he's one of

the new bowlers starting that night. Danny goes over to introduce himself and asks if he can help him with his equipment.
The guy was so floored that he tracked me down just to tell me
how much he appreciated the effort. That was two years ago and
this guy has been one of my regular bowlers since.

Mossontte firmly believes that stories like this are the main reason for his success, so he bases his hiring policies on one simple principle: "You can teach almost anybody to do anything, but you can't
teach them personality."

The philosophy has translated into long-term success. League
bowlers are the lifeblood of any bowling alley, and Mission has more
league bowlers than any other bowling alley in the area—twice as
many as some of its nearest competitors. The demand for a spot in
one of Mission's leagues is so strong that Mossontte is able to charge
nearly a dollar more per game than the competition—and this at a
time when some alleys look like ghost towns on most weeknights. In
a survey of bowlers in the San Fernando Valley area of Los Angeles,
Mission Hills Bowl came out on top in customer satisfaction—way
on top—driven in large part by exceedingly high scores for its employees.

Like many industries today, the bowling business is dominated
by two giant consolidators—AMF and Brunswick—that own hundreds of bowling centers across the country. In Mossontte's opinion,
too many companies make the mistake of looking at labor only as an
expense, and accordingly have hiring policies that focus on finding
the lowest-paid employees who are physically capable of performing
the job. In contrast, Mossontte considers his employees an asset and
bases his hiring decisions almost exclusively on what that person can
do to improve the experience for his customers.

The first thing companies do when revenues drop is try to re-
coup their losses by cutting labor costs. Mossontte believes this philosophy only puts the company into a downward spiral because

lower-caliber employees will only cause more customers to defect to competitors. To emphasize the point, he notes that in 2001 AMF was forced to file for bankruptcy protection.*

"Sure, I could find someone to hand out bowling shoes for minimum wage," Mossontte says, "but I'm not going to find a superstar for that kind of money. And even if I did, they're just going to leave when they find a better paying job somewhere else."

So what does Bill Mossontte look for when he's hiring?

"I want people who genuinely like working with people—the type of person who is going to go the extra mile to make sure my customers are happy, not because I tell them to, but because they *want* to—you know, it's just the way they're wired. That's why I pay Super Danny like I do. Look, I'm not trying to exaggerate. It's not as if half my customers are going to walk out in protest if Danny left. But I do know that Danny [and my other employees] are the reason my customer satisfaction is so high, and that's the only reason this place is filled every night."

CHANGING YOUR HIRING PHILOSOPHY

At most companies, the lowest-paid employees are the ones who have the most face time with customers. Retail salespeople, cashiers, call center operators, receptionists; the list goes on and on of entry-level employees who effectively serve as the touchpoint where your customers meet your company.

In the previous chapter, we discussed how customer satisfaction results not only from the policies, procedures, and processes that are put in place by management, but also from the personal interaction that takes place between an individual employee and a customer. A chief operating officer can put the best telephone system in place, hire enough operators to handle the traffic, and make sure the phone

*AMF subsequently emerged from Chapter 11 in March 2002.

list is up to date, but unless she walks downstairs and answers the telephone herself, there isn't a thing she can do to control that all-important first contact.

Although management has no direct influence over these individual customer contacts, it can at least control the hiring process, making sure that those contacts are made by employees who can be trusted to do the right thing for customers each and every time—employees who are not only technically capable of handling the job, but employees who will bring a smile to customers' faces the same way that Super Danny Joyce does with everyone he meets at Mission Hills Bowl.

Every company sets its own criteria and agenda when it comes to hiring, and it's impossible to offer a formula for hiring that works across multiple companies and industries. Identifying the "right" employee reminds us of a quote by Supreme Court Justice Potter Stewart in a landmark pornography case in 1964. Stewart wrote in his now-famous decision that although he could not *define* pornography, "I know it when I see it."

So it goes with hiring great employees. The successful companies just seem to know them when they see them. And the companies that top our satisfaction surveys spoke loud and clear that their hiring policies are founded on the following key tenets:

- They focus on personality rather than the technical skills of the potential employee with whom their customers will spend most of their time.
- When necessary, they will pay above market average—sometimes well above—to attract the absolute best candidates from which to choose.
- They attract career-minded individuals who will care about the long-term satisfaction of their customers by making it widely known that they are a company that believes in promoting from within.

- They search out creative employee benefits that create a more desirable working environment.

The first of these tenets is undoubtedly the most crucial. Nowhere was there more universal agreement among our satisfaction leaders than in their unwavering solidarity that the road to customer advocacy begins with who you hire to man your front lines. This fact can be distilled into the simple overarching principle that it's easy to find people who are technically capable of carrying out the duties of most entry-level customer-facing jobs, so the real key is hiring those few special individuals who naturally care about—and relate well to—others.

We recently completed a project for Nissan Motor Corporation that validates this philosophy. Much like Toyota, Nissan builds a high-quality product but receives low scores for customer satisfaction with the buying process. After years of low scores, Nissan asked us to look deeper into the problem.

The first thing we discovered was that not all Nissan dealers (or their employees) are created equal. Depending on which dealership customers drive into, they might have a buying experience that was so smooth and professional that it would give any Lexus dealer a run for its money, or they could have one of those experiences that makes some people equate car shopping with a trip to the dentist.*

This got us thinking. If some dealers consistently provide great customer satisfaction while others don't, perhaps there were a few fundamental processes that separated the satisfaction leaders from the also-rans. Find these keys, and Nissan dealers would have a road map to higher customer satisfaction.

To test this theory, we put six high-satisfaction and six low-satisfaction Nissan dealers under the microscope, breaking down

*Variances between individual dealerships is a problem for all automobile manufacturers, not just Nissan. J.D. Power and Associates' various studies of new-vehicle buyers already show significant improvement among Nissan dealers.

everything they did into the tiniest parts. We reviewed their financial statements, their advertising, their merchandising. We interviewed everyone from the owner and the managers on down to the individual salespeople. We even sent in teams of mystery shoppers to record all the processes and interactions from the perspective of the customer.

What we found opened our eyes. Each dealer conducted business in essentially the same way across more than 90 percent of the processes we investigated regardless of whether it was a high- or low-satisfaction dealer. The real difference—the root cause that drove their customer satisfaction profiles—wasn't *how* each dealer went about selling cars, but *who* it employed to do the selling.

A quick debriefing of the mystery shoppers made it abundantly clear that the high-satisfaction dealers employed salespeople who were simply better communicators. And by "better communicators" we're not saying that they were smooth operators who could sell ice to Eskimos. Quite the contrary. One of the things that made these people better communicators was that they knew when to speak and when to stay quiet and listen. They used a more consultative and empathetic sales approach. They asked questions. They took the time to find out if their customer needed a third-row seat, and then tailored the product demonstration around those needs. To everyone involved in the analysis, the best salespeople were those who seemed, by nature, born to be helpful. It is as much a part of their DNA as their eye color or whether they are right- or left-handed.

Greg Dexter, the president of North Bay Nissan, and the highest rated of the high-satisfaction dealers we analyzed, just shrugged and said that he didn't need to wait for our report to know that it all comes down to the hiring process. Dexter points out that car dealers are in a unique position to hire customer-oriented salespeople if they really want to. This is because many car companies not only measure the customer satisfaction of each of their dealers but provide an individual customer satisfaction report for each salesperson as well.

Dexter says that the first thing he asks for when interviewing a prospective salesperson at North Bay Nissan is their CSI report:

> The good candidates are proud of their scores and will bring the report up themselves before you even have a chance to ask. Don't get me wrong, we're in business to make money too. It's just that I believe the best way to do it is by making my customers as comfortable as possible so they're with us for the long haul.
>
> I know it sounds like a cliché, "we care about the customer" and all that, but it's part of our DNA and culture here. Let me correct that, customer satisfaction *is* our culture. We've won many customer service awards from Nissan, and we have higher satisfaction scores than any other dealer in the area. But the real proof that it pays to hire lower key "people-oriented" salespeople is the fact that according to Nissan's own data we have a very high closing rate. And we do that by trying to hire salespeople who just like working with people.

What about the fast-talking hucksters wearing loud ties and shiny white shoes who reflect the popular stereotype of car salespeople? Dexter acknowledges the stereotype, but adds, "I could employ fast-talking high-pressure types if I wanted, but this type of selling just doesn't work anymore. Between the Internet and everything else, customers are just too smart for that today. So when the top salesman from the dealership down the street comes looking for a job, he doesn't get past the first five minutes of the interview if he has a bad CSI report. End of story, I don't care how much experience he has."

SHOW ME THE MONEY

Greatness doesn't come cheap. We found that Nissan's best dealerships paid a premium to hire these great communicators—twice as much, in fact, as those in the lower satisfaction control group. This shouldn't come as a surprise. Car salespeople work on commission and are therefore paid to perform. If great people skills translate into more sales, then these salespeople are generating more profit for their employer and deserve to be paid accordingly.

This may be fine for commissioned salespeople, but what about the more commonplace customer-facing jobs for which you can't directly link one individual's performance to profits? To the best companies, it isn't the amount of the transaction that matters, only that each and every customer contact provides an opportunity to drive the customer experience, to determine whether it is an advocate or assassin who walks out the door.

For example, there is a fast-food burger chain on the West Coast where new employees must actually prove themselves peeling potatoes and slicing onions for three months before they earn the right to ask customers if they want fries with their burger. The chain is so fanatical about its customer image that its starting hourly pay is $9, which ensures that even the guy who throws out the trash will greet every customer with a smile.

The Irvine, California–based chain is called In-N-Out Burger, and its devoted legions of fans will attest to its place among fast-food outlets. The company is almost over the top in customer service. But over the top or not, you can't argue with success. In J.D. Power and Associates' survey of restaurant satisfaction, In-N-Out not only scored higher than every other fast-food restaurant chain in its market, it also scored higher than all the higher-priced quick-dining restaurants that offer table service and other high-touch amenities.

We asked Carl Van Fleet, In-N-Out Burger's vice president of strategy, how they did it, and like so many of the satisfaction leaders, he said it comes down to the people you hire and the fact that In-N-Out is willing to pay to hire the best:

> We're out there competing with everyone else in our industry
> for that same 20-year-old. Not every applicant is willing to put

our customers' interests first. We want people who don't just wipe down a table, but take the time go back over it to make sure they didn't miss a spot. When they take a customer's order they may say "thank you," but we want someone who will smile so that our customers know they really mean it.

By starting our associates at $9 an hour we have a few advantages. First, we are fortunate to have a tremendous candidate pool; this allows us to hire associates who help us let our customers know this isn't just a fast-food place. We are proud of the tremendous job our associates do. More important, our customers appreciate our associates as well. We know this because it is the ratings for our associates that drive our high satisfaction scores.

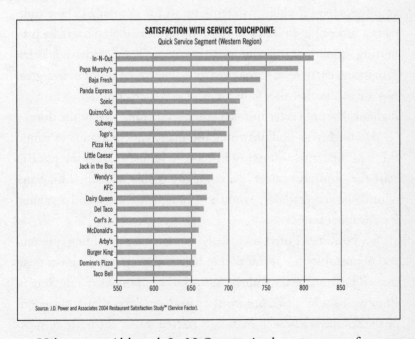

SATISFACTION WITH SERVICE TOUCHPOINT:
Quick Service Segment (Western Region)

Source: J.D. Power and Associates 2004 Restaurant Satisfaction Study℠ (Service Factor).

He's correct. Although In-N-Out received strong scores for taste and various other attributes, its score for courtesy and friendliness of staff was off the charts by market research standards. Customers rated its employees so high that we have absolutely no doubt that people drive out every day saying to themselves, "Now that's the way to run a business." In other words, they leave as advocates.

YOU MEAN IT'S NOT ALWAYS ABOUT THE BENJAMINS?

Great employees with advocate-building attitudes are not going to be swayed simply by the promise of higher compensation. The best employees, like the companies that employ them, are thinking long-term: where will I be five or ten years from now? This means that the carrot must be more than money; it must be about career-building opportunities.

The companies that top our surveys take advantage of this trait and organize themselves in such a way that even the most junior employees have the ability to move up within the ranks. These companies succeed in building a legion of motivated employees by promoting from within—and they mean it. They understand that promoting entry-level employees to management is not only a great way to ensure that they hire the best managers, but it also brings a higher caliber of career-minded entry-level applicants to the door.

Although you wouldn't think too many college graduates would think of the rental counter of Enterprise Rent-A-Car as the place to start their business career, the company is able to staff its branches with dedicated graduates who show integrity, energy, and a passion for customer service.

So, how does Enterprise do it? They do it by providing the very real opportunity for promotion to higher-paying management positions. They don't make empty, pie-in-the-sky promises. Sandy Rogers, Enterprise's senior vice president of strategy, notes that 100 percent of the company's branch managers started out at the bottom, picking customers up at their home, office, or repair shop; getting cars ready for rental delivery; calling on accounts; and everything else that might otherwise repel most up-and-coming college graduates. It doesn't stop with branch managers. All the general managers and nearly all the corporate officers—including the chairman, CEO, president, and COO—began the same way.

We asked Rogers whether this policy limits their ability to hire great managers that apply from outside the Enterprise family: "Sure. It means that sometimes we have to walk away from someone who looks like they might make a great branch manager," Rogers says. "But you've got to understand that you're stepping into dangerous territory if you start making exceptions. Our founder, Jack Taylor, made a commitment to put his employees and customers first. He promised our employees room to grow within the company, a chance to make their entry level job the stepping stone to a career. If you are going to tell the world, and more important your employees, that you stand for something, you better back it up by following those rules every time."

Enterprise isn't alone in this philosophy. In-N-Out Burger, Staples, Mission Hills Bowl, and many other satisfaction leaders have similarly impressive records of providing career paths to entry level employees who demonstrate the ability to do right by customers.

HIRING THE BEST WITHOUT BREAKING THE BANK

Other companies find they can cost effectively attract a higher caliber of customer-facing employee by offering unique benefits. At JetBlue, the two prime directives are: (1) cutting costs, and (2) setting the standard for friendly customer service. On the surface it would seem that these goals conflict with one another—you can be low price or high service, but not both.

CEO David Neeleman understands that being a low-cost provider does not justify poor service. If it did, airlines like People's Express would still be in business. Like our other satisfaction leaders, Neeleman is a staunch believer that customer satisfaction begins by hiring people with great personalities. But he is also a realist. He understands that as a discount airline, JetBlue cannot afford to pay its flight attendants the same as pilots, or reservation agents the same as management. Therefore, across most jobs, JetBlue pays only at or below the industry norm.

This does not mean that JetBlue has had to compromise its hiring standards. Despite its salary constraints, the airline employs a workforce that is outgoing, happy, and decidedly union-free. JetBlue pulls off this little magic trick by searching out programs that employees see as valuable, but which in fact cost very little to implement—or in some cases which actually save the company money.

This is really nothing different than a basic ROI of CSI analysis, except here the company is balancing the employee's, instead of the customer's, perception of value. Nothing frustrates David Neeleman more than when people plod along the same old path in a never-ending cycle of business as usual without ever stopping to think about the possibilities of looking at a problem with new eyes and a clean sheet of paper.

One of the first things JetBlue did was decide that its reservation agents (today over 1,000 strong) would work from an unusual location—their own homes! The next time you call 1-800-JET-BLUE to book a flight, the person on the other end of the line may be leaning back on their couch with a laptop computer perched on their knee while wearing their favorite robe and fuzzy slippers.

Neeleman couldn't be happier with the result. "We actually sponsor one day a month where we allow other companies, including competitors, to come in and take a look at how we do it," he says. "We think it's been a great thing for humanity, for the environment, for so many things—well, maybe it hasn't been so good for the people who make business clothes."

He points out that his turnover rate is down to 6 percent, far below the industry average. More important, JetBlue now has access to a higher quality workforce by being able to offer customer-facing employees the opportunity to work out of their own homes.

Another JetBlue innovation is a flexible work schedule that allows flight attendants to sign up as a two-person team. This team is free to divide up the flight schedule between them. JetBlue doesn't care which of the two team members shows up for a scheduled flight as long as the shift is covered. This allows the company to have their pick among an entirely new pool of job candidates who may not want to work full time.

Because the program is so flexible, flight attendants are willing to compromise on wages. And, because each member of the team is working only part time, JetBlue does not need to pay the same health insurance premium it does for full-time flight attendants. Neeleman also says that the program prevents the type of burnout that accounts for much of the surly behavior exhibited by flight attendants on some other airlines.

CHOOSING THE RIGHT CANDIDATE

Once you've done everything necessary to bring these top candidates to your door, you are still faced with the task of choosing the one or two who will do the best job of representing your brand. By following the advice laid out earlier, you'll find the task of choosing actually becomes more difficult because you will have more people applying for each position. Unfortunately, despite all our poking and prodding, the satisfaction leaders who universally advocated the need to hire on the basis of personality and empathy are no better able to articulate *how* they go about choosing these individuals than Justice Stewart was able to define pornography. Most experienced, successful bosses simply know the right candidates when they see them, spend time with them, and get a strong sense of the person behind the résumé.

At first this lack of a formalized, time-tested approach seemed almost unthinkable. After all, these executives had not only been able to articulate answers to every question we threw at them, but they did so with surprising consistency, almost as if they had been cut from the same mold, or at least mentored by the same business professor.

The more we thought about it, however, the more we realized that perhaps this inability to define a requisite personality in some formulaic way wasn't such a bad thing. If the main objective is finding an employee who has that certain spark, shouldn't that spark be just as evident during the interview as it is when that person is manning the cash register?

Despite the amorphous nature of the eureka moment, there are many valuable options available to help employers identify the best candidates. For example, at Cactus Petes, prospective casino employees are asked to go out onto the casino floor and interact with customers.

Jeanene Higgins, a human resources director for Ameristar, and the person responsible for hiring the customer service superstars at Cactus Petes, says, "I strongly suggest to all my managers that they actually take the candidate into the casino. We'll send them out on the floor and give them an assignment. They will be told, 'That guest looks lost, go help him.' Then we view how they handle that situation." For Higgins, there is no substitute for seeing how someone will react in a real world situation as opposed to listening to how they *say* they would react.

Staples and Enterprise Rent-A-Car provide an exception to the others. Both of these companies provide managers standardized assessments to help them separate the wheat from the chaff. Although they were in a minority among the companies we examined, both companies swear by the results. And to be fair, it isn't as if the other companies came out against these tests, but just like Justice Stewart, they preferred to put their trust in the instincts of their people who will make those decisions.

Enterprise's assessment covers six attributes: leadership, persuasiveness, work ethic, flexibility, communication, and customer service. Marie Artim, assistant vice president of recruiting, explains,

"We typically have twenty or more applications for every hire, so the assessment is just one more piece of the puzzle to help our managers pick the right person."

Artim points out that the assessments are only a guide; they are not life and death. And it's not as if any candidate will be shown the door based on the assessment results alone. Instead, these assessments are just one more tool that companies increasingly use to help them identify the next Super Danny Joyce.

One thing successful executives agree on is that the hardest part of the hiring process is remaining focused on just who you are trying to hire in the first place. In other words, don't get sidetracked by the hotshot candidate who talks a great game but is unlikely to fit into a culture where the customer really does come first. A great education, ten years' experience in a similar position, or an IQ that qualifies for Mensa are all impressive but will likely have nothing to do with determining if a person has the empathy and personality to make every customer encounter a memorable one.

Like finding the right mate, it is one thing to make a good choice and quite another to make the relationship work. As we will see in the next chapter, great employees must be empowered and encouraged to deliver that greatness to customers. There is little value spending the time and money it takes to hire well if a company is not going to provide the freedom and incentive to do the right thing.

11

TRUSTING EMPLOYEES TO DO
THE RIGHT THING

VSP is one of the nation's largest and most successful providers of group vision insurance. Like most health-care companies, its portfolio of clients ranges from small, locally owned businesses to major corporations. Linda Stevens, senior account executive at VSP's Indianapolis office, says, "We appreciate all our clients—big and small—but it's those one or two opportunities we get each year to sell a really big client that can make our year."*

So, when Linda received the biggest request for a proposal her office had seen all year, it would normally be a time for celebration. But celebrations would have to wait because the deadline for completing this proposal was fast approaching, and the prospect made it clear there would be no extensions. One problem was that much of the information Linda needed to finalize the bid resided in VSP's corporate office in California, and she had only twenty-four hours to get those documents, finalize her bid, and deliver the proposal.

Getting the documents from corporate wouldn't pose a problem

---

*Interestingly, this story comes from a manager at VSP, which is in and of itself a leader in customer satisfaction, having earned the top spot in the J.D. Power and Associates 2005 National Vision Plan Member Satisfaction Study.[SM]

given the wonders of overnight package delivery—in this case UPS. Unfortunately for Linda, even the best package delivery company can not deliver a package if the address label isn't filled out correctly, and as Murphy's Law would have it, the one time she really needed something overnight, someone had made a mistake filling out the label.

Linda arrived at the office early expecting the package to be waiting for her. When it wasn't there she became nervous. That nervousness escalated when Scott, her regular UPS driver, arrived empty-handed at 10 A.M.

"I told Scott how important the package was and he said he would look into it. I knew there wasn't much he could do so I called the UPS customer service line and found out that the package was undeliverable because the driver didn't have the complete address, and would be sent back to the UPS operating center later that day. This was very concerning. Without that package there was no way I could meet my deadline. It had been a long time since I'd had an opportunity to bid on a contract this big, and to think I wasn't even going to be in the running because of a stupid address labeling mistake was unbelievably frustrating."

Linda then told us, "It was about an hour later that I looked up and saw Scott walking through the door with a big smile on his face and an even bigger package in his hands."

It turns out that Scott had also called the home office and found out the location of the truck Linda's package was on. He delayed his regular deliveries and arranged to meet up with the other driver in a parking lot somewhere between the two drivers' routes. When they met, Scott tore through that driver's truck until he found Linda's package, and then drove straight back to her office to deliver it.

Going to these heroics was in no way part of Scott's job description. In fact, by taking it upon himself to delay his regular deliveries to track down and retrieve Linda's package, he took a very real but calculated risk that he might cause a problem with one of the other customers on his route.

Scott's dilemma is similar to those faced by employees every day who may want to do the right thing for their customers but are prevented from taking action because of strict policies that do not allow them to make decisions without first seeking approval from a higher central authority. This means that even the best employees, the ones who really do want to go the extra mile to help a customer in need, are faced with a decision that often means choosing between helping their customer on one hand and job security on the other.

We spoke to UPS to ask whether Scott's decision to delay his deliveries to help Linda put him at risk. "Absolutely not," came word back from John Beystehner, COO for UPS. "We firmly believe in empowering our drivers on a range of issues, many of which will inevitably fall out of the direct line of business at hand. Our drivers are our most visible and powerful brand asset, and the level of trust they bring to their customers is both the bedrock of our brand and our foundation for the future."

Sound like just another executive pontificating about his company's focus on the customer? Of course it does. But at UPS it's not just empty talk. UPS not only came out on top in J.D. Power and Associates' most recent small package delivery satisfaction study, it came out on top across all three subcategories: domestic air, ground, and international delivery.

With 88,000 drivers on the road every day working in a business where minutes are crucial, and while being physically disconnected from their chain of command, UPS understands they have to trust their drivers' judgment if they want to provide the best customer service. While it doesn't mean that every driver is going to make the right decision every time, the key is creating an environment where UPS drivers know that as long as their decisions are based on a good-faith effort to do right by their customers, they should never fail to act out of fear of losing their job.

Beystehner points out that by giving their drivers both the authority and the accountability for their actions, the drivers become entrepreneurs, almost the owners of their routes. And, like owners, they begin to see the direct link between performance and rewards.

As great a job as UPS does in customer satisfaction, there is no rest for the weary. Federal Express performs nearly as well as UPS in customer satisfaction as these companies (and others) compete to divide up what was once essentially a monopoly held by the U.S. Postal Service.

YOU HIRED THEM FOR A REASON

Empowering frontline employees to act on their own to keep customers happy is critical, or at least that is the mantra of the satisfaction leaders we interviewed for this book. What good is owning a Thoroughbred if you are going to hitch it to a cart? But giving away this type of control isn't always easy.

Bill Mossontte of Mission Hills Bowl notes, "For me the hiring is the easy part. I don't run a multinational corporation, so I'm right here all the time. For me the hard part is letting go and avoiding the temptation to micromanage everything they do. You've got to keep telling yourself you hired them for a reason, and then give them the freedom to go out there and do what's right, even if it means making a mistake now and then."

Of course, the larger the company is, the more important—and challenging—it is to empower your employees to act on their own. It is well chronicled that one of the greatest challenges successful small companies face is the day they grow to the point that the original entrepreneur is no longer able to manage the everyday details of the enterprise. It is at this point that companies need to let go of some of their precious control and delegate more decision-making authority down through the ranks.

But what about organizational theorists who scream, "Deviation breeds chaos"? In a very real sense they are right. Empowering frontline employees, especially those in lower paying, entry-level positions, with the authority to make decisions on their own is a scary proposition. That's why the issue of empowerment needs to be handled very carefully. But, as dangerous as empowerment can be in individual situations, it is nowhere near as dangerous as an institutional policy where any deviation from the norm is discouraged and must be run through multiple layers of the organization before exceptions are granted.

In today's fast-paced society, nothing will frustrate your customers faster than having to wait while helpless employees seem unable to carry out what appears to be the simplest of tasks without receiving approval from above. Mind you that we are not talking about the type of deviation exhibited by Scott the UPS driver. What Scott did was go above and beyond the call of duty to make Linda Stevens an advocate for life. No, we are talking about the very real risk of having an otherwise good customer turn into an assassin before your eyes as she is inconvenienced by what appears to be paralysis on the part of your frontline employees. Remember, any encounter with an otherwise satisfied customer can result in two very different outcomes. Make the wrong choice and you've created an assassin, but make the right choice and you may have an advocate for life.

We received a story from a business traveler that illustrates this point. He had flown three hours to New Orleans, rented a car, and driven north through the Louisiana swamps to Baton Rouge. He hadn't made a hotel reservation, but knew the town well enough to know that this shouldn't be a problem. It was getting close to the end of the business day back home, and more than anything he needed to find a hotel that offered Internet access so that he could handle what he knew would be an unpleasantly long string of e-mails:

> I planned to go over to a Marriott I knew, but when I got off the freeway I saw a brand new AmeriSuites Hotel with a giant banner out front that read free high-speed Internet access. Why pay

$9.99 for Internet at the Marriott if I could get what I needed for free? So, to make a long story short, I went in, confirmed they had a room with an Internet connection available, and went up to my room to call into the home office. After the call I looked at the desk for the Internet connection. Nothing. I spent the next ten minutes like a kid on a scavenger hunt looking for the connection. At one point I even got down on my hands and knees to look under the bed—why I thought the connection might be down there God only knows.

I finally went downstairs and asked the woman who checked me in where the Internet connection was. "It's wireless," she says. "But my computer isn't set up for wireless," I replied. "Don't you have a standard Ethernet connection I can plug into?" She couldn't have been more polite, but had absolutely no idea what I was talking about.

I asked if she could open up the business office for me just so that I could take care of my e-mails. No, she said, it's closed and she's not allowed to open it up after hours. I asked about the computer in the office behind the desk, and she said that she isn't allowed to let guests use that computer.

Now this is the really good part. I can see I'm not going to be able to log on at this hotel so I ask her to go ahead and cancel my room so I can go over to the Marriott. "Only my manager can cancel a transaction," she says—even though she acknowledged that I'd been there less than an hour, and had spent most of that time trying to get onto the Internet. She tells me I have to check out, pay for my room, and then she will check with the manager when she sees him next if they can reimburse me for any of my charges.

All I can say is I'm going to stick with hotels that I know from now on, and I will never—and I mean *never*—set foot in an AmeriSuites again. I know it probably isn't fair to judge them on this one experience, but I don't care. The hotel itself was brand new, looked great, and I really got the feeling the desk clerk felt bad about my situation. But no way am I going to stay someplace where the staff is so afraid of their own shadow that it seems like they can't even go to the bathroom without permission.

We checked our data, and AmeriSuites definitely isn't the worst when it comes to customer satisfaction, but we wouldn't call it a satisfaction leader either. Just as this customer pointed out, the chain receives high praise for the quality of its guest rooms, but falls down in some of its people skills—perhaps enhanced by what appears to be a lack of authority to do right for customers when a problem arises.

The first big danger when your employees are unable to act is time. Whenever a problem is bumped upstairs you create a delay. This is especially problematic in situations like the AmeriSuites story, where it was apparent that the customer was in the right, and once someone with authority reviews the situation they are going to do what the desk clerk should have been able to do on her own— terminate the room reservation. The problem is that by the time the company finally rectifies the situation, your customer has been left seething and your best hope is that they haven't gone out in the community to trash your brand.

Our annual Sales Satisfaction Index Study that measures how satisfied people were with their new-vehicle purchase experience finds that even at car dealerships, one of the biggest differentiators of customer satisfaction is the level of empowerment the dealer affords its salespeople. To illustrate this we held all other variables constant and measured customer satisfaction independently based on whether a salesperson had the authority to quote prices directly without having to run off to check with a manager. In cases where the salesperson had this authority, more than half (54 percent) of all buyers gave their dealer the highest possible satisfaction rating. But when a salesperson needed to get permission to quote a price, the number of people giving the highest rating dropped to 35 percent. And if a salesperson needed to bring in another salesperson or manager to talk prices, the top box rating dropped further to only 27 percent.

People just like dealing with people in authority. This probably explains why the highest satisfaction scores come from people who bypass the frontline salesperson altogether and walk in asking to deal directly with the manager. Nearly two-thirds (60 percent) of these customers give their experience the highest rating.

EMPOWERMENT IN A REMOTE CUSTOMER SERVICE SETTING

As companies become larger, and transactions become more complicated, customers are challenged with the job of even finding someone in a position to solve their problem. The problem is exacerbated when your customers must deal remotely through your call center or Web site. Customers will cling to any live person like a port in a storm, pleading for help and begging not to be transferred to yet another department where they will be forced to relive their problems all over again from the beginning.

Sit down and talk to people about why they dislike being transferred to customer service centers in India or other far-off lands. The problem isn't so much concern over the loss of American jobs, or difficulty understanding an accent. The real problem is that these offshore call centers typically give their employees zero authority to take any action that falls outside the narrowly defined norm. Try asking for their supervisor, and the answer is almost always the same: "We are sorry, sir, but we are not authorized to do what you request." Ask to be transferred to someone at the home office who does have the authority and you will be told, "We are sorry, but we are unable to do that." These offshore operators begin to sound like a bad sci-fi movie from the sixties where the robot says "unable to compute." Meanwhile that little assassin inside of you is building strength, just waiting for the opportunity to blast the company at the first opportunity.

Just ask Dell, a company that once stood at the pinnacle of customer satisfaction. Although Dell is still a very successful company, it's been widely reported that it has lost much of its luster on the service side of its business, much of which is attributed to overseas call centers that seem to have about as much empathy for its customers as the Grinch had for the children of Whoville. Instead, Dell's success is now tied primarily to its distribution model (i.e., the sales touchpoint) and not service.

One of the consumer stories we received illustrates why Staples earned our highest recognition for call center performance. Dennis had ordered office furniture from Staples, but right before it was about to be delivered he needed to make a last-minute change. Knowing that time was of the essence, Dennis called the customer service line to see if there was anything they could do. The operator, knowing how people hate telephone transfers that result in voice-mails—or worse, the dreaded disconnect—offered to stay with Dennis until she reached the right department that could handle his problem. A good thing too, because the line kept ringing busy. Rather than telling Dennis to call back later, the operator took down his information, handled the changes on her own, and called Dennis back to tell him the situation was resolved.

We realize that this story may sound trivial. We also realize that just about every company can reach into its archives and find similar stories of such heroics. But before you discount the import of this story, please consider two things. First, the experience was significant enough that Dennis took the time to write and tell us about this operator. He even began his story with, "I'm sure you'll get lots of horror stories, and I've got a bunch, but I'd like to focus on a positive experience I recently had with a telephone customer representative at Staples." More important, our research shows that Dennis's experience wasn't just a one-time anomaly. Staples does this time after time, which builds legions of advocates like Dennis—one of the primary reasons the company has grown to its current level of dominance.

LOVE FOR SALE

The Staples and UPS stories reflect one type of empowerment—giving employees the freedom to deviate from their normal job descriptions to go above and beyond the call of duty to help their customer. The cost to the company is their time, along with the risk that by going off on their own you must trust that they won't—for lack of a better term—do something *stupid* that gets you into trouble.

There is an altogether different empowerment issue that companies must face involving situations in which redeeming a customer's trust may require an outlay of hard cash: a round of free drinks at Mission Hills Bowl while you wait for the mechanic to fix a broken pinsetting machine, a cash voucher to a JetBlue customer whose TV went on the fritz midflight, or WaMu reimbursing a customer for losses associated with a check that bounced because of a delay at the bank. The stakes are raised when deciding how much authority to give your employees to dole out actual cash to keep a customer happy.

Although we can't provide you with a formula for determining where to draw the line, we can tell you with confidence that the companies that earn the highest satisfaction draw that line quite differently than the rest. There of course must be guidelines, but the only way to provide the best customer service is to allow your employees to use their best judgment within those guidelines.

Above all else, your employees must understand that they should never fail to act out of fear for their job. At times your employees' best judgment may turn out to be not so good after all. In such situations everyone must see that you applaud the effort to do right by the customer, while simultaneously counseling the employee so that they use better judgment the next time around.

So how do you calibrate those guidelines to determine when (and for how much) your company should pay to make a customer happy? Every company must make that decision on its own, but our experience suggests the following golden rule: Your employees must avoid getting caught up in the heat of the moment. Don't get caught up in a battle with an angry customer where winning the argument becomes more important than the bigger goal of customer satisfaction.

Teach your employees to stop, reflect, and put themselves in the shoes of the customer. Does this customer truly feel entitled to compensation, or are you facing a customer who is just trying to get something for nothing? Of course, the most important question is *Did you screw up?* For if the customer's frustration is due to your own actions—be it a mistake, a broken promise, or a premature product breakdown—then both fair play and good long-term business strategy dictate that your company should rectify the problem, even if such rectification will cost money.

Good companies, those looking for long-term growth, don't ask if they are legally obligated to pay. And the best companies, the ones that top our studies, enforce this long-term growth strategy by allowing their employees to make things right without making the customer jump through multiple layers of corporate hoops.

We asked the satisfaction leaders how often they found employees going too far, spending too much of the company's money to satisfy a customer. "Very rarely," they answered in unison. In fact, most discussed the frustration that despite all their emphasis on doing right by the customer, they find that many employees don't go as far as they should to fix a bad situation.

Of course, there were a few stories in which an employee took it upon himself to open the company checkbook a little too far, the most extreme of which was offered up by David Neeleman from Jet-

Blue. The airline had 160 passengers waiting at its Long Beach, California, terminal one evening for a flight to New York. Unfortunately, while the passengers were waiting patiently at the gate, their plane was not, having been delayed in route to the point that it wouldn't land until the next morning.

Not to worry, the employee in charge of the Long Beach gate was well aware of JetBlue's policy never to strand passengers, so he simply walked down to the United terminal and asked if they could accommodate his passengers on their flights. "No problem," came the reply, "that will be $1,000 per ticket." And just like that this employee wrote what essentially amounts to a check for $160,000 to United Airlines.

Although Neeleman notes that the heart was in the right place, he would have preferred that this employee take a minute to think about his options before opening the company checkbook. It turns out that while this employee was booking his passengers on United, JetBlue had a spare plane sitting just a few hundred yards away, and even a spare crew available to fly it!

Neeleman points out that the employee was not rebuked for his actions. He received some counseling—and probably more than a little ribbing from his coworkers. But as Neeleman says, "He was trying to take care of his customers and you can't fault him for that."

THE EMPATHY FACTOR

The JetBlue story is important for another reason. It illustrates that a company does not always need to spend whatever it takes to put the customer in the same position as if the problem never occurred. Neeleman points out that even if the other plane hadn't been available, not every passenger absolutely had to get to New York that evening. Some would have felt fully compensated with a heartfelt apology, a nice hotel room for the night, and a $200 travel voucher.

We were surprised by how many of our satisfaction leaders already knew one of the more subtle nuggets contained in our data-base. For many people, the deeper-rooted need when problems arise isn't compensation, but just for someone at the company to feel their pain, to really care about their plight. Empathy, it seems, is com-pensation enough for many consumers.

In a particularly hair-raising example of what not to do, we share a story about a flight aboard Frontier Airlines in which passengers became angry when they were told that the last people to board the plane would have to check their carry-on bags because no more space was available in the cabin. What ensued was a virtual shouting match between the passengers and the flight attendants. The reason this seemingly minor inconvenience escalated was the lack of empathy ex-pressed on the part of the attendants. Rather than just grabbing bags and boldly pronouncing "FAA regulations expressly require the air-line to check any luggage that doesn't fit in an overhead bin," the at-tendants should have shown a little empathy. They could have quietly asked for volunteers who had other items checked, which meant that they would need to wait in baggage claim anyway. They could have told passengers that they were going to check their own carry-on items to help make room for a few extra bags. Basically, they could—and should—have done anything other than hide behind rules and regulations that gave them the right to pull off passengers' bags. When it comes to your customers, it's not about what you have the right to do, but asking what's the right thing to do.

Too many times companies that empower their employees to do good watch those employees take the easy way out by trying to buy their way out of a bad situation. Don't just automatically offer a $25 gift certificate to every customer who walks up with a legitimate beef. Take the time to really listen to your customers when they complain. Sure, for many customers the correct, and perhaps only, course of action is incur the cost to make the problem go away. But, for others, by listening and trying to find the root cause of their discomfort, you will not only be able to do a better job of building advocacy, you may be able to save money in the process.

LEARNING FROM THE TRAGEDY OF 9/11

Though 9/11 was a day of unspeakable tragedy and sadness, something wonderful happened that day as well. Human decency and a spirit of compassion and caring superseded business interests then and in the days that immediately followed. It is for this reason that we debated even presenting the following story about Enterprise Rent-A-Car and of the heroic efforts its employees went to on that day to take care of their customers.

On one hand we felt the story was perfect for this chapter because it dealt with employees taking extraordinary measures—on their own—to help customers, even though they knew their actions would cost their company hundreds of thousands of dollars. On the other hand, we were concerned that by including this story we would somehow trivialize the heroics of so many individuals at so many companies across the country that day. Therefore, please read the following story in the context in which it is presented, and take from it the belief that the world will be a better place, not just for consumers, but for society in general, if we think back to the spirit of that day—a day of unity when we were more concerned with doing what was right than worrying about the cost or imposition of helping others.

As the events unfolded that day, no airport was shut down faster or tighter than Dulles near Washington, D.C. One of the hijacked jets had been flown into the Pentagon just a few miles away, and for hours there was concern that another jet was still unaccounted for and heading for the city. Amid the chaos and confusion, prospective airline passengers found themselves stranded, with all flights cancelled, and even the rental car facilities at the airport closed.

Despite the fact that Avis, Hertz, and other competitors had shut down, Enterprise's airport location remained open for business. As word spread though the airport that Enterprise was open, people began trekking on foot to the company's Jefferson Davis Highway location, sometimes climbing over a four-foot-high fence as a shortcut to the facility. It didn't take long before there were hundreds of people crowded in and around Enterprise's modest office, hoping to rent a car so they could drive back to their homes and loved ones.

The manager climbed up on the counter and told the swelling crowd, "Folks, let me explain what we've got going on here. I've got 100 cars and there are a lot more of you than I have cars. So here's what we'll do. I've got a gentleman up here going to Atlanta. How many of you are going to Atlanta or that direction? Let's work together and get paired up so we can get you all home, because that's our goal."

And so it went. Within a couple of hours the Enterprise staff had organized the rental of all the cars and created a massive carpooling plan designed to get everyone home, or at least close to it. When the cars were gone, two newly hired management trainees, acting on their own understanding of the company's customer service culture, actually drove one remaining stranded traveler all the way to South Carolina in one of their own personal cars.

While this is an amazing story of how a few employees took it upon themselves to go above and beyond the call of duty in a time of crisis, there is an important footnote to this of which you are probably not aware. For all its greatness, Enterprise Rent-A-Car has one operational flaw. The company is *not* set up to do one-way rentals. Enterprise's entrepreneurial business model is predicated on each local operation buying, maintaining, and disposing of its own fleet. On this day Enterprise's managers across the country ignored the rule and sent literally thousands of vehicles out across the country where they would eventually have to be picked up and driven back to their original fleets. The cost was staggering. But to this day the executives at Enterprise look back at its employees as heroes, individuals who took the company's motto to heart, and acted without prior authority in a manner they believed was consistent with the company's philosophy of always doing what's best for the customer.

FINAL THOUGHTS

Please consider this one final comment about empowerment. Recall that there was one company we initially planned to hold up as a satisfaction leader, but its scores dropped precipitously while we conducted our investigation. We interviewed the CEO, not knowing of the impending drop in CSI score. During that interview he told us that although their company previously provided great freedom and authority to even their lowest level employees, they have changed that policy in favor of one that requires much more centralized control and supervisory review. This turned out to be the only company we interviewed that was moving away from employee empowerment to a more controlled approach. A coincidence? You decide.

12

TURNING BAD CUSTOMER ENCOUNTERS INTO WINS

There is no better recipe for customer advocacy than building products that work perfectly right out of the box, or providing such good service that customers don't think twice about whom to call. But if this doesn't sound like your company, all is not lost. Although it may not always seem like it, customers understand that problems will arise from time to time and have a surprisingly large capacity for forgiveness.

Indeed, time and time again our data shows that customer encounters in which a problem is resolved quickly and efficiently receive higher satisfaction scores than situations in which there was no problem at all. Obviously, every individual has a different level of patience and understanding and repeated mistakes will eventually turn even the most saintly into assassins. But screwing up can turn out to be a good thing if amends are made impressively.

Regardless of how much we as consumers plan or how many precautions we take, there is always the risk that someone, somewhere, will mess up. A missed deadline here, a product breakdown there; all you can really be sure of is when that inevitable problem arises, it is likely to come at the most inopportune time, the time when you can least afford it. For example, consider this story that one of our clients shared with us about his much-anticipated honeymoon trip to Bermuda:

We chose Bermuda because of its tropical beauty and its reputation for wonderful hospitality. My travel agent said she knew the perfect resort on the island's south coast, a place called the Stonington Beach Hotel. She said she could put us in a room right on the beach with a view we would never forget. That sounded good to me so I told her to book it, but not before emphasizing one instruction: "Please make sure there are no surprises. It seems like all I ever get when I'm traveling these days are surprises and the surprises always turn out to be bad." I told her, "This is my honeymoon. I don't care what gets messed up on my next business trip; just make sure this one is perfect."

After an uneventful flight, we arrived in Bermuda, found a shuttle waiting to take us to the hotel, and the only surprise was that the place looked even better than in the brochures. When the bellboy took us to our room, we were impressed. It was beautifully furnished and had a large picture window. The first thing I did was throw back the drapes and all I can say is that my agent was right, I wasn't about to forget the view anytime soon. Instead of a beautiful panorama of the ocean, there stood two giant mounds of dirt. Instead of palm trees, there were several pieces of heavy equipment and a small contingent of construction workers who were standing so close that they might as well have joined us for tea. My bride saw the veins start to bulge in my neck and forehead. She thought I might keel over right there from apoplexy. Here was my dreaded surprise and it was worse than I could have imagined.

As our client relayed this story, we sat there quietly thinking that this is a classic example of how customers become assassins. The big question was whether the problem arose from an innocent breakdown in communication, or from the hotel intentionally failing to mention the construction to travel agents (i.e., a decision to place short-term revenue ahead of customer satisfaction). One thing we did know is that by taking the first ten minutes of a meeting to share his story, our client was a dyed-in-the-wool assassin hell-bent on completing his corporate hit. He wanted to make sure that none of us ever visited this hotel, and probably hoped that we would share his nightmare tale with others. And so he continued:

I stormed back to the hotel front desk and, through clenched teeth, tried to make myself very clear. "I've had this trip planned for a month. You knew it was my honeymoon. Why didn't someone tell me I was booking a room in the middle of a construction site?" I could feel my blood begin to boil when she apologized but told me that the hotel was completely booked and there wasn't another room available.

It was then that she did something completely unexpected. Instead of telling me that there was nothing she could do and we would just have to live with it, she immediately instructed the concierge to call all the other top hotels in the area to find us a room with an ocean view. She didn't fight with me at all. She even agreed that this wasn't acceptable.

Have you ever been so keyed up about being wronged that getting some kind of revenge becomes more important than resolving the original problem? Well, I was close to that state. Having her eliminate all resistance and envelope me in empathy really took the sting out of my anger. I suddenly felt really bad for coming down on this woman like a ton of bricks. I actually found myself telling her that it was all right, that she didn't have to find us another hotel. "Okay then," she replied, "let's see what we can do to make this right for you."

She looked at her computer and said that if we could put up with our current room for the first two nights, she would move us to a private bungalow right on the water for the remainder of the week. The bungalow was far from the construction site and would give us enough privacy to make up for having to share our first two days with some of the local hardhats.

I wasn't pleased but I also wasn't interested in ruining our honeymoon. We accepted, and we were glad we did. The bungalow was beautiful. More important, for the rest of our time there, every time we saw the desk clerk, she went out of her way to make sure we were happy and to see if there was anything she could do for us. By the time we checked out, I was feeling the kind of calm one feels after a week in paradise. But the hotel still had one more surprise up its sleeve—and for once this was a nice surprise. When I received the bill, I saw that she had deducted a thousand dollars from the total. I was stunned. She pointed out the change and said it was their way of showing how sorry they were for the inconvenience. She wanted to make sure we left with good memories from the Stonington Beach.

The discount was really just the icing on the cake. Everyone at the hotel had already showed me through their actions that they felt bad for what had happened. They really didn't need to give me the discount. No, I didn't give it back . . . I'm not crazy. But I've probably repaid it many times over by telling everyone I know about what happened and how it was resolved. I know of at least three or four couples I've convinced to stay there. That's pretty amazing if you think about how I was ready to torch the place when I first found out about the construction next to my room.

TURNING LEMONS INTO LEMONADE

Granted, not every customer encounter affords such an elaborate remedy for a bad experience. Agreeing to pay for your customer's dry-cleaning bill after your waitress spills red wine on a white cashmere sweater is not likely to placate the customer, regardless of how apologetic one might be. Yet in most instances, such as the honeymoon debacle, there is a great opportunity for redemption.

Sticking with the hotel example, imagine that you've just been asked to answer a satisfaction survey about a recent hotel visit. As you think about how satisfied you were with your stay, you look back to all the touchpoints in which you interacted with the hotel personnel. How professional was the staff? What about the physical quality of the room and common areas? Were you *satisfied* with each of these elements, or were any of them so outstanding that you were moved beyond satisfaction into the realm of advocacy? Or was the opposite true? Did you have a problem during your stay that required attention?

Not surprisingly, hotel guests who experienced one or more problems during their stay rate their overall experience more than a hundred points lower than those that didn't have any problems (749 vs. 612). This seems obvious. Poor television reception, a noisy ice-

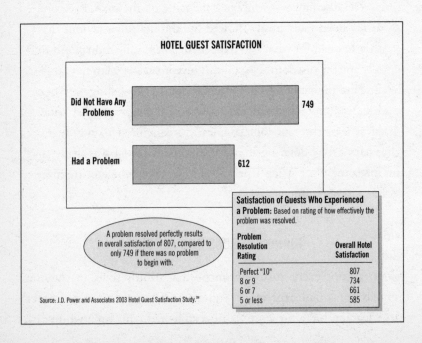

HOTEL GUEST SATISFACTION

Did Not Have Any Problems — 749

Had a Problem — 612

A problem resolved perfectly results in overall satisfaction of 807, compared to only 749 if there was no problem to begin with.

Source: J.D. Power and Associates 2003 Hotel Guest Satisfaction Study.℠

Satisfaction of Guests Who Experienced a Problem: Based on rating of how effectively the problem was resolved.

Problem Resolution Rating	Overall Hotel Satisfaction
Perfect "10"	807
8 or 9	734
6 or 7	661
5 or less	585

making machine, or a cold, overpriced room service meal are certain to have a negative impact on how you feel about your stay when you answer your survey.

But not everyone who has a problem is destined to give a low rating. The determining factor isn't whether you had the problem, but how the hotel made you feel about how it resolved the problem. For example, if the hotel scores a "perfect 10" for problem resolution, *overall satisfaction for the entire stay is more than fifty points higher than for guests who never had a problem in the first place!* Do a poor job fixing the problem, however, and overall satisfaction drops below 600, well below the level of apathy and into the depths where assassins breed like rabbits on a warm spring day.

Now let's view the issue from a different angle. Instead of looking at the impact of problem resolution on customer satisfaction, let's look at how it affects brand loyalty. Specifically, how likely are automobile owners to indicate they will repurchase the same brand of automobile shortly after they pick their vehicle up from a dealer's service department?

First, we must separate service customers into two buckets: (1) those who brought their car to have a *problem repaired,* and (2) those whose cars only needed *routine maintenance.* Not surprisingly, if you ask someone how likely they are to buy the same brand of car again right after they were forced to make an unscheduled trip to the dealer for repairs, their likelihood of saying they are going to purchase the same brand goes down (28 percent of repair customers versus 34 percent for customers who only needed to bring their vehicle in for routine maintenance).

Once again, however, the way the dealer handles the repair provides the key to potential loyalty. Customers who rated their dealership a "perfect 10" for fixing their problem were actually more likely to plan on repurchasing the same brand than those who didn't need any repairs (46 percent versus 34 percent)!

One Jaguar owner summed up his feelings this way:

I'm absolutely in love with everything about my car except the fact that it's been in the shop four times during the last year. Every time I have another problem I say, "That's it, I'm going to dump the Jag and buy a Honda." But then I call Ray, the service manager at Jaguar of Thousand Oaks, and he takes care of everything. He's always able to get me in no matter how busy they are, and as soon as I drive up he brings around a new Jaguar for me to use as a loaner. When I come to pick up my car, he takes the time to sit down with me and go over what went wrong and everything he did to fix it. He even details my car before I pick it up. The funny thing is that despite all the problems I've had with the car, I'm actually putting off buying another car just because I know I'll never find someone who will take care of me like Ray.*

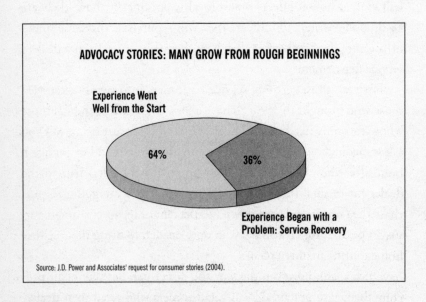

ADVOCACY STORIES: MANY GROW FROM ROUGH BEGINNINGS

Experience Went
Well from the Start

64%   36%

Experience Began with a
Problem: Service Recovery

Source: J.D. Power and Associates' request for consumer stories (2004).

*This story helps explain why J.D. Power and Associates surveys large numbers of customers as part of our studies. Although this particular Jaguar owner experienced numerous problems with his car, on average, the owners of late-model Jaguars report significantly fewer problems than the industry average. Although our research shows that most people still equate Jaguar with the "old days" when reliability was terrible, over the past decade Jaguar quality has improved dramatically under the ownership of Ford.

Stories like this got us wondering. How often is the genesis of advocacy rooted in the fires of adversity? We have countless testimonials in our files from consumers who spoke with reverence about companies to which they were so loyal that it would require an act of Congress to get them to switch brands. We went back over each of these stories looking for just one thing. How many of these relationships began with a problem that the company turned around in such a manner as to spawn this customer's devotion and advocacy?

Of all the stories we gathered, more than a third read like our client's honeymoon story. You start out assuming you are reading an assassin's diary and then the company does something to turn around the entire encounter. It isn't until you've finished the story that you fully comprehend the depth of commitment that the customer has to a brand. And although problem-free advocacy stories still outnumber recovery stories nearly two to one, it is amazing to see how many advocates were just a breath away from going the other way if it hadn't been for an employee who had the ability to empathize with their plight and turn around a bad situation.

THE CURSE OF PERFECTION

It's fairly easy to understand why some of the strongest customer bonds begin with a little adversity. Recall the story about how Lexus decided to recall the first 8,000 vehicles it ever sold. Put yourself in the shoes of one of those customers. Sure, you're not happy when you first hear your new car has to be recalled. "Maybe I should have bought a Mercedes instead of this new unknown brand," you might have said. But then you read the personalized apology letter that accompanies the recall. The next day the dealer comes and picks the car up for you. He returns it not only repaired but washed and with a full tank of gas. You even find a nice gift waiting for you on the seat as Lexus's way of apologizing for the inconvenience.

Who is more likely to go to bed that night thinking nice

thoughts about their vehicle—the Lexus owner who just had this exemplary recall, or the Mercedes owner who just experienced another day of trouble-free driving? Sometimes trouble-free products and service run the risk of leaving a company out of sight, out of mind. A little hiccup now and then serves to remind your customers how lucky they are to do business with you. We are not advocating the creation of small problems to serve as customer wake-up calls. Companies know that perfection is an elusive goal and the wake-up calls tend to appear on their own.

We can almost think of customer satisfaction as an emotional pendulum. Gravity keeps the pendulum centered at rest, a position that points directly toward apathy. When a customer experiences a problem, a force is applied to the pendulum moving it to the left. The more severe the problem, the more the pendulum is pulled up and away. If the problem is severe enough, the pendulum is pulled all the way into assassin territory.

Now let's assume the problem is suddenly fixed. Freed from the force pulling it to the left, the pendulum comes swinging down past the center and up into the land of advocacy. Human nature is much like a pendulum. A conflict suddenly resolved brings with it a rush of good feeling, which is why some of the strongest customer bonds begin with adversity.

Unfortunately, real-life customer situations are more complex than simple pendulums. If they weren't, the only thing companies would need to do to create advocates would be to design in a few ready-made problems, and then prepare their staff to become heroes by charging to the rescue. Even if you could rig the game, you would be playing with fire and customers can usually sniff out a scam pretty quickly. Remember, a problem must be well resolved before you create advocacy. And well resolved means more than just fixing the problem itself. Your customer must know with certainty that you recognize the error of your ways and that you are doing everything possible to make amends. They want to feel the empathy that allows them to walk away feeling emotionally uplifted—that the pendulum is swinging up into the zone of advocacy.

Making lemonade out of lemons is easier said than done. Recall that hotel guests who gave the hotel a perfect 10 for fixing their problem were more satisfied than guests who didn't have any problems to begin with. What we didn't mention in that example is how difficult it is to fix a problem perfectly in the eyes of your customer. In fact, only 15 percent of guests felt that their hotel had resolved the problem perfectly, compared to nearly half who expressed outright displeasure at the hotel's problem resolution skills.

The same is true in the car repair example. Only a small percentage of customers rated their repair experience a perfect 10. And while a perfect repair experience garnered higher loyalty than not needing any repair at all, just dropping the repair experience down one notch to a 9 on a 10-point scale produced much lower levels of loyalty—46 percent of survey respondents said they would remain loyal when they rated their repair experience a perfect 10, but loyalty plummets to 28 percent when the repair is rated a 9. In other words, the margin of error when it comes to customer expectations is razor thin. And you don't want to be the company that is one blade short of a sharp edge.

In the long run, the lesson to manufacturers and service providers is clear—it is better to make quality the highest priority right from the start. There is, however, a forgiveness cycle that can save the day if something goes awry. Recovery shouldn't be thought of as a last resort but as a second chance to ratchet up satisfaction levels into the stratosphere. Remember, to err is human; to fix it superbly is divine.

13

BUILDING A COMMUNITY, OR HOW TO TURN YOUR CUSTOMERS INTO FANS

Remember Groucho Marx's famous quote: "I don't want to belong to any club that will accept me as a member." While Groucho was certainly a comic genius, he probably needed to brush up a little on his theories of human psychology. That's because most people do in fact want to belong to a club of like-minded individuals who share their same passions and desires. It's human nature, and goes a long way toward explaining everything from the phenomena of NASCAR to Trekkies and Deadheads who still get together long after the object of their passion has ceased to exist.

High-satisfaction companies understand the power of building a community around an organization or brand. Communities lead to loyalty, and loyalty is a key component of profitability.

Take the Houston Texans. As a National Football League expansion franchise in 2002, the Texans had the advantage of starting with a brand-new stadium and a rabid, ready-made fan base hungry for a professional football franchise. But none of that guarantees long-term success in the fickle world of professional sports. Countless new franchises in professional sports have squandered similar opportunities.

It wasn't that long ago that the National Basketball Association (NBA) added two new basketball teams, the Charlotte Hornets and Vancouver Grizzlies. Like the Texans, each team opened its doors to sellout crowds of adoring fans. Once the novelty wore off, however, the reality of low fan satisfaction kicked in, and the crowds began to dwindle. Before you knew it, it seemed as though there were as many players on the court as there were fans in the stands, forcing both teams to pack up their sneakers and skulk off in search of a new home city.

The Texans, however, stand in stark contrast to these other teams. That's because the Texans knew long before they played their first game that their viability as a profitable sports franchise had as much to do with fan satisfaction as it had to do with its win/loss record. That's a good thing too, because as of this writing the Texans haven't had a winning season yet!

Although we're pretty sure its fans wouldn't mind if the team found a way to win a few more games, its losing ways haven't done much to hurt fan satisfaction. In a study we conducted to measure fan satisfaction, the Texans came out on top, so far on top, in fact, that we did a double take when we saw the data. Turns out the Texans not only topped all the NFL teams in fan satisfaction, they beat every other Major League Baseball team and NBA basketball team to boot! Not bad for an upstart with a losing record that plays just down the highway from one of the most storied NFL franchises of all time, the Dallas Cowboys.

The Texans' management gives much of the credit to their early decision to build a community among their fans. They wanted to provide fans with more than a football team and a comfortable stadium; they wanted to capitalize on the type of synergy that develops when your customers feel they are part of something bigger. Arrive at Reliant Stadium at 8 A.M. on game day and you will encounter an awe-inspiring sight. Though kickoff isn't until noon, the main parking lot next to the stadium is teeming with activity, turning itself into a small city with 10,000 enthusiastic residents, 1,000 barbecues, and more beer than anyone can count.

As the number of revelers swell throughout the morning, you can walk among the RVs and pickup trucks and listen to fans debate everything from recent trade rumors to the menu selection at the snack stands. Sure, everyone's having fun, but at the same time these fans are forming a bond they will remember long after the final whistle blows. It is this bond, and the feelings that go with it, that will dominate their thoughts when it comes time to decide if they want to reorder season tickets for the next year. Traffic jams, long lines, and missed field goals all become inconsequential when your customers feel part of the team.

Although tailgating is a tradition as old as the game itself, there is one important difference at a Texans tailgate party. Whereas many NFL franchises do everything possible to *discourage* tailgating, the Texans actually *encourage* it, and have even taken the tailgating experience to an unprecedented level.

According to Jamey Rootes, the Texans' senior vice president, the team saw a fertile opportunity to demonstrate the importance of its customers by actively encouraging tailgating and by making tailgating an integral part of the game day experience. Tailgating was not allowed on the Astrodome campus for Houston Oilers games, and research conducted by the team identified tailgating as a key component to a world-class football game experience. Rather than making it difficult, the team mounted a campaign to welcome the tailgaters, putting portable toilets out in the parking lots, having stadium personnel out among the tailgaters to foster the camaraderie and to direct traffic and coordinate access to the area, and setting up game day contests to choose the best tailgaters for each game. At season's end, all winners are invited back to compete to become the top tailgater for the year at the team's final regular season game, dubbed Fan Appreciation Day.

What the Texans successfully fostered is a community of zealots and missionaries. "Our mission is to create raving fans," Rootes says. "We established this at the front end and it means we have to go out and seek opportunities to improve the lives of our customers. You don't wait for the calls to come, you don't wait for interactions. You seek out opportunities to have contact with the customer base, ask them how we can make their lives better, and then we go out and make those things happen for our fans."

Tailgating is just one of a long list of customer satisfaction initiatives that landed the Texans atop our study of sports franchises. Given that the team has already sold 62,000 season tickets in a 70,000-seat stadium, it is not hard to imagine the outpouring of support that will occur when the team begins to contend for a championship.

THE TATTOO SAYS IT ALL

The granddaddy of all community-building efforts surely goes to Harley-Davidson, the Milwaukee-based motorcycle maker that specifically set out to create a community around its brand by forming the Harley Owners Group, or HOG. Since its early efforts, HOG has grown into a massive global community with nearly a million members! What binds these people together is a passion that transcends a product. It is a lifestyle.

The club's Web site proclaims: "We are more than a motorcycle club. We are your brothers and sisters. And we share your boundless passion for an American legend and the lifestyle it has created throughout the world."

HOG is a conduit to the Harley experience. Members get perks such as the ability to rent Harleys in other cities while traveling. But mostly, HOG fosters gatherings of the faithful. It sponsors countless rides around the United States and the world in order to bring Harley lovers together and allow them to share the experience. It has formed affiliations with many charities to help soften the brand's image as the bike of choice of the Hells Angels and other outlaw motorcycle gangs. And it creates new revenue streams for Harley—tie-ins for clothing, merchandise, and other Harley paraphernalia—that not only benefit the company's bottom line, but also create a positive halo around the brand.

In the case of Harley-Davidson, the passion and commitment of its customers literally saved the company in the 1970s when product quality was so atrocious that serious riders felt the need to keep a second bike as a spare, just in case. Demand spiked as the company fixed these quality problems in the 1980s, but then production shortages meant that customers were greeted with the prospect of waiting over a year to take delivery of their new motorcycle—not a good situation considering the Japanese motorcycle dealer across the street could provide immediate delivery of a bike that cost less and performed better from an objective point of view. As production capacity increased during the nineties, the stars aligned, and both customer satisfaction and shareholder value have steadily improved to the point that this brand that was once associated with outlaws and no-goodniks is now a darling of Wall Street.

The important thing to remember is that when you are talking about a community, *objectivity* has nothing to do with it. Perhaps this is why thousands of people—customers and employees alike—rush out to permanently tattoo the company's logo on their bodies, thereby transforming them into walking billboards for the brand.

IT DOESN'T HAVE TO BE OUTLAW TO BE COMMUNITY

You are probably thinking it's easy to create a community of owners if you have a product that breeds passion like motorcycles or a professional sports team. But what if you sell toothbrushes or laundry soap? Who's going to join a club for mundane products such as these?

It's a fair question and we freely acknowledge there is an inverse relationship between the sexiness of a product and the effort and creativity required to build a community. That's okay, because when we talk about building a community we're no longer talking about blocking and tackling. Building a community is *not* the low-hanging fruit of customer satisfaction. We've graduated from Satisfaction 101 and moved into the advanced courses where the customer satisfaction leaders really begin to strut their stuff. Besides, if it were easy, every brand would have a community of owners. And while the challenges are great, the payoff is even greater, because a community of customers provides you with the very real opportunity to differentiate your brand from the pack to reach unprecedented levels of loyalty.

You would be surprised how many decidedly nonsexy products have built successful communities where customers not only stay in touch with the company, but interact with each other. Consider Saturn automobiles launched by General Motors in the early 1990s. When it comes to sexy, Saturn got the short end of the stick. One pundit even dubbed Saturn's styling as a cure for insomnia.

But that's just fine with GM, which didn't set out to turn heads. Instead, General Motors created Saturn as a way to win back import buyers by redefining customer satisfaction, and it all began with the dealership experience. Saturn dealerships featured a no-pressure, no-games, and generally no-nonsense approach to selling. They didn't even use the term *dealer* for the place you go to buy a Saturn—you were invited to visit your local Saturn *retailer* instead. Like Lexus, Saturn also took a proactive stance by immediately recalling the slightest defects, regardless of cost, and making customers feel like they weren't forgotten the minute they drove away from the dealership.

The net result is that Saturn is only one of two new domestic brands introduced over the past fifty years that is still in business—HUMMER is the other—a span of time that has seen brands such as AMC, Edsel, Tucker, and many others all come and go. Saturn achieved its success by reestablishing a relationship of trust between a car company and its owners, which resulted in not only a plethora of customer satisfaction awards, but also in one of the highest rates of owner loyalty in the industry.

At the heart of Saturn's program to establish a relationship of trust were its efforts to open up the lines of communication and establish a community where dealers, customers, and the manufacturer acted as a team to serve a common goal. Dealerships sponsored regular barbecues and new-owner clinics in which customers sat down with mechanics in a nonthreatening environment to learn more about their cars.

In late June 1994, nearly 40,000 Saturn owners, some from as far away as Alaska, Hawaii, and Taiwan, converged on Spring Hill, Tennessee, home of the first Saturn plant, for a company-sponsored "Homecoming" weekend of family events and tours of the factory. Dubbed "Saturnstock" by the business press, this outpouring of community and commitment to a car was unprecedented. Having Harley riders traverse the entire country to Daytona Beach in order to commune with fellow bikers was one thing, but getting 40,000 compact car owners to take a similar journey was beyond comprehension. While the faithful gathered in Spring Hill, another hundred thousand Saturn owners participated in local events around the country.

But even Saturn's efforts in building a community pale compared to those of Staples. That's right, Staples, the king of office supplies—arguably the least sexy of all products on the planet—found a way to connect with customers by hosting a contest to come up with ideas for new or improved office products. The winner got a patent for his idea and a deal with Staples that the product would be sold at Staples stores under the Staples brand.

The winning entry in 2004 was a combination lock that used letters instead of numbers for the combination. Dubbed the "Word-Lock," the inventor believed that it is far easier to remember a word than a series of numbers. He tried to sell it to Master Lock but they were not interested—their loss to be sure. Other contenders included a rubber band that comes with an attached paper tag making stacks of material easier to identify, and a palm stapler that can be used on vertical surfaces with one hand.

Although this was only the first year for the contest, dubbed Invention Quest, Staples generated thousands of entries and seemingly struck a chord among customers and would-be inventors who had great ideas but lacked an outlet to share them. The contest was so successful that Staples plans to turn Invention Quest into an annual event. And why not? Staples not only got some great product ideas, the contest turned into a huge marketing bonanza as well. Donald Trump even featured the contest on his hit television show *The Apprentice.* But most of all, Invention Quest gives Staples the opportunity to reach out and connect with its customers.

THE RULES OF COMMUNITY

Saturn and Staples demonstrate that any company, regardless of the product being sold, can create a community. But take note: a community can also be destroyed if a company fails to live up to the characteristics that spawned the community in the first place. Saturn was initially created to be a company that conducted business independent of General Motors' usual bureaucracy; its tagline even read "A different kind of car company." In an age of badge engineering, where it seems like all that's required to turn a Chevrolet into a Pontiac is to swap the grille, Saturn was unique. Saturn vehicles shared very little in common with the other GM lines. They were built in their own plant in Tennessee, and even the corporate brass kept their offices far from Detroit so as not to be seduced back into the bureaucracy that General Motors tried so hard to break.

Just as Saturn was beginning to win the trust of its customers in a way that very few companies have, the accountants at GM began to think about all the money they could save by folding Saturn back into the regular corporate structure. Slowly but surely new Saturn models began to look a little more like Chevrolets, and the dent-resistant plastic panels that previously adorned all Saturn vehicles were changed back to steel. Even its dealers seemed to be changing as Saturn's customer satisfaction, once the envy of every auto company around the globe, begins to show signs of weakening.

As we've often said in this book, you cannot sell customers a bill of goods. They know the difference between the real thing and when they are being conned by glitzy marketing and empty promises. High-satisfaction organizations build communities by embracing a few crucial rules:

- Never underestimate the emotional power of human nature and the desire to belong. We all want to belong to something. Companies that create this sense of belonging and purpose make themselves more attractive and more likely to gain the benefit of the doubt from customers in weathering negative economic or product news.

- Reach out to your customers, and don't wait for them to contact you. Smart companies proactively create and sustain a steady line of communications with customers. Communities offer the best way to do that in an unobtrusive, valued way. Never trick yourself into thinking that "no news is good news." No news means silence and silence can be deadly.

- A strong community around a brand constructs a barrier to entry for competitors because your customers are emotionally invested and thus less likely to defect.

- If the product or service quality fails to consistently meet its own high standards, the community will dissipate faster than it was formed.

- Building a sense of community does not require formal clubs and mandatory joining. Companies can foster a community spirit in many ways that inspire an emotional connection, a sense of team that induces customers to feel they are on your side, sharing both the good and the bad.

To illustrate this last point, consider JetBlue, where passengers are treated to a sight they won't see on any other airline. Once the pilots complete their postflight checklists, they climb out of the cockpit to help the flight attendants clean up the plane. By taking on these tasks, JetBlue not only cuts out costly maintenance crews, they show that every employee, regardless of rank, plays for the same team.

They also make a conscious effort to make you feel like part of this same team. Just before landing, the flight attendants get on the microphone and announce that JetBlue is committed to maintaining lower fares and that one important way to do that is to keep costs down. They boldly ask each passenger to help out by cleaning up their own area. Sure, other airlines have a flight attendant walk down the aisle with a trash bag, but JetBlue really makes a show of it. And they do it for a purpose. This seemingly insignificant request, in conjunction with the pilots helping out, creates a communal feeling among customers that "we are all in this together and if they win, we win."

SIZE DOESN'T MATTER AFTER ALL

You don't need to be a big national corporation to create a community. You only need to be creative. Perhaps this is why small businesses often do the best job of building communities. Frequently these entrepreneurs don't even realize the benefits of what they've done; all they want to do is make the place a little more fun to work.

Look around you. No matter where you live you will find numerous examples of entrepreneurs getting close to their customers. In West Concord, Massachusetts, for example, Debra Stark's Natural Gourmet is a small natural foods and supplements store with a passionate customer base. Like the products she sells, a community sprang up organically around her store. People like to come to Debra's store, and she built upon that feeling by instituting a series of regular events that include lectures, product demonstrations, and gatherings of customers who want to share issues ranging from menopause to serious illness.

She also added the element of fun. The store hosts countless parties and celebrations throughout the year for its loyal customers. On the Saturday before Thanksgiving, for example, Stark hosts an annual pajama party for customers. Come in between 6 A.M. and 9 A.M. in your pajamas and you'll receive a 20 percent discount off everything in the store. There is free food to sample and a warm atmosphere of camaraderie around the shoppers. From all this, a de facto Natural Gourmet community has evolved; customers share stories, meet at the store to shop and participate in activities, and spread the word as enthusiastic advocates.

STAYING AT THE TABLE

Given the power of communities, it is not surprising that every business, from Starbucks to BMW, seeks to enroll their customers in one group or another. But vanity credit cards and frequent buyer programs do little to foster the kind of loyalty that true communities achieve. This is because a real community includes that intangible element that is difficult to orchestrate: emotion.

Blackjack players, for example, are generally not considered a sentimental lot. But at Cactus Petes, the Ameristar casino in Jackpot, Nevada, the sense of belonging for regular customers is carefully cultivated. At the tables where the dealers know the customers by name and encourage friendly exchanges, it is common to see players lose their stack of chips but immediately dip into their wallets so that they may remain part of the group that has embraced them. We were able to quantify the benefit of community at Cactus Petes with a simple experiment. That quantification isn't so easy in most other applications, a fact that probably explains why so few businesses take advantage of this great opportunity to build customer satisfaction and commitment to the brand.

14

THE INTERNET: FILLING THE INFORMATION VOID FOR CONSUMERS

In terms of its impact on the human condition, one could argue that the Internet stands alone in the sheer number of ways it touches our lives. Take e-mail as an example. By combining the real-time speed of the telephone with the "respond at your own pace" convenience of a letter, the Internet has revolutionized everything from the way grandparents stay in touch with their grandchildren to how managers communicate with employees. Shopping is another venue that has changed dramatically. Online stores not only provide the convenience of 24/7 shopping from home, they offer the type of selection that would break the bank of all but the largest traditional brick and mortar retail locations.

As wonderful as these conveniences are, the Internet's greatest advancement is its ability to collect, collate, and deliver vast quantities of information with a level of speed and efficiency that makes the invention of the printing press seem almost trivial by comparison. From kids researching term papers to mothers diagnosing their family's ailments, the Internet not only replaces the *Encyclopedia Britannica,* but it is transforming the role of all media, from television to magazines to even our public libraries.

For consumers, the Internet has become a potent magnet. A recent study by Pew Internet estimated that two-thirds of all Americans now use the Internet regularly, and three-fourths of them go online to research a product or service before buying it.

This infinite supply of information offers consumers not only knowledge but something they generally lacked in the past: power. A vastly informed customer base shifts the advantage to the consumer, and the impact of this tectonic shift is wreaking havoc with old and battered notions about customer satisfaction. P. T. Barnum's old saw, "There's a sucker born every minute," must be recast for the new millennium. On the Internet, a potential sucker is *enlightened* every minute.

The Internet has become what Malcolm Gladwell dubbed "a tipping point," especially when it comes to the quest for information. The Internet "epidemic," as Gladwell describes the emergence of "big changes that follow from small events," may well be the biggest change in the history of the consumer experience. Never before has there been such an unlimited, cost-effective open channel between customers and businesses. And perhaps more important, never has there been this level of communications among consumers who are willing and anxious to share their knowledge and experience with anyone who can tap into the Web.

The implications for customer satisfaction are enormous. Prior to the Internet's burgeoning popularity, a company could survive even if it provided poor quality or service. It could accept the low rates of loyalty that accompany poor quality as long as there was a pool of potential new customers who didn't know any better. Today, purchase decisions are increasingly dependent on a company's past performance as measured from the customer's perspective.

Although it seemed like risky business, a company could ask itself: Could we save enough money by lowering quality standards so that it more than offsets the loss of repeat business and word-of-mouth advertising? Unfortunately, too many organizations faced with a tough economy chose just this route. The long-term viability of such a strategy, already doubtful, has run smack into the reality of the Internet.

Perhaps this is why Internet customers are statistically less loyal. By providing information, the Internet effectively reduces the cost (i.e., risk) of switching brands. Rather than repurchasing the same brands over and over again, Internet consumers are more likely to look at every purchase as a fresh start, an opportunity to evaluate brands with a clean sheet of paper.

As the Internet swells, it begins to eliminate that pool of potential new customers who didn't know any better. Good news travels fast, but bad news travels faster, farther, and with more impact. Companies can no longer count on advertising to mold their brand perceptions. Ford can tell us that Quality is Job One, and BMW can tout itself as the Ultimate Driving Machine, but all it takes is one slip and the Internet will spread the news about a company's poor performance so fast that even the most seasoned spin doctors will be hard pressed to keep up.

We recently conducted an experiment to illustrate how the Internet impacts the decision process of consumers. The impetus of this experiment stemmed from an alarming finding in our NewAutoShopper.com Study, which is specifically developed to help companies understand how the Internet is shaping the automotive landscape. General Motors, which sells about five million vehicles each year, accounts for nearly 30 percent of the U.S. market. But among consumers who searched an online bulletin board for information before they made a purchase, GM's share drops to only 16 percent. Toyota, by comparison, benefits from this open exchange of information—so much so that it sells nearly as many vehicles to this group of Internet consumers as all the General Motors brands combined. We wondered what people could be finding on these bulletin boards to have this much impact on each brand's fortunes.

To find out, we went online and posted messages on a variety of automotive bulletin boards posing as a new-vehicle shopper. The message was simple: we were in the market for a midsize car and had narrowed our choice to the Chevrolet Malibu or Toyota Camry. We hadn't purchased a new car in years so we turned to the community of Internet users to help us decide which would be the better vehicle. Soon after our posting, the replies started pouring in. In total we received forty-nine responses from people expressing an opinion about whether we should buy the Camry or the Malibu.

Of these, only eleven favored the Malibu while thirty-eight urged us to buy the Camry. Malibu endorsers did not exactly heap praise on the Chevrolet, but suggested the car will get you from point A to point B for a little less money than the Camry. Those endorsing the Camry, by comparison, spoke with great passion, some making quite powerful—and even colorful—arguments as to why they would never recommend a Chevrolet, General Motors, or in some cases any domestic-built vehicle.

The point of this experiment is this: put yourself in the place of someone about to plunk down $20,000 on a new car. After reading such lopsided responses, you'd feel like you would be taking one heck of a risk buying the Malibu. That is, of course, if you feel you can trust this faceless community who responded to your message.

THE NEW WATER COOLER

It wasn't that long ago that our personal sphere of influence was limited to family, friends, and a few coworkers we met around the water cooler. This was a good thing for companies with poor customer satisfaction. With the burgeoning influence of the Internet, that tiny sphere of influence now encompasses the world. Experts are everywhere and no credentials are required! Anyone with a modicum of skill using the Internet can voice their opinion on any of the thousands of bulletin boards; just look at our Camry experiment. And for those who really have an axe to grind, all it takes is a little technical skill and a few hours of spare time to create your own Web site to serve as a bully pulpit to get your point across.

According to *Business Week* in May 2005, there were 9 million Web logs (or *blogs* as they are called) on the Internet, with 40,000 new ones popping up every day. "How does business change when everyone is a potential publisher?" *BusinessWeek* asked. "A vast new stretch of the information world opens up. For now, it's a digital hinterland. The laws and norms covering fairness, advertising and libel? They don't exist, not yet anyway. But one thing is clear: *Companies over the past few centuries have gotten used to shaping their message. Now they're losing control of it.*"

Even staid, old economy giants like General Motors have gotten into the blog business. Perhaps they've decided it's easier to join a trend rather than fight it. Go to GMblogs.com and you will find a place where senior GM executives such as product guru Bob Lutz hold refreshingly frank and open discussions with their customers. Sure, GM sometimes uses the blog as an opportunity to tout itself, but it also acknowledges many of its sins of the past, and solicits the opinion of the community to help it avoid making the same mistakes again in the future.

An entire subcategory of Web sites has emerged devoted solely to allowing consumers to vent their frustrations at specific companies. All one has to do with nearly any company name is add the word "sucks.com" and do a Google search. More times than not, up will pop a Web site posted by disgruntled customers venting their frustrations and anger. Even Enterprise Rent-A-Car, a company that consistently tops our satisfaction surveys, or Starbucks, a company with millions of devoted customers, aren't able to escape the Internet's ability to amplify the voice of a single angry customer. Just go to FailingEnterprise.com or Starbucked.com to see a corporate assassin's handiwork in action. The use of the Internet for this purpose is so prevalent that Bush campaign supporters fired a preemptive shot against would-be Internet pundits by registering dozens of potentially derogatory domain names such as Bushsucks.com and BushBlows.com.

And for those who are angry but just not so angry that they are ready to go out and create their own Web site, there are countless preexisting sites just waiting for your post. Some are specialized—such as RoadBikeReview.com—but others such as BadBusinessBureau.com are there to receive any complaint about any company you feel has done you wrong. Thinking about hiring a particular software design firm but want to avoid problems? Just do a search and see if anyone has posted a complaint about that company. If you find a couple of horror stories, regardless of whether or not these stories reflect a true picture of that business, we expect that you'll change your plans and look elsewhere.

Sites such as these simply serve as a clearinghouse for complaints, a place to vent your anger. They don't, nor do they pretend to, provide both sides of the equation—the good and the bad. For this we turn to those review sites whose specific purpose is to help consumers choose which products and services perform best.

Consumer review sites can generally be placed into three categories:

- Sites where customers express their opinions in the form of a short narrative about their experience
- Sites where customers express their experience in the form of a numerical rating
- Sites that provide their own expert opinion about the product or service

Our Malibu versus Camry experiment provided an example of the first—postings from people who purported to have an opinion about which car we should buy. What we received was a stream-of-consciousness diatribe from anyone and everyone with an opinion, or perhaps just an axe to grind. The subscription site offered by *Con-*

sumer Reports would be an example of the latter, where *Consumer Reports'* panel provides recommendations based on their own independent tests. Our own site—jdpower.com—focuses on the second, aggregating the voice of thousands of consumers into a simple rating system that allows viewers to directly compare the customer experience with company A versus company B.

Some consumer review Web sites combine all three methodologies. For example, in the world of photography there are many sites providing vast quantities of information designed to help anyone from soccer moms to professional photographers make the right purchase. One of the most comprehensive is dpreview.com. Any digital camera worth knowing about is posted and reviewed, not only by their own panel of experts, but also by consumers who comment on their own experiences.

Besides the objective listing of a camera's attributes and the subjective views of owners, the site posts actual test photographs from each camera. A prospective buyer can compare the same photograph taken by any number of cameras to get an irrefutable look at the varying quality of the digital images prior to making a purchase. To make the experience complete, the site even lists prices at various retail outlets so that a buyer can find the best deal. In other words, this virtual experience truly embodies the phrase "one-stop shopping." Here's how one consumer used dpreview.com to select a camera:

> I wanted to buy a digital camera that was easy to use but also of high enough quality that I could enlarge a picture and get a quality print. The first thing I did was read the reviews in the photography magazines, but I always felt I had to take what I read with a grain of salt. It seemed like the magazines had only nice things to say about each camera, brought on no doubt by the fact they rely on the camera manufacturers for advertising. So then I went to several local camera stores to check out what was available. What a mistake! I either got stuck talking to some

kid who knew less than I did, or someone who talked over my head with all sorts of techno-jargon. I finally chose a Pentax 750Z at one of the camera shops mostly, I'm embarrassed to admit, because I liked the way it looked. By that time I had pretty much given up being able to actually determine which camera was best, so I figured at least I could have one that looked good.

But the Pentax cost about $500, so I went home to sleep on it. That was my first good decision. I went online that night to see if there was anything more I could learn about the Pentax and came across a site called dpreview.com that offered a side-by-side review of all the cameras in this price range. After reading the reviews, I realized that the Pentax probably wasn't the best of the bunch. Sample photos from comparable cameras such as a Panasonic Lumix were far sharper and I discovered in reading the reviews that the Pentax took longer to reach the ready mode for picture-taking than comparable cameras. So I began looking at the reviews for the Panasonic and found that about the only complaint its owners had was that the lens cap wasn't tethered to the camera making it easy to lose. I thought, if that's the biggest complaint, sign me up. I ordered the Panasonic that night on the Internet and it's been a great camera. However, if it hadn't been for this Web site, I wouldn't even know Panasonic made cameras, let alone how good they are.

This story carries an important message: review sites serve not only as a tool of exclusion but also a tool of inclusion. We normally think of the shopping process as one where the consumer initially establishes a consideration set of brands, and then goes on to narrow their choice until only one brand is left. The Internet, through the combination of positive and negative feedback, helps facilitate that narrowing process. But, just as in the case of our Panasonic camera buyer, these Web sites can also provide information to place a brand on someone's consideration set to begin with. This is especially important to smaller, less well known brands that don't automatically jump to mind when you are in the market.

Pick any industry and you will find examples where the Internet impacted the sales of a new product or service. For example, golfers use the Internet to share their ravenous appetite for information about the latest clubs. When Callaway, makers of the hugely success-ful Big Bertha series of drivers, introduced its new C4 driver in 2001, Web sites such as GolfREVIEW.com were abuzz with anticipation. The C4 represented the most important breakthrough since the eighties when club makers began making drivers out of metal instead of wood. The C4 was unique because it was the first driver built from composite carbon graphite. Despite the fact that it carried a list price of over $500, the C4 was a fast seller, at least in the beginning.

But after the initial success, word quickly spread online and the reviews began taking on a decidedly less favorable tone. Golfers complained that the club did not make the expected loud "thwack" sound when it struck a ball. Instead, the graphite head made barely a whisper on impact. And worse, even though the club helped novice golfers hit the ball straighter, it didn't necessarily help them hit it any farther, and distance is what sells in today's highly com-petitive golf market. Internet posts about the club's perceived short-comings were everywhere, and it didn't take long before sales began to plummet. Before you knew it, golf shops were taking their C4's off the shelf and dumping them into the discount club barrel for less than a fourth the original price.

Would sales of the C4 have tanked without the Internet? Of course, but it would have taken longer. And that's the point about the Internet. In terms of what it does—facilitate communication—the only thing that's revolutionary is the speed at which it occurs.

Paul Wassem, president of ConsumerREVIEW.com, which op-erates GolfREVIEW.com, said, "The Internet is another form of word of mouth, but instead of telling your experience to one person at a time, our sites give you access to thousands of people ready to make a buying decision. That's our role in the marketplace, and if it means we help make people make better shopping decisions, that's a good thing for society—even if it isn't good news for companies that provide second-rate products."

THE INTERNET GOES LOCAL

To date, consumer review sites concentrate on higher ticket items such as cars, cameras and pricey home electronics. This is understandable—the more expensive a product or service, the more the customer has to lose by making a wrong decision. The payoff associated with buying right justifies the effort required to conduct a thorough Internet search.

This is changing. It won't be long before these review sites will blanket every customer satisfaction scenario one can imagine, from everyday products such as staplers or laundry soap to local services of every kind. All it takes to make this a reality is: (1) finding enough people willing to share their experiences online, (2) demand from consumers to understand the experience of others, and (3) Web sites that are sufficiently well organized to allow targeted searches without having to pour through hordes of superfluous information.

Surprisingly, it is the last of these three that provides the greatest challenge. A few years ago doing consumer research online could be a frustrating experience, requiring you to read through dozens of opinions to find something relevant to your situation. Today's review sites are much better organized, allowing people to target their search to their own specific needs. Zagat, the company famous for providing restaurant reviews, provides a glimpse into the Internet's local potential. Visit Zagat.com and you can tailor your search to not only your own neighborhood but for whatever type of cuisine your stomach is craving. In fact, the site has worked so well that Zagat recently expanded its scope to include other venues such as hotels and bars.

I READ IT ONLINE, THEREFORE IT MUST BE TRUE

Unfortunately, the Internet isn't always the utopian environment that it might seem at first glance. The very freedom and openness that allows Internet users to plug into the collective experience of others may ultimately prove to be its Achilles' heel.

How do we know that some of those glowing reviews weren't posted by corporate shills attempting to bias opinions about their business by posting favorable reviews? Or just the opposite might be true; a competitor could be using the site to trash another company by posting negative reviews.

Although shilling is a very real concern, it is relatively less so when we are talking about big companies such as automobile makers or hotel chains. The sheer volume of feedback about Mazda or Marriott is so great that it overwhelms the few comments from shills that might appear online. Also, should a major corporation be caught posting phony endorsements while posing as customers, the public relations disaster that would follow would far outweigh the benefits of a few positive comments.

The danger of shilling becomes more real as these sites are used to review smaller and more localized companies. If an electrician receives only a few ratings, all it takes is one or two phony posts to throw off the entire picture. Even with a trusted site such as Zagat, you can never be too sure if the ratings are truly representative of a restaurant's actual customers, or if a few unscrupulous restaurateurs have set out to rig their own results. And to make the problem worse, readers aren't always told whether a company's rating is based on hundreds, dozens, or just a few customers. The best defense is, once again, reaching the critical mass at which so many people are providing feedback that the comments of a few shills become relatively meaningless.

Even if shilling didn't exist, and every reviewer provided their honest opinion, there would still be a question about the validity of those opinions. Remember, with the Internet, everyone is an expert with an opinion, whether fact-based, biased, or just plain wrong. Take our Malibu versus Camry experiment as an example. Just because most people opined that we should buy the Camry doesn't mean that the Camry is necessarily a better car *in fact*. Peel back the layers of the onion and you will notice that much of the anti-GM rhetoric expressed by these responders was linked to their own personal experiences of the past, some before the current Malibu was even on the drawing board. These legacy perceptions do not take into account the reality that the quality gap between GM and Toyota continues to narrow each year. In fact, our own Initial Quality Study found that the Chevrolet Malibu has improved to the point that it now has fewer problems than any other vehicle in its segment.

Even the sites that provide so-called professional opinions are not above scrutiny. After all, how are we supposed to know whether the views expressed within are by a true panel of qualified experts or just some teenager in his garage giving you his opinion? Designing a professional-looking site is now so simple and cheap that almost anyone with the right software can build a slick-looking Web site. This is the reason there will always be a place for companies such as *Consumer Reports,* J.D. Power and Associates, and other branded research firms that consumers know they can trust and rely upon for accurate and unbiased information.

As real as these concerns are, the totality of the information contained on today's review sites is directionally accurate, and its value far outweighs the alternative of not having access to the information at all. More important, consumers do not seem overly concerned. In fact, we've seen that the Internet has a high trust factor, not unlike the feeling that people once had about newspapers, i.e., if you read something in a newspaper, it must be true.

We find, for example, that people put much more trust in what they read on independent Web sites than the information put out directly by a manufacturer or its ad agency. The key word is independent. For if consumers believe a Web site is independent, they don't think it has an agenda, and therefore the information must be accurate. Further, if a site has a professional look to it, the perception is that the people who created the site must know what they are talking about.

WHAT'S GOOD FOR THE GOOSE IS GOOD FOR THE GANDER

Imagine Googling your own name and the first hit that pops up is a story written about you by the waiter you stiffed the night before. Sound preposterous? Just log onto bitterwaitress.com or waiter-rant.net, where angry waitresses and waiters are airing their grievances and naming names of customers who have ticked them off with bad tips or rude behavior.

"Grievances, including friction between kitchen and dining room staff, rapacious management and near-universal bitterness over tipping, are being revealed with gusto on the Internet by restaurant staff members," *The New York Times* reported. "As a customer, to read [these Web sites] is to wonder nervously, 'Could they be talking about me?'"

If the Internet provides a free forum for consumers to air their opinions, why shouldn't businesses be allowed to do the same? At least that's the view of an increasing number of business owners and employees who feel that customers are unfairly using them as verbal punching bags on the Internet. And they are just beginning to realize they have the power to fight back.

Of course, businesses need to do more than just sit back and watch how the Internet speeds up the court of public opinion. In the next chapter we discuss how some companies embrace the power of the Internet to proactively shape those opinions and improve the experience of their customers.

15

TAKING CONTROL OF THE ONLINE EXPERIENCE

Ironically, the companies that are most impacted by the Internet's information avalanche have often been the last to understand and embrace its power themselves. For some the Internet was an enemy, an evil force that stole away the power they previously held over customers. It facilitated the telling of lies—allowing customers to spread half-truths and innuendo to millions in the blink of an eye. For others, the Internet was something they couldn't control, and this more than anything else made them uneasy.

While no company can ever hope to control the flow of information on the Internet—though some still try, and most secretly wish they could—companies must at least do everything within their power to make sure they use the Internet to effectively communicate their own message to consumers. Yet, as difficult as it is to believe, most companies still don't get it when it comes to creating a positive customer experience online.

There seems to be a direct correlation between the size of a company and the difficulty managing its Internet presence. For many big, traditional corporations, the Web was an intimidating proposition and most came at it quickly but without careful strategic forethought. Word came down from on high, "Get us on the Web, and do it *now*." Before you knew it, the company created a separate Internet department or even a new dot-com subsidiary and threw boatfuls of cash at the task, all without taking the time to stop and listen to what this new generation of customer wanted.

The rush to the Web led to a myriad of problems. For one, customers often felt like they were dealing with two completely different companies, depending upon whether they entered through the front door or the cyber door. The dot-com side of the business simply lacked a cohesive connection back to the mother ship. A customer who bought a blouse at a retailer's Web site could not return it at an actual store, and no one at the store could answer any questions about the Web site. The overall look and feel of the company's Web site might be so different from the company's traditional marketing that online visitors found themselves flipping back to the home page asking, "Am I even dealing with the same company?"

By failing to listen to their customers, most companies missed the one thing that customers want most—the ability to connect to a real live person. According to a survey of 1,000 people about their online customer service experience by the Society of Consumer Affairs Professionals in Business, based in Alexandria, Virginia, the top complaint was the inability to find a human being to help them. Even some of the largest sites make it difficult to find a telephone number to call for a human voice if a customer has a question that cannot be answered on the site.

Although the problem improves with each new generation of shopping site, it continues to be a source of frustration for those going online to answer a question or handle a complaint. While some sites offer real-time interaction, an instant messaging type of connection to a service person, too many won't respond to queries for hours or even days. By then, most users will abandon all hope as well as the Web site.

One frustrated traveler told us the saga of his suitcase that set out on its own adventure to an unknown destination after he got off his plane. The airline gave him a Web site where he would be notified as soon as his wayward bag arrived. Every few hours he dutifully checked the site, and each time the answer came back the same: the bag had not yet arrived. Two days later he arrived back at the airport ready to catch a flight home and went down to the baggage claim area to notify the airline where to send his bag when (and if) they ever located it. "No need to do that," came back the response from a surprised baggage agent, "it's right here." It turns out his bag hadn't gone to the wrong city after all, but had just caught the next flight, arriving at his destination only two hours after he did. Unfortunately, the airline's Web site hadn't been updated for two days! Our traveler noted that when the agent said that he should have just called to check on it, it took every ounce of restraint not to say something that was sure to land him on the government's do-not-fly list.

In this, the Internet is akin to dealing with call centers. Customers must take it on faith that somewhere, someplace, a real live person is going to take their inquiry and actually do something about it. This creates stress, and stress provides a downward vector on satisfaction.

The best Web sites create a complete circle around the customer's experience, whether it is in the store or online. The next generation, those who have grown up at the keyboard with the Internet as an intrinsic part of their lives, will not tolerate the current shortfalls. The Internet to them is speed and expectation. Information and delivery must flow in an integrated fashion and companies that continue to think of the Internet as a separate channel will be the losers. The days of in-store versus online, in which one channel has no record of interaction in the other, must be a thing of the past. There must be one view of the customer. And in order to create the best online user experience, a company must know who its audience is. This is a tough assignment for big companies that serve many masters, but the beauty of the Internet is its ability to measure success literally by the keystroke.

Another common mistake that comes from not listening to the voice of your customer is the notion that it takes a computer geek to design a Web site. Sure, they may have mastered the elusive seventh level of Dungeons & Dragons, but they probably don't have a clue about your customers! When it comes to your Web site, most of your customers just want to get from point A to point B with as little fuss as possible. Bells, whistles, and trick graphics are fine for computerphiles, but you need to be very careful about how you apply these tools to your Web site. The problem is analogous to what often happens when a company puts its engineers in charge of product development and design. They tend to get too caught up in what technology will allow them to do, and lose focus of what your customers want you to do.

A few years ago we launched a new study where everyday Internet users worked with a variety of Web sites to evaluate their content and functionality. We were looking forward to the results, because this was just around the time site designers were beginning to flex their creative muscle. So you can imagine our surprise when the automaker Kia, which featured one of the most pedestrian sites ever to grace the Web, came out near the top in user satisfaction. How could this be? Technologically, the Kia site was like playing a thirty-year-old game of Pong in the age of PlayStation2.

It turns out users didn't care that the Kia site didn't feature animated cars that talk to you when you scrolled your mouse over their image. They weren't concerned that they couldn't download the company's commercials, or read engineering comments about every feature. What they did care about were things the Kia site did right: vehicle options were clearly labeled and displayed using large black print against a clean white background, the home page focused on guiding visitors to all the key information, and the site was mercifully uncluttered with promotions and other extraneous information. In statistical terms, when we correlated overall satisfaction against everything a site could (and couldn't) do, we found that ease of navigation trumped everything else.*

Nothing, and we mean *nothing*, turns Internet users off quicker than a confusing Web site. It's the virtual equivalent of going to the grocery store and not being able to find the frozen food section. In fact, it's much worse. If a customer walks into a store, they've invested enough of their time just getting there that they're likely to put up with a little frustration before they turn around and walk out the door. No such investment occurs in cyberspace. One moment of frustration and all it takes is a twitch of a finger on the mouse and your customers are out the cyber door and off to a competitor.

Just one example of the type of problem users complain about comes at the point you least want to screw up: the order form. On most sites, the order form contains many fields that must be filled out accurately or the purchase won't be consummated. Neglect to fill in a required space and a prospective customer may discover upon hitting the "Submit" button that not only does an error message pop up, but the page returns and all the boxes he had filled in are now blank and must be filled in once again from scratch. No wonder at least half of all Internet orders are never completed!

Surveys show that the quit rate at Web sites is highest at the inflection points where a customer does not know how to proceed and there is no way to get help. Anyone who has tried to use the ubiquitous Help menus on Web sites will attest to the frustration levels of finding an answer to your specific question. Where do customers get stuck? What is the first question on the list of FAQs? If a question is getting asked over and over again, why not fix it so that it need never be asked again?

---

*Over the past few years Kia has continually upgraded its site with additional high-tech features such as 360-degree viewing. Despite these additions, Kia managed to keep its site very simple and intuitive to use, a fact that resulted in a first-place ranking in the J.D. Power and Associates 2005 Manufacturer Web Site Evaluation Study.℠

But for those who get it right, the payoff is huge. Every year we conduct a pre/post test to determine how the Web experience changes a customer's likelihood to purchase a brand. And every year the results come back the same. If a customer has a good experience at your Web site, they become more likely to go out and shop for your product in a retail setting than they were before they went online. But if they have a poor experience—unable to find the information they came to get, technical difficulties, etc.—they are less likely to do business with you in the physical world.

The importance of easy navigation doesn't mean you should go out and begin de-contenting your Web site. There's nothing wrong with innovation; just don't let your creative streak get in the way of functionality. The trick is providing information in layers. When describing your product's features, make sure the key information is out there on a single page. Avoid the temptation to splash every detail out there on the first layer. Provide too much information at once and your customers need to scroll through reams of information they may not care anything about. But for those who do care, provide the means for them to drill down to increasingly deeper levels of information and detail. In short, create a Web site that works for both types of customers: (1) those seeking quick access to basic information, and (2) those who want to take a deep dive into everything you do.

Always remember that your Web site serves an intrinsically different purpose than every other form of advertising. Radio, television, and print share one bond in common—each is intrusive in nature. Their purpose is to stop you in your tracks and grab your attention away from whatever you were doing. Humor, catchy jingles, and sexy models all find their way into corporate advertising for this singular purpose.

Your Web site is designed for an entirely different purpose. It doesn't come to the customer, the customer comes to it, more often than not looking for specific information. As we said before, there is nothing wrong with adding a little pizzazz to your Web site; just don't forget that your site's purpose is to provide information to those actively seeking it. Entertainment is secondary; educate, don't obfuscate.

It seems clear to anyone monitoring the world of commerce that the Internet is already inextricably interwoven into the game. There's no going back, and within ten years the notion that companies didn't incorporate cyberspace into their strategic plans will seem as foolish as selling buggy whips as the age of automobiles got underway.

16

MANAGE THE STORE, NOT THE SCORE

As companies increase their focus on customer satisfaction, senior management ups the pressure on branch management and field personnel to deliver ever higher customer satisfaction scores. And since human beings, by nature, are reward-based creatures, it is increasingly common for companies to reinforce their commitment by tying employee compensation to the results. On one hand, the focus from above is a good thing. As we said in chapter 8, improving customer satisfaction begins at the top.

Unfortunately, the message that begins at the top sometimes becomes distorted along the way until front-line managers become more concerned about improving their *score* than they are about improving their *store*. Instead of working to fix the underlying processes causing a less than optimum customer experience, some managers take what they believe is the easy way out and directly ask customers to give them favorable scores when they fill out their satisfaction survey. This, needless to say, is a problem.

For example, we recently received a heartfelt two-page letter from a gentleman who had filled out a customer satisfaction survey a few weeks earlier and all but begged us to find his completed survey and delete it from our records. Before he left the store, the salesman confronted him and told him how each salesperson's pay depended on getting perfect survey scores, even going so far as showing him pictures of his wife and kids to help ratchet up the guilt factor.

When he received his survey in the mail, he agonized over what to do but finally filled it out just as his salesman had requested—perfect "top box" scores right down the line. As soon as he dropped the survey in the mail, regret set in and ultimately he felt anger at both his salesman for putting him in this position and himself for succumbing to pressure. Ironically, our protagonist told us in his letter that the salesperson didn't need to resort to strong-arm tactics. Up to that point he had had a good experience, and probably would have provided favorable answers to the survey anyway.

While you may be able to use guilt to get a few customers to provide higher scores, this approach will actually lower your scores overall. We find in our research that people do not like being pressured, and the mere act of asking someone to fill out a survey a certain way frequently causes an otherwise satisfied customer to provide a less favorable rating. Unfortunately, this fact doesn't seem to stop salespeople from trying.

Never forget—the goal is to create customers who are truly advocates and not simply to find a way to coerce customers to hand in a favorable survey. This is why we emphatically tell our clients to concentrate on the underlying processes and behaviors that impact customer satisfaction. Do that and the score will take care of itself!

Some managers have gone beyond polite coercion and have actually been caught cheating in an attempt to rig survey results entirely. A few automobile dealers, for example, were caught bribing customers with offers of everything from a free tank of gas to free oil changes if the customer would just bring their blank survey into the dealership, presumably so that the dealership could fill it out *the right way*. Fortunately, automobile manufacturers and the vast majority of dealers reject such behavior and are working diligently to weed out dealers resorting to such unethical practices.

When another large, national service organization began using a telephone customer satisfaction survey to determine if managers would receive a bonus, the branch managers at a few of its problem locations found an innovative solution around the problem. Whenever those managers had a "problem customer," they conveniently mistyped the customer's telephone number into the computer; you can't conduct a telephone survey if you don't have the right number. This went on for months before the secret to their newfound success leaked out. For this reason, we always recommend that if a company is going to rely on a telephone survey, it should calculate the percent of "wrong numbers." If one branch has an overly high percentage of wrong numbers, we bet there is more than careless typing at work.

As a firm that has built its reputation on measuring the customer experience, our position is that no company should ever make any attempt to sway or bias a customer's survey results in any manner— other than just providing the best possible service to begin with. Having said that, we see an increasing number of clients take what at least on the surface appears to be a more palatable approach to this issue. At the end of an encounter, the customer is told about the survey and then asked if there was anything about their experience that would prevent them from giving the highest score. If the answer is yes, the customer is invited to discuss the situation with management to rectify the problem. Although we don't endorse any attempt to influence survey results, at least this latter approach gives the customer a sense that your company not only cares, but provides the opportunity to address deficiencies.

PAY FOR PERFORMANCE

The reason employees feel the need to beg customers for favorable ratings is because companies increasingly tie those ratings into each employee's compensation package. In particular, companies pay bonuses specifically for high scores or look at survey results when deciding whether an employee should get a raise or promotion.

Tying monetary incentives to customer satisfaction scores is a double-edged sword. On one hand, any psychologist will tell you that the fastest way to get someone to conform to a desired behavior is to build a reward system around that behavior. While this may be fine for getting your child to eat broccoli, incentivizing customer-friendly behavior is more problematic. After all, what are you really paying them for? Are you paying your employees to treat customers better or are you paying them for higher survey *scores*? Your goal is the former, but your employees may focus on the latter; and this is why we find so many resorting to begging customers to mark perfect scores on their surveys.

Given the arguments on both sides, which path should companies choose? To answer the pay/not-pay debate we once again turned to our satisfaction leaders, hoping to find a consensus. Unfortunately, unlike their position on most issues, our leaders were all over the map on this one. On one end of the spectrum we have companies like Staples that pay direct bonuses to customer-facing employees based on customer satisfaction. Other companies, such as Enterprise Rent-A-Car, don't pay for performance per se but require branch managers to reach certain customer satisfaction targets before they will be considered for promotions or recognition awards. Still others understand the importance of money as an incentive, but only apply these monetary incentives to senior managers and executives. The reason, as discussed above, is they don't want customer-facing employees to feel tempted to beg customers for scores.

Finally, there are some, such as JetBlue and In-N-Out Burger, that steer clear of incentivizing customer satisfaction altogether. Employees are taught from their first day on the job that customer satisfaction is more than a buzzword, and employees are expected to act accordingly as a condition of employment. While this may sound all

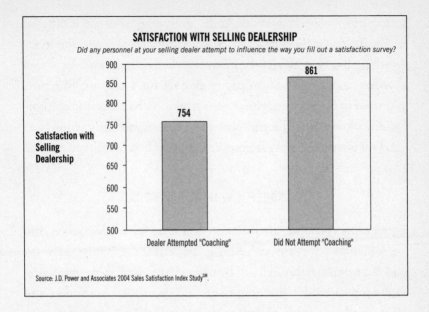

SATISFACTION WITH SELLING DEALERSHIP

Did any personnel at your selling dealer attempt to influence the way you fill out a satisfaction survey?

Source: J.D. Power and Associates 2004 Sales Satisfaction Index Study℠.

well and good in theory, any company that follows this path must be fanatical in its hiring practices. Everyone brought on board must be the type of person who will be internally motivated to do right by every customer. Hire the wrong people—those whose only motivation is the almighty buck—and employees will take the path of least resistance, a path which rarely leads to customer advocacy.

David Neeleman points out that just because JetBlue doesn't pay directly for customer satisfaction doesn't mean that there aren't any monetary rewards. He notes that every employee takes part in profit sharing, and since his company's fortunes are inextricably linked to customer satisfaction, his employees see the payoff every day in the financial section of their local newspaper. While this may seem like a bit of a throwaway answer at first, the reality of it hits home when you compare the profits of JetBlue against the other major airlines.

In truth, there is no silver-bullet answer to this question. Some organizations thrive by tying compensation to satisfaction scores. Others find such behavior counterproductive. Our idealistic side wants to believe that employees will always look to the best interest of the customer, but our pragmatic side keeps reminding us of the realities of human behavior. Therefore, we do not feel we are in a position to say which path is best. What we can say with conviction, however, is that if your company decides to pay employees for survey performance, you need to be very careful how you structure the program. Employees must know that the end goal is great customer satisfaction, and you will not tolerate *any* attempts to unfairly bias the survey results.

BE CAREFUL WHAT YOU ASK FOR

By focusing corporate attention on customer satisfaction scores, did we somehow let a very powerful genie out of the bottle? As we've said many times throughout this book, our goal is to emphasize some crucial truths: listening to the needs of your customers and creating advocates by striving to deliver upon those needs are paramount to long-term profitability. We never meant for companies to take their eyes off these basic truths by focusing their attention exclusively on the scorecard. But some do.

This is precisely why we said back at the beginning of the book that if your company understands the link between satisfaction and profits, you are already 90 percent of the way toward success. Until a company truly believes down deep in its corporate soul that satisfaction is the key to its success, that company will be forever chasing a carrot in the form of a customer satisfaction score that, by itself, is as meaningless and worthless as the paper it is written on.

Another simple truth that successful companies embrace is the notion that efforts to improve satisfaction and build advocacy must be transparent to the customer. Remember, customers aren't stupid. They can sense disingenuousness in a company the same way an animal senses fear in its prey. They will know if your employees seem more concerned about which box they check on a survey than they are about the actual customer experience.

You don't want your customers to feel that you are artificially trying to earn their satisfaction. Instead, your efforts should be seamless, making your customers feel as if their special experience is simply a reflection of who you are. In romance and in business, it is tough to buy love. While there may be a few short-term benefits to such behavior, it is most certainly not the path to a long-term relationship built on mutual trust.

And if that's not enough, please consider the following. If your customers believe that all you care about is how they fill out a survey, what's to keep them from turning the tables against you? If a hotel guest keeps getting reminded about the survey she will receive when she checks out, that hotel shouldn't be surprised when that guest turns around and says, "Tell you what, you want a perfect score so bad, how about you throw in a free gym pass and we'll talk about it."

If you are thinking this wouldn't actually happen, you have to understand that we are seeing the beginning of customer coercion just like this across many industries. And why shouldn't customers look for something in return for high satisfaction ratings when employees put so much emphasis on the survey? This is just one more reason why companies will find it more profitable to focus on real customer satisfaction initiatives than horse-trading with aggressive, cynical customers.

One only needs to look on eBay to watch it in action. EBay asks buyers to fill out a feedback form about their experience. Potential bidders use this feedback before they bid to feel confident they are dealing with someone who won't just take their money and run, or fail to provide an honest description of the merchandise. Remember, unlike traditional auctions, eBay auctions run online, which means that buyers must purchase merchandise essentially sight unseen. A string of negative feedback forms is tantamount to a death blow for eBay sellers.

Ask anyone who is a frequent seller on eBay and they will share horror stories about buyers who immediately pull out the feedback card as soon as the slightest disagreement occurs. We've even heard stories where buyers attempt to renegotiate deals by threatening negative feedback if the seller refuses to play ball.

No one ever said dealing with customers was easy. After many years in the automotive sector, we can say with complete confidence that customers are just as likely (if not more likely) to make unreasonable demands or tell white lies than are the salespeople with whom they're dealing. The same is true for the restaurant industry—just ask any of the servers who became so fed up that they posted their experiences on bitterwaitress.com.

The difference, of course, is that until a customer crosses that invisible line of decency where you have no alternative but to show them the door, it is your employees' job to smile, take it, and do everything within their power to soothe the angry beast in front of them. Why? Because you need the customer more than she needs you. Because you need to make sure that that person walks out the door willing to walk over burning coals to come back to your door. Because you need them to go out and proselytize your brand in a way that no amount of advertising could ever do. And the only way you can do that is by listening to your customers and doing everything possible to make sure they walk out that door an advocate, regardless of whether they ever receive or answer another survey as long as they live.

17

VOICE OF THE CUSTOMER

Earlier in this book, we told you two crucial truths about customer satisfaction: it is driven from the top down, and the real heavy lifting is done by your lowest-paid employees, who fight the battle for customer satisfaction every day on the front lines. Although this *top-down/bottom-up* approach is crucial, the companies that top our surveys embrace one other important element: they incorporate the voice of the customer in everything they do, from product design to service delivery. Even their facilities are continually revamped and fine-tuned around customer feedback.

There are two critical elements required to achieve that level of greatness. The first is information. An army can have the wisest generals, the best trained infantry, and even the latest weaponry, but if it doesn't have the fuel to get to the front lines, then the war is lost before the first shot is fired. In today's competitive business environment, information serves as the fuel that powers the customer satisfaction machine. Without information, companies have no idea which way to turn, or how to apply resources to maximize their return on customer satisfaction.

The second is infrastructure. Even if your company collects the right information, it needs to have an infrastructure in place to analyze, disseminate, and finally act upon that information. Information collected, but never used, is the same as not having collected the information in the first place. We call this building an information infrastructure around the *voice of your customer* (VOC).

Companies must do three things in order to reach the pinnacle of VOC integration:

- Collect the right information from customers;
- Properly analyze that information and make sure it gets into the hands of the people who are in a position to use it; and finally
- Properly act upon that information.

To illustrate what we mean, let's consider what happens to companies that plow forward in product or service development without integrating the voice of the customer.

THE BEST PRODUCTS THAT NOBODY NEEDED

Today, the average household owns 2.6 television sets—one for almost every room in the house.* It wasn't that long ago that the industry didn't measure the number of sets per household, but instead measured the percentage of homes that owned a television. Back in the early fifties, just owning one of these magical boxes bestowed its owners with celebrity status, guaranteeing a steady stream of neighbors who suddenly couldn't get enough of Mom's meatloaf.

Of course, watching television in those days was quite different than it is today. Even on a good day shows like *Texaco Star Theater* looked as if they were shot through the middle of a snow storm. TV

*Source: Nielsen Media Research.

images would sometimes flicker and fade so badly that you couldn't tell Lucille Ball from Milton Berle. Dad would scamper up to the roof in what seemed like a never-ending wrestling match with his new arch nemesis, the antenna. But down in the living room nobody seemed to care. Just to be able to catch a glimpse of one of those early TV images was magic enough.

It didn't take long for television images to improve. Tubes gave way to solid state. Black and white gave way to color. And those old ugly antennas that once dominated the residential skyline gave way to cable.

But for all these improvements, one constant remained—the networks ran on their schedule, not yours. When it came to television, there were no second chances. A late night at the office or an unexpected knock at the door meant missing your favorite show. That is, at least until 1975 when Sony introduced the first Beta Max video recorder.

For the first time, everyday consumers could record their favorite television shows and play them back whenever they wanted. Even though those first Beta recorders sold for around two thousand dollars, sales were brisk and Sony had a hard time keeping up with demand. Sony sold 30,000 Beta Maxes during the first year alone, a year we might add that Sony had the home video recorder market essentially to itself.

Of course that kind of monopoly never lasts, and the following year JVC introduced its own video recorder using what ultimately came to be known as VHS. Executives at Sony openly scoffed. Not only were the VHS recorders late to market, they knew their Beta format was technically superior. Compared to Beta, VHS required larger and bulkier tapes. More importantly, Beta produced an image that to the trained eye was sharper than anything that came out of a VHS machine. This last fact was important to Sony. Being an engineering-driven company, Sony always strived to market the best possible products. To Sony, performance equaled customer satisfaction, and it believed consumers would naturally continue to choose Beta over the inferior VHS machines.

But a funny thing happened on the road to market dominance. Sales of competing VHS recorders began to rise, and by 1980 recorders using the VHS format were outselling Beta two to one. It turns out that in Sony's quest for miniaturization and superior picture quality, it didn't take into account the fact that consumers might want to record something that lasted longer than an hour. Sure, the picture quality of the competing VHS players may not have been as good, but you could easily record a movie or football game without having to change tapes—something that was difficult to do if you were out for the evening! Sony's hands were tied. The Beta format was such that they couldn't just stuff more tape into a cassette to make it play longer. At least for the time being Beta tapes would be limited to one hour.

Though there were other competitive issues that hampered Sony's efforts to control the market, the fallout from this single failure to properly understand how their customers would use their recorders led to the ultimate demise of the entire Beta format, causing Sony to forfeit what would have been billions of dollars in profit.

One problem facing Sony was the fact that when it came to video, movies were the name of the game—a fact that is quite ironic when one considers those first home recorders had the movie executives shaking on their Hollywood sets. "Why," they asked, "would people continue to buy tickets to the movies when they could just rent one for half the price and watch it in the convenience of their own living room?" They even took the matter to Congress, arguing that video recorders facilitated copyright violations.

As we all know, this initial fear was short-lived. Kids still needed a place to go on dates, and parents still needed an excuse to have a night away from the kids. Movies were bigger than ever, and it wasn't long before the studios' fear turned to greed. Movie rentals not only gave them a second round of profits for successful films, but also provided a market for weaker films that never had a chance in the theater—the term *straight to video* became synonymous for a third-rate movie that no one would pay to see in a real theater.

As the movie rental business grew, the companies producing rental tapes saw the popularity of Beta fading. This was great news to them. After all, Beta tapes were not only more expensive to purchase, they were technically complex and typically required more than one tape to cover the length of a movie. It wasn't long before only the most popular movies were released on Beta.

Suddenly, buying a Beta machine meant you took a big risk that your favorite movies wouldn't be available for rental. The whole scenario spun out of control for Sony, and although they were ultimately able to produce Beta tapes that could record a full-length movie, the damage was already done. Beta, despite producing a better image than VHS, was dead, a victim of Sony's engineering arrogance that it felt it knew what was best for consumers.

The Beta Max debacle is not an isolated incident. The marketplace is littered with products and services that never stood a chance because their parent company either didn't make the effort, or somehow turned a deaf ear to their customer.

J.D. Power and Associates was born from the ashes of just such a miscalculation by McCulloch, the one-time leading maker of chainsaws. Although no one would ever accuse chainsaws of being the most civilized tool in the shed, today's chainsaws are actually quite refined compared to the industrial behemoths that dominated the market during the early sixties. For serious lumbermen, McCulloch was the brand to own. And since lumberjacks were the prevalent buyers of chainsaws, this meant McCulloch dominated the market.

McCulloch, much like Sony, was a company that cared deeply about its customers, and dedicated itself to providing what they defined as the best products on the market. To make sure they kept building the best, every year McCulloch, through a cadre of in-house researchers that included our founder, J.D. Power III, would go out and talk to lumbermen. They would watch how their saws were being used, often running for hours on end felling some of the largest trees ever produced by Mother Nature. And every year these professionals would say the same thing, just keep making the saws as durable as possible and they will keep buying them. Keep in mind there was no such thing as an electric chainsaw back then. Every saw was built around a crude two-stoke gasoline engine that belched smoke and screamed like a wild banshee, neither of which mattered one iota to professional lumberjacks.

The problem, as Mr. Power saw it, *wasn't* that McCulloch lost contact with its customers. Instead, the problem was *who* the company defined as a customer in the first place. Mr. Power and his contemporaries inside McCulloch's research department understood there was another market for their chainsaws just sitting there ripe for the picking. By completely ignoring the growing segment of residential chainsaw owners, McCulloch not only failed to understand the needs of residential users, it never fully realized the potential size of the residential market. Unlike the professional lumbermen of the Northwest, residential users cared about things such as weight and noise. While their professional counterparts used these saws to clear entire forests, private homeowners were more concerned with pruning a few branches and cutting firewood, a fact that gave them an entirely different set of needs.

Fortunately for backyard lumberjacks everywhere, not every company ignored their cries for a more civilized saw. Enter Homelite, a manufacturing company with a forty-year history of building a variety of products, from pumps to generators, specifically built for residential use. Although Homelite wasn't an expert in saws, it at least understood the needs of the residential customer. So, after studying the market, Homelite introduced the world's first lightweight chainsaw in 1963, calling it the XL12 because it weighed only twelve pounds.

McCulloch dismissed the XL12 as nothing more than a toy. Not the case for husbands whose wives were nagging them to clean up the jungle outside that once passed for a backyard. Sales soared, and by 1965 Homelite passed McCulloch as the leading chainsaw manufacturer.

ORGANIZING YOUR COMPANY AROUND VOC

It seems so fundamental. How could a company like McCulloch ignore the needs of residential customers when designing its saws? Or how could Sony not understand that people might want to record shows that last longer than an hour? As incredible as these miscalculations seem, we see companies make these kinds of blunders all the time.

A small company such as Mission Hills Bowl doesn't need to worry much about VOC infrastructure. That's because the owner Bill Mossonnte personally serves as judge, jury, and executioner. He's out there on the front lines every night talking to customers, personally deciding which comments warrant further action. For Mission Hills Bowl, being a customer satisfaction leader only requires a customer culture spawned from the top, and employees who are willing and able to translate that culture into a friendly customer interface.

Not so for larger organizations where the need for establishing a proper infrastructure around VOC is mission-critical. It doesn't matter how dedicated a company is to satisfying its customers if the information about those customers never makes it into the hands of those who need to know. And just as we've measured the link between a company's customer satisfaction and profitability, we've also measured the link between a company's VOC infrastructure and its customer satisfaction. Remember, it all begins by listening, and listening begins with knowing what information to collect.

COLLECTING THE RIGHT INFORMATION

Without information, there is no need for a VOC infrastructure. We could write an entire book just on the subject of collecting VOC information, but for now just ask yourself if your company possesses the information to answer each of the following four questions. Keep in mind that we're not asking if it *uses* this information, but only if this information is collected.

- Do you know how satisfied your customers are relative to those of your competitors?
- Do you measure how well each individual branch or department satisfies its customers?
- Do you understand your customers' needs (i.e., what it takes to make them happy and, more important, get out of their chairs and go out and do business with you)?
- Do you know how closely customer satisfaction is tied to your bottom line (i.e., its impact on loyalty, word of mouth, etc.)?

The first question is easy, provided you are in a large-scale industry such as automobiles, hotels, or airlines. J.D. Power and Associates, various consumer publications, and in some cases even the government already collect this information for you. The big question for you is how effectively you use this data.

If this information isn't publicly available, you must find a way to answer this question for yourself, because trying to manage customer satisfaction without knowing where you stand relative to your competition makes about as much sense as setting sail without a compass. Your customers have basic expectations, and you will make very different tactical decisions if your customers are soaring through the zone of advocacy, or mired in a land of hostile assassins.

The second question—do you measure branch performance—is

particularly important to service organizations that touch their customers through hundreds or. even thousands of different customer-facing employees. The quality of the deliverable depends on the quality of the encounter. This introduces variability, and variability is the enemy of customer satisfaction. And since branch profitability is closely tied to branch satisfaction, measuring (and then minimizing) variability is of the highest priority. One-size-fits-all solutions don't cut it anymore. You need to know which branches to leave alone, which just need some fine tuning, and which ones need complete restructuring.

The third question—needs assessment—is perhaps the most important, and applies to every type of business from retailers to manufacturers to service organizations. Understanding the needs of your customer provides a filter through which every decision must be screened. Developing a new product or service? Every phase of that process must begin and end with customer needs. Features, options, pricing strategy—they all depend on the wants, desires, and concerns of your customers. Just ask Sony and McCulloch, which failed to understand these needs. Or consider the market successes of our satisfaction leaders:

- JetBlue: found that the payback in passenger satisfaction with its leather seats more than offset the cost of installing those seats
- Enterprise Rent-A-Car: identified the market opportunity for picking up customers at their home or office
- Mike Diamond Plumbing: because customers didn't see a big difference in the technical skill of plumbers, differentiating itself on neatness and a "Smell Good" promise became the key to market success; and
- Washington Mutual: struck gold focusing on the unique needs of the traditionally underserved small investor.

Even your facilities need to be designed around the voice of the customer. This fact came through loud and clear as we interviewed our customer satisfaction leaders, and explains why our leaders fundamentally modified their facilities in ways that set them apart from the competition.

- Washington Mutual: redesigned its branches to look and feel more like a traditional retail store than a bank
- Scottrade: bucked the traditional reasoning of online companies and actually began expanding its bricks and mortar presence to help stay in touch with customers
- Westin Hotels: created and marketed the Heavenly Bed after determining that the bed would provide its hotels with the biggest bang for the buck

If this all sounds like something straight out of Introduction to Marketing 101, it is. But, as basic as these concepts are, this is just the sort of blocking and tackling companies frequently take for granted. Just stop for a minute and ask yourself how well your company really understands its customers. Maybe we should rephrase that—after all, both Sony and McCulloch *thought* they understood their customers. So, the real question therefore is: does your company actually collect this information from customers or simply assume it already knows the answers without having to ask?

And when you set out to collect VOC, don't make the same mistake as McCulloch. Your customers are more than just those advocates who do business with you over and over again. Your customers include disgruntled former customers who have long since defected to the competition, and even include those who chose never to do business with you in the first place. When you stop and think about it, you can learn a heck of lot more about how to grow sales from your *noncustomers* than the ones who do business with you already. Collecting VOC is not a meeting of the mutual admiration society.

Do that and you'll find yourself designing chainsaws exclusively for mountain men wearing flannel shirts.

The final question—understanding the link between satisfaction and profits—is simply a restatement of the theme that courses throughout this book. Satisfaction is not an end goal in and of itself. Satisfaction costs money, and just like any investment, you need to be able to evaluate the return on investment for any improvement strategy. Recall our example from an earlier chapter where a call center properly concluded that the cost associated with improving customer satisfaction by reducing wait times was not justified by the minimal expected return in loyalty and other financial metrics. Every business must make this same ROI of CSI analysis, and to do this you must first collect and synthesize every piece of information that defines your own unique link between satisfaction and profitability. How closely is customer satisfaction tied to the loyalty of your customers? What is the impact of satisfaction on word of mouth, and how dependent is your business on the recommendations of others?

LEARNING TO LISTEN

Our clients often come to us thinking the only way to collect this information is to write out a long list of questions, get on the telephone, and ask their customers one by one in the form of a formal survey. Make no mistake; surveys play a crucial role in gathering VOC, and doing them right is much more difficult than it seems. However, VOC does not live by surveys alone. And since there are plenty of books and companies that can help your company conduct a proper survey, we will forgo the discussion on survey technique and focus instead on some of the other ways you can collect VOC information.

Every day your customers provide a steady stream of anecdotal feedback; all you need to do is learn to stop and listen. Warranty records, letters of gratitude, and even a screaming tirade to a service rep are all pieces of the puzzle. The better able you are to collect, synthesize, and mine all of these disparate inputs, the better you will understand your customers.

Smaller companies are less likely to have large research budgets, and therefore must rely more heavily on anecdotal feedback. When a customer complains, don't get defensive; savor it as an opportunity to receive free and unfiltered feedback.

Companies must also learn to observe, because what your customers *do* sometimes speaks volumes compared to what they *say*. Every year, observational research plays an increasing role in understanding customer behavior. The next time you are at the supermarket and the checker asks you to swipe your loyalty card, instead of thinking how nice it is to get that loyalty discount, think about how much the contents of your cart just told the store about you—you rarely purchase the same brand of salad dressing twice, you like to stock up by buying in bulk, and unless you've developed some very strange eating habits it would appear that you recently acquired a dog.

The most well-known and perhaps longest-running consumer study of all time, the Nielsen ratings, falls squarely into the category of observational research.* Television networks don't call you and ask whether you *liked* that show you just watched. Once a show makes it onto the network's schedule, they don't really care all that much about satisfaction, but only that you are watching. Because as long as you're *watching,* the advertisers are happy, and when the advertisers are happy the network is happy. As such, Nielsen became the standard by which networks decide which shows will be renewed in the fall, how much money sixty seconds of advertising will command, and whether the cast of *Friends* was each worth a million dollars per episode. And it all comes without asking a single question about whether people like the show.

Of course, the Nielsen ratings are a rather blunt instrument—

*The Nielsen Ratings are produced by Nielsen Media Research.

the television is either on or it isn't. Nielsen doesn't know if the whole family is glued to the set with rapt attention, or if it's only on to provide a little white noise while you go about your daily chores. That's where TiVo comes in, that magical remote control that allows you to stop live television in its tracks, answer the doorbell, and play it back when the intruder is gone. Imagine you're watching the U.S. Open and out of the corner of your eye you think you see Tiger Woods' caddie giving a one-finger wave to a noisy photographer. Was it your imagination, or did he really do that on national television? No worries; just hit the replay button on your remote and have another look. Play it back in slow motion just to be sure, and then hit fast forward and skim through that boring interview with some player you've never heard of.

Sure, TiVo may be a godsend to couch potatoes, but be forewarned; these features are not just there to allow you to become master of your own universe. Part of TiVo's business is to work directly with television outlets to provide important feedback on the viewing habits of its customers. For example, TiVo is able to tell Jay Leno which jokes people played over again, and which ones hit so flat that viewers decided to switch channels in time to catch Letterman's Top Ten list. Now that's what we call real-time VOC; it's almost like having a market researcher sitting with your family taking notes. What's the most replayed moment in TiVo's television history? Here's a hint—it came during the Super Bowl. But it wasn't a game-winning catch, or even one of those outlandish Super Bowl commercials. According to TiVo, it was Janet Jackson's wardrobe "malfunction" that took place during the halftime of the 2004 game.

Staples takes listening to the voice of its customers quite literally. Once each month Staples' customer care professionals sit side by side with senior executives to listen to live calls coming into the company's toll-free customer support line. These "Voice of the Customer" sessions allow each employee to hear what customers are actually saying, the good, the bad, the ugly, completely unedited and unrehearsed. Data are great, but sometimes you just need a little dose of human reality to put all those numbers into context.

Whether it's in the form of a survey, monitoring behavior, or just getting out on the floor mingling with your customers, the key is to learn as much about them as possible. Who are they, what motivates them, and how do they feel about doing business with you vis-à-vis the competition? The more information you collect, the more ammunition you have to help you hit your targets. Of course, as we will see in the next section, ammunition is worthless unless you have a good targeting system.

VOC DATA IS A TERRIBLE THING TO WASTE

So you've done your due diligence and collected everything there is to know about your customers. While this puts you ahead of the game, the battle is far from over—you still must find a way to use the data. VOC—like a mind—is a terrible thing to waste. Let it just sit around unused and your VOC information is doing about as much good as that gym membership that seemed like such a good idea at the time. And, as crazy as it might sound, we estimate that most companies use less than half the VOC information they collect, and some waste nearly all of it.

In our experience, VOC data typically goes unused for two reasons:

- Raw data sits without being properly analyzed, or
- VOC information is never transferred to those who are in a position to act upon it.

One reason clients fail to analyze the information they collect is the simple fact that it is easier to *collect* VOC information than it is to *interpret* it. To some degree this is a function of resources, but is typically more closely related to the underlying problem that many companies just don't understand the value of VOC, or why they collected it in the first place. Companies sometimes collect things such as customer satisfaction and demographics because they think that this is the type of thing big companies do.

Once collected, however, nobody knows what to do with it, so it sits untouched and unanalyzed. When a user group asks for the data, the research department sends it out raw, disjointed, and without context. No one should be surprised when the recipient spends a few minutes looking at it, shakes their head in frustration, and shoves it off into the corner never to be used again.

This brings up an important point. Every program to collect VOC must begin by asking yourself *why* you need the information, *who* within the company needs that information, and *what* are the decisions they need to make from it? Never begin the process the other way around. Don't collect the information first and try to find a use for it later.

It is always disappointing to walk into a client's office only to find a report we delivered last month still sitting in a corner collecting dust. We ask the client if they were satisfied with the results, and just like the diner who had an *OK* meal the night before, the answer comes back sounding something like, "Oh ya, sure, it was fine." Ouch! Straight to the land of apathy, do not pass go, and most certainly do not collect two hundred dollars. It's not that these clients are dissatisfied per se; it's just that there isn't much to get excited about when you never dig into the data. Companies often hold the mistaken belief that data, once collected, will somehow jump off the page of its own volition, providing the magic bullet that will cure all that ails it. Needless to say, it doesn't work that way.

Rather than sit around and sulk when a company fails to use the information it paid us to collect, we try to take our own advice and consider their apathy as valuable feedback. We've significantly beefed up our own analytical capabilities in response. Before we take on a new project we now do everything within our power to convince clients to expand our role beyond data collection to include data analysis. We've found this is the most reliable way to make sure the data gets used. Because, if it doesn't get used, we won't create an advocate, which means we are less likely to be asked back to repeat the study again next year. At some of our larger clients we've even begun installing our own analysts on site, sometimes at our own expense. Their primary job is to continually mine the data on behalf of their host client, always on the lookout for solutions to what keeps them up at night. Sure it costs money, but as we said before, what good is data if nobody uses it?

THE POLITICS OF VOC

Even when the data gets analyzed, it sometimes stagnates within the department responsible for collecting it—not a good thing when one considers that the department that collects VOC is probably at least three floors down from the department that needs it. Information about customer needs doesn't get into the hands of designers. Branch satisfaction data stays at corporate and never finds its way to the desk of the branch manager. Or marketing fails to provide usability data to product engineers, thereby resulting in wonderfully engineered products that nobody wants.

The reason that data fails to get into the right hands frequently comes down to an ineffective VOC infrastructure. We will address this in a moment. Sometimes, however, there are more nefarious forces at work. The individual collecting the information may pronounce themselves as gatekeeper, and hoard the data like a wizened miser, doling it out in dribs and drabs to serve their own personal agenda. We've even been chastised by middle managers who became livid upon learning that we had the audacity to meet directly with the senior executive who commissioned a study, rather than delivering the results to them so that they could put their own spin on the findings that would ultimately make it to the top.

For example, we once provided a series of reports to the American subsidiary of a large European company, only to learn that the COO of the American operation immediately locked up every report in his office away from what he called the "prying eyes" of his corporate superiors across the Atlantic. This not only gave him complete control over how the information would be used, it eliminated the need to answer for a number of quality issues that he personally felt were red herrings that had very little to do with his company's recent decline. Once this particular executive departed, the information floodgates opened, and user groups both in the United States and abroad that were previously kept in the dark suddenly had complete access to all their VOC information—not just those parts that met the COO's personal agenda. The company began shifting its focus to the voice of the customer and the root causes of its customer satisfaction issues. The net result is that over the past few years this company has turned the corner, and is seeing a rise in both customer satisfaction and sales.

But the best—or maybe we should say worst—example of gatekeeping comes from Hyundai, which very nearly failed in the United States because senior executives were kept in the dark. When Hyundai first came to the United States in 1986, consumers flocked to the little car that featured European styling at a price thousands less than just about anything produced here or abroad. Hyundai sold 250,000 cars in its first full year in business. To put this achievement into perspective, consider that it took Volkswagen eleven years selling the Beetle before it even reached the 100,000 plateau. Hyundai was barreling headlong down the road to success—that is until it hit a speed bump of its own making.

Despite everything going for it, Hyundai had one small problem. The cars began falling apart before their customers' eyes. Transmissions were failing before the cars barely broke a sweat. Customers would get a new transmission under warranty, but this too would fail. The early Hyundais were just as frustrating for their owners even when they were able to crawl out of the garage. Nagging problems such as trim pieces that would fall off at inopportune times or upholstery that wore out prematurely kept drivers well acquainted with their service department.

When J.D. Power and Associates conducted its first long-term reliability survey of the Hyundai it finished thirtieth out of thirty-four brands. You may be thinking that thirtieth isn't that bad, after all four brands finished worse. Unfortunately, these four included AMC, Merkur, Peugeot, and Yugo—all of which turned tail and stopped importing vehicles to the United States soon thereafter.

For a while it looked as if Hyundai might face the same end. Sales steadily declined until 1998, when the volume plummeted to less than 100,000. The cars were taking such a beating by the press that many insiders questioned whether Hyundai should follow suit and pack up and go home.

The tragedy of the early Hyundai story is that its quality nightmares were not due to a lack of engineering or manufacturing skill. Quite the contrary, Hyundai was well equipped to produce quality products—if it chose to. Hyundai's problems instead were directly the result of failing to understand the needs of the American consumer.

We went to Korea to deliver the results of our study, but were immediately shuffled off to lower level managers who simply did not want to listen to bad news. These managers refused to even acknowledge they had a quality problem, and most certainly did not want us giving such a message to their superiors. Time and time again they would tell us that they priced their cars so low that quality shouldn't be an issue. They blamed their troubles instead on mistakes made by their U.S.-based (and staffed) sales and marketing division. More than once they even blamed the fact that there were too many women drivers in the United States.

In 1996 we once again went to Seoul with yet another dismal quality report. But something was different this time. Instead of meeting with junior executives, this time we were granted an audience with Chairman Chung Ju-yung. This meeting confirmed our suspicions; as unbelievable as it seems, the senior leadership had never been made aware of our reports, nor the fact that we had been able to directly tie these problems to their sales decline.

The response from Chairman Chung was both immediate and powerful. He immediately sent us out to the factories to personally deliver the message to those in charge. With Chung's directive, changes began at once. For one thing, Hyundai commissioned J.D. Power and Associates to help them understand the American consumer—until then Hyundai had only looked at (but not acted upon) the results of our customer surveys.

Our role at Hyundai was very specific. We were not going to take over the production line. What we did do is change the corporate culture so that above all else it integrated the voice of the customer (VOC) as a filter from which all decisions were made. As we said before, Hyundai already had some of the best engineers. All they needed was to break the information barrier that prevented VOC information from reaching those executives who were in a position to turn the ship around.

In the decade since making this cultural shift, Hyundai improved across a wide range of VOC metrics including customer satisfaction and loyalty. Initial quality has improved 59 percent since 1998, far more than any other brand sold in America. Most importantly, sales rebounded accordingly. In 2004 Hyundai sold more than 400,000 vehicles—more than Volkswagen and Mitsubishi combined. More importantly, people now buy a Hyundai because they *want* one, not just because it's the *only car they can afford.*

The lesson from this story is simple: break down any political silos that exist between the collectors and the users of VOC data. Do not allow something as critical as VOC to be spoiled by the personal agendas of a few, or in Hyundai's case, middle managers who were so afraid to bring bad news to their superiors that they nearly allowed the company to fail.

LEARNING TO SHARE

Although there is no excuse for intentionally withholding information, the more common cause of VOC stagnation simply comes down to poor infrastructure. This results in an information gridlock that is every bit as detrimental as a power-hungry gatekeeper. A company collects great information, but it doesn't know how to use it—which includes who in the company needs it. And so it sits in the hands of the collector. Meanwhile, managers in other parts of the company toss and turn at night agonizing over upcoming decisions, completely unaware the information they need already exists. Remember, the purpose of VOC is to help consumers make better decisions. Have the right information, and every decision becomes a no-brainer.

Companies need to structure the dissemination process around these decisions—and the people who make them. We cannot begin to tell you how often we receive a call from a senior executive asking for our opinion on various aspects of customer behavior, only to tell them we already delivered a report on that subject to someone else in their organization two months prior. It is an ongoing disconnect between those who know and those who need to know, and the magnitude of the problem is directly proportional to the size and complexity of the organization.

A classic example comes from a hospital on the East Coast. We conducted a one-time exhaustive survey of their discharged patients as part of J.D. Power and Associates' Distinguished Hospital Certification Program that focuses on the patient experience. Mortality rates and infection reports are of course important, but it's the soft side of the experience—bedside manner, atmosphere of the room, and of course that dreaded hospital food—that really drives patient satisfaction. And from a business perspective, it's these soft side attributes that cause someone to choose one hospital over another.

We delivered our report to the hospital, and unbeknownst to us that report remained with the hospital's certification team. It wasn't as if there was anything untoward going on. The certification team commissioned the study for a specific purpose, and just didn't think about the fact that other departments might be able to use the data. Imagine our surprise when we received a call from the quality assurance folks at the hospital asking us to do a survey of patient satisfaction very similar to the reports we had just delivered. Once the caller got over his embarrassment of not realizing that someone three doors down the hall already had everything he needed, we're pretty sure he began thinking of all the ways his department could spend the money it just saved.

It bears repeating that this is far from an isolated story. In fact, during our research for this book we discussed the issue with our client teams and found that you couldn't spend too much time out in the field without running into companies whose left hand didn't know what the right was doing. Take a hard look at your own organization and we are pretty sure you will find valuable information just sitting around unused for no other reason than your company lacks a proper VOC infrastructure. The problem is so significant that we've even established an entire practice area at J.D. Power and Associates dedicated to helping clients learn to share.

HAVE YOU DRIVEN A UTOPIAN TURTLETOP LATELY?

The year was 1955, and although Ford Motor Company's newest car wouldn't roll down the assembly line for another two years, the company was already hard at work coming up with a name. Initially, the task of naming the car fell to Ford's long-time advertising agency, Foote Cone & Belding. Long lists of names were generated, tested, and ultimately run by Ford executives to gauge their reaction. A few of the agency's favored names included Pacer, Citation, and Ranger. Although each tested well with consumers, Ford's executives were underwhelmed. They wanted a name befitting what Ford planned to hail as the first totally new car in twenty years.

In frustration, Ford hired Marianne Moore, a popular poet at the time, to come up with just such a name. Ms. Moore may have been a great poet, but she had a lot to learn about marketing. A few of her more interesting suggestions included: *Mongoose Civique, Resilient Bullet,* and *Utopian Turtletop.* Thankfully, Ford had the wherewithal to see these suggestions for what they were—a disaster waiting to happen. Unfortunately, in their frustration at being unable to choose among Foote Cone & Belding's recommended names, someone suggested they end the debate by just naming the car after Henry Ford's only son—Edsel Ford. And while the name *Edsel* made sense to Detroit insiders who understood the historical significance of the name, it made absolutely no sense to American consumers who were repulsed by everything about the car, from the name on down to what some considered phallic styling. In the end, the Edsel would go down in history as one of the biggest product disasters of all time, and the word Edsel is forever etched in our vernacular as being synonymous with failure.

At least Ford can't say it wasn't warned. Not only did it choose to ignore every name its agency tested and later recommended, Ford's own market research warned it to stay away from the Edsel name. Among other things that Ford's research determined through word association testing, people associated Edsel with such things as "pretzel" and "schmedsel." Even with the best VOC information about pros and cons of each possible name, and a process that put that information directly in front of Ford's official naming committee, there was no guarantee that the company would actually listen to its research.

VOC IS NOT A FOUR-LETTER WORD

Market research sometimes gets a bad rap. We've heard them all: design by committee, turning control of the company over to a focus group, and dozens of others suggesting that making decisions through market research somehow shows a weakness of character, or a lack of initiative to make big decisions on your own. If this were the case, we'd live in a world where the most successful companies would be the ones that swim against the tide and take the position that they and they alone know what's best for customers. It's the type of story that makes for great headlines: "Lone Maverick Breaks All the Rules and Comes Out Smelling Like a Rose."

But real life is rarely this romantic. Corporate profits are directly correlated to customer satisfaction, and satisfaction that rises to the level of advocacy is only achievable by exceeding customer expectations. And this is only possible by understanding those expectations and needs upfront, *before* you take action.

Relying on VOC to make decisions isn't weak, it's efficient. Even leaders with that innate ability to wake up one morning with a great idea that transforms their company don't do so in a vacuum. They come up with these ideas by first knowing their customers and then using that knowledge to develop products or services to fill unmet needs—not the other way around.

As we've seen throughout this book, customer satisfaction has many faces. Sometimes it's found in a product that provides new features that make the user's life a little easier. Sometimes it just means hitting the "on" switch for the thousandth time and getting the same result you did the first time out of the box. And sometimes satisfaction is nothing more than a warm smile that lets a customer know you care. Whatever the face of satisfaction, there is always one constant: the companies that understand and leverage the voice of their customers not only earn J.D. Power and Associates' most coveted awards, they earn the hearts and long-term commitment of consumers everywhere. Because, when it comes to your customers, perception is reality, and ultimately your company is nothing more than what your customers say it is.

MEASURE YOUR OWN VOC PROFICIENCY

Are you really hearing the voice of your customer? To answer this question, J.D. Power and Associates has developed a simple on-line assessment to evaluate your company's VOC proficiency to determine whether it is maximizing the benefit of true customer satisfaction. Just log on to **jdpower.com/VOC/test** and follow the prompts. The whole process takes less than fifteen minutes, and the results will show you how well your company performs relative to other organizations in areas such as:

- The quality and depth of information your company collects from its customers
- How effectively it analyzes and disseminates the VOC information it collects
- Its ability to use VOC information to develop, improve, and market its products and services
- The extent to which your company is dedicated to maximizing customer satisfaction at every level throughout the organization

Because VOC proficiency is an enterprise-wide activity, we invite others from your company to log on to take the same assessment. As more employees log on, we will continuously increase the depth of your company's VOC profile. We hope that companies will use the resulting information to help them maximize their VOC proficiency, not only for the benefit of their customers, but for their bottom line as well.

ABOUT J.D. POWER AND ASSOCIATES

Established in 1968, J.D. Power and Associates is a global marketing information firm that conducts independent and unbiased surveys of customer satisfaction, product quality, and buyer behavior. Today, the firm's services include industrywide syndicated studies, proprietary (commissioned) tracking studies, media studies, forecasting and training services, as well as business operations analyses and consultancies on customer satisfaction trends. On April 1, 2005, J.D. Power and Associates became a business unit of The McGraw-Hill Companies.

The firm has expanded to serve a number of industries outside of automotive, including travel and hotels, telecommunications, marine, utilities, health care, homebuilder, consumer electronics, and financial services. The firm has also expanded internationally, bringing the language of customer satisfaction to consumers and businesses in India, Japan, Taiwan, China, the Philippines, Indonesia, Singapore, Thailand, Malaysia, South Africa, Canada, Mexico, the United Kingdom, Australia, New Zealand, Germany, and France.

J.D. Power and Associates includes more than 800 professional analysts, statisticians, economists, consultants, experts in demographics and consumer behavior, and administrative support personnel. Headquartered in Westlake Village, California, a suburb north of Los Angeles, the firm has five U.S. offices and international locations serving Canada, the United Kingdom/Europe, and the Asia Pacific region. J.D. Power III is the founder and Stephen C. Goodall is the president.

ABOUT THE MCGRAW-HILL COMPANIES

Founded in 1888, The McGraw-Hill Companies is a global information-services provider meeting worldwide needs in the financial services, education, and business information markets through leading brands such as Standard & Poor's and McGraw-Hill Education. The Corporation has more than 280 offices in thirty-seven countries.

INDEX